Warn

Do not attempt to buy or read this book unless the intended reader can correctly identify three of the music-related (band/label/album/product) logos below.

A
BC
DEFG
HIJKL
MNOPQR
STUVWXYZ

(answers at the very back of the book)

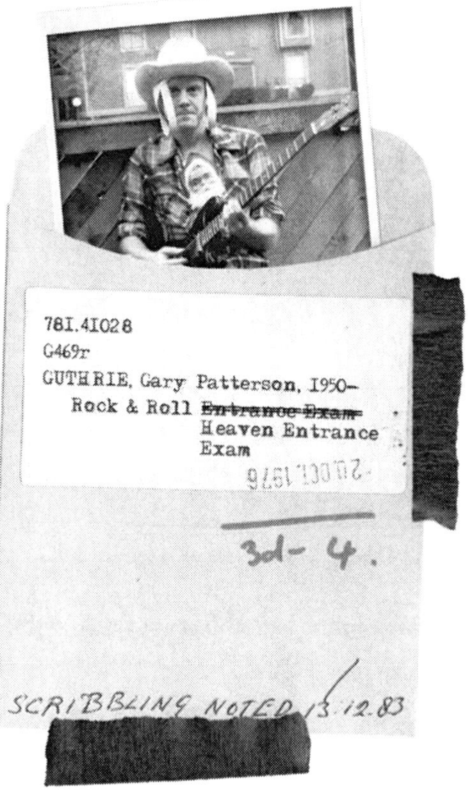
781.41028
G469r
GUTHRIE, Gary Patterson, 1950-
Rock & Roll ~~Entrance Exam~~
Heaven Entrance Exam
3d- 4.
SCRIBBLING NOTED 13.12.83

A Nest of Eggs

Rock and Roll Heaven Entrance Exam

Second Edition

Cover design: Trigger Black

Edited by: Max Bozeaux, Speed Franklin, and B.J. McAllister

DISCLAIMER: There are absolutely no references to Head East's *Flat As a Pancake* is this document.

Table of Contents

ROCK
AND ROLL
HEAVEN
ENTRANCE
EXAM

Introduction

SOMEWHERE IN THE MID-60S, there must've been something in the credits of an LP cover that raised a profound eyebrow of curiosity. Maybe it was seeing Joe Osborn pop up as the bassist on album after album, or finding Paul & John as background singers on a Stones song. Whatever it was, it started me on a zealous path of reading liner notes and credits on both albums and 45s.

At my very first rock concert – Paul Revere & the Raiders at Freedom Hall in Louisville – I tasted my first "I gotcha" when Keith Allison, one of the warm-up acts, introduced "Summer Rain" as a "song *I* just wrote". Of course I knew that Keith was BS'ing the crowd because it was *Johnny Rivers* who had just released the song, but having one-up'ed a star of TV's *Where the Action Is* gave me great pride and, in a flash, I was terminally hooked on useless knowledge – a condition cemented later that year when I won a television from Imperial Records in their contest for Rivers' *Realization* album.

To be honest, my journey has been a little over the top. I put myself in more situations than most music buffs would allow*, but the fervor of music is hard to beat. Still, to this day, I find myself noodling around the 25¢ bins at Half-Price books connecting dots on everything from Lester Flatt to Dirk Hamilton albums because of the little hidden slants that can give a recording a whole new meaning.

To those of us who fancy music trivia, it's as important as the periodic table is to a chemist. I have to admit it doesn't improve our lot in the world order, but being the go-to guy for the oddball music question offers up a nice little kick.

We trivia geeks all have our niche. I have friends like Sean Ross who can absolutely slay me on regional chart records and I dare not even attempt to get into the same box as Gary Moore when it comes to Zeppelin or Pink Floyd trivia. *My* specialty? The parallel universes of Useless and Interesting.

This collection of (useless/interesting) trivia questions is far from being "mass market" or for the faint of fortissimo. It's really just my little throwdown; something you can use to test yourself, expand your horizons, or shut up your annoying know-it-all chums. Heck, you can turn it into a drinking game for all I care.

There's everything in here: brain busters, WTFs, curveballs, even some creampuffs just to give it balance. Nonetheless if you're a one-genre pony or don't know squat about labels, lyrics, who Pattie Boyd slept with, or what polk salad looks like, you may be flat out of luck. Sure, the book's mostly marquee names and Classic Rock in nature, but there's a little

Disco, Country, Punk, Soundtrack, Glam, some passing fancies, and a sufficient amount of Pop and R&B to see how well-versed you *really* are.

The slant that makes this different from other trivia books (or so I hope) is that the *answers* offer the real "interestingness", if you will. Whether the questions give you fits or you find 'em a walk in the park, there's been a little extra elbow grease applied to the details to offer some new enlightenment.

Before I close, let me make a suggestion: many of the answers are a tad abridged so if you come across something interesting, go out and find out more on your own so you get the whole story. Follow the tangents... go to iTunes or Amazon or YouTube (a great resource because they play some of the hard-to-find tracks all the way through) and listen to the parallels... Google wildly, read more at artist websites/fansites, AllMusic.com or Wikipedia. True music discovery requires *some* involvement, you know.

Enjoy.
Gary Guthrie

Oh, yeah – the asterisk...

- Ran away from home (from Sonora KY to Philadelphia PA) in the Fall of '67 because of a dust-up with my parents over The Who's appearance on *The Smothers Brothers.*
- Had tongue tacos with Ted Nugent, crawfish pie with Tony Joe White, oysters Bienville with Eddie Rabbitt, and something weird from waaaaaaay south of the border with Johnny Rivers ... got my butt beat in

softball by John Denver ... given the evil eye from Billy Joel for daring to bring up Attila ... accidently mistook Linda McCartney's leg for a table leg when I was blindly trying to secure a microphone cable ... wound up on the poster inside of *Venus and Mars* (I assume not part of a reverse chastisement for feeling Linda McCartney's leg) ... rescued by Charlie Daniels from a "moment" in the Casablanca Records suite at an industry convention ... attended Wilson Pickett's funeral (Aretha and Solomon Burke were on the program but disgracefully failed to show) ... had to lie to Alice Cooper's manager about the whereabouts of my wedding because the word leaked out that Alice was going to have his Cyclops character crash the nuptials ... told to "f*ck off" on the radio by Mick Fleetwood and John McVie when pressing them for an apology for standing up a stadium-full of fans in San Antonio.

- Produced a Canned Heat and John Lee Hooker concert in college, only to have the Heat's road manager run off with the gate proceeds in the middle of the show ... did the same thing with Mudcrutch, Boz Scaggs, Melissa Manchester, John Hammond Jr., the Meters, and Hall & Oates with much better results.
- Got fired from the campus radio station at Murray State as the result of a coup staged by some classical accordion freak who convinced the Board of Regents that we were soiling the university's image with all the rock 'n roll we were playing ... Got canned from a radio station in Benton KY after I made a 20-foot loop out of the breakdown in Zeppelin's "Whole Lotta Love", added every sound effect I could find, and stretched the song out to 19 minutes.

- Used to drive to Muscle Shoals, Alabama, just to see if I could find anyone of note hanging out in public. Oh, and one trip to Black Oak, Arkansas, proved there was no need to return, trust me.
- Went to the first Atlanta and Texas Pop festivals where I had the serendipitous moment of sitting at a picnic table with Janis Joplin.
- Had a daily TV show built on music videos and cheesy camera tricks called *The Now Explosion* at WDXR-TV in Paducah KY, in 1971. Note: I use the term "music videos" lightly – there were only a handful like CCR, Cornelius Brothers & Sister Rose, John Kay, et al available. Most of the time, we did things like throw paint on a lazy Susan and do camera zooms in and out.
- Went to Cobham, England and applied to be a roadie for the Moody Blues ... worked lights for Poco on part of their 1971 tour.
- Yeah, and that Streisand/Diamond 15 minutes in the sun.
- Yadda...

■ ■ ■

ROCK
AND ROLL
HEAVEN
ENTRANCE
EXAM

Questions

1. What group spent more weeks in the UK Singles Chart* than the Beatles? *(between '65 and '69)
    a. Dave Clark 5
    b. Dave Dee, Dozy, Beaky, Mick, and Tich
    c. Pretty Things
    d. Gerry & the Pacemakers

2. The story line of "Stoner cab driver picks up old girlfriend and gets huge tip" belongs to what song?
    a. Rolling Stones/"Limousine"
    b. Harry Chapin/"Taxi"
    c. Wings/"Back Seat of My Car"
    d. Neil Young/"Needle and the Damage Done"

3. With which famous artist's niece does the narrator of Bob Dylan's "When I Paint My Masterpiece" have a date?
    a. Rembrandt
    b. Picasso
    c. Botticelli
    d. Goya

4. There were two songs from Broadway musicals that hit #1 on the singles charts in the '60s/'70s... Which two?
   a. The Cowsills/"Hair"
   b. Three Dog Night/"Easy to Be Hard"
   c. 5th Dimension/"Aquarius"
   d. Louis Armstrong/"Hello, Dolly"

5. Sandy Denny sang on which Zeppelin song on their fourth LP?
   a. "Battle of Evermore"
   b. "Goin' to California"
   c. "Tangerine"
   d. "All My Love"

6. Sticking with Led Zep's fourth album, what do the symbols shown on the label/sleeve represent?

7. Rosanne Cash is the offspring of Johnny Cash and which one of these ladies?
   a. Bonnie Owens
   b. Sylvia Flye
   c. June Carter Cash
   d. Vivian Liberto

8. John Lennon's first wife's name was what?

9. Which member wrote the title song of Crosby, Stills, Nash, and Young's *Déjà Vu* album?

10. Who played the guitar solo on the Drifters' "On Broadway"?
    a. Jerry Reed
    b. Phil Spector
    c. Johnny Rivers
    d. Wes Montgomery

11. Springsteen once opened for Anne Murray. T/F?

12. What singer is the subject of Roberta Flack's hit "Killing Me Softly with His Song"?

13. What song was on the Sun Records flip side of "That's Alright, Mama" by Elvis Presley?
    a. "Baby, Let's Play House"
    b. "Blue Moon of Kentucky"
    c. "Milk Cow Blues Boogie"
    d. "Mystery Train"
    e. "Good Rockin' Tonight"

14. Paul Revere & the Raiders were mainstays of *Where the Action Is* but hosted their own Dick Clark-produced program when *Action* folded. What was the name of that show?

15. He/she had/has a 5 ½ octave vocal range...
    a. Lou Christie
    b. Eddie Holman
    c. Jon Anderson
    d. Minnie Riperton

16. Who took Syd Barrett's place in Pink Floyd?

17. Steely Dan and the Eagles "fought" each other in the lyrics of what two songs?
    a. "Everything You Did" vs. "Hotel California"
    b. "Gaucho" vs. "Hotel California"
    c. "Haitian Divorce "vs. "The Greeks Don't Want No Freaks"
    d. "The Fez" vs. "The Last Resort"

18. At the Stones' 12/6/69 gig in Livermore, California, what ensued during "Under My Thumb"?

19. When KISS' members released their solo albums in 1978, which one scored the highest chart position? Frehley, Simmons, Stanley, or Criss?

20. Which Beatle had the first trans-Atlantic (U.S. & UK) #1 single as a solo act and what was the song?

21. The only Byrd allowed to play his instrument during the recording of "Mr. Tambourine Man" was who?

22. True/False time for Blondie's *Parallel Lines*...
    a. It was produced by Mike Chapman, the cat who produced the Sweet, Suzi Quatro, and the Knack T/F
    b. Features King Crimson's Robert Fripp on guitar on a coupla tracks T/F
    c. The album charted better in the U.S. than the U.K. T/F
    d. They cover a Carl Perkins tune T/F

23. Bill Haley's first group was called…
    a. Bill Haley & His Comets
    b. Bill Haley and the Saddlemen
    c. The Palaminos
    d. The Haley Family Band

24. Who inspired Bowie to write "Jean Genie"?

25. Name the Stones song on which Lennon and McCartney sang backing vocals.

26. Match the musician with the movie they were in...

a. Kris Kristofferson	1. *Performance*
b. Bobby Darin	2. *Bram Stoker's Dracula*
c. Ricky Nelson	3. *Alice Doesn't Live Here Anymore*
d. Tom Waits	4. *Rio Bravo*
e. Mick Jagger	5. *Capt. Newman, M.D.*

27. The Doors' first recording deal was with...?
    a. White Whale
    b. Warner Bros.
    c. Elektra
    d. Columbia
    e. GNP Crescendo

28. Norman Greenbaum was sort of a one-hit wonder *twice!* Of course you know "Spirit in the Sky" but he was a part of *another* group who were one-and-done. Who were they and what was the song?

29. Time for a comprehensive Motown mofo. Get at least half of these right...
    a. What was the Supremes original name?
    b. Marvin Gaye did duets with what four Motown chick singers?
    c. There were four Hollywood film/TV stars who recorded for Motown. Who?
    d. The Beatles said their favorite girl singer was a Motown artist and even invited her to tour with them. Who?

30. What 80s/90s rocker's cousin produced the first Talking Heads album (*Talking Heads 77*)?
    a. Jon Bon Jovi
    b. David Lee Roth
    c. Michael Stipe
    d. Axl Rose

31. The very first *white* artist signed to Island Records would be who?
    a. Nick Drake
    b. Robert Palmer
    c. Julian Cope
    d. John Martyn

32. Why does Dennis Edmonton never have to work another day in his life?

33. Who's the only artist to have separate Top 10 singles as a solo act, as half of a duo, a third of a trio, a fourth of a quartet, and a fifth of a quintet?

34. In Simon & Garfunkel's "7 O'clock News/Silent Night" (the one where Paul & Art sing "Silent Night" and someone reads the news under it), name at least *one* news item the newscaster reads.

35. Who wrote "Everybody's Talkin'"?

36. Joni Mitchell has a thing for bassists. Namely?
    a. Charles Mingus, Larry Klein, and Jaco Pastorius
    b. Stanley Clarke, Charlie Haden, and Larry Klein
    c. Jaco Pastorius, Phil Upchurch, and Duck Dunn

37. Name *one* connection between Donovan ("Mellow Yellow", et al) and the Beastie Boys...

38. Foghat was the result of a defection of three of what group's members?
    a. Jethro Tull
    b. Brownsville Station
    c. Ten Years After
    d. Savoy Brown
    e. Toe Fat

39. Carlos Santana's brother had a big hit fronting a band on Warner Brothers. Name the brother, the group, and the song.

40. Name one '60s/'70s member of "27 Club" besides Janis Joplin or Jimi Hendrix.

41. Dr. Nichopoulos' license to practice medicine was suspended after Elvis died, but permanently revoked when it was learned that he had also dispensed drugs to what other rocker?

42. What was Cat Stevens' last Top 40 hit before he changed his name to Yusuf Islam?
    a. "Oh Very Young"
    b. "Ready"
    c. "Another Saturday Night"
    d. "Remember the Days of the Old Schoolyard"

43. What drummer played for King Crimson and Yes… *and* Genesis?

44. What 70s pop star played drums on the Shirelles' "Will You Still Love Me Tomorrow"?
    a. Carole King
    b. Kenny Loggins
    c. Henry Wayne Casey (KC/Sunshine Band)
    d. Barry White
    e. Billy Joel

45. Which of the following U.S. #1s didn't even hit the Top 40 on the U.K. charts?
    a. Ohio Players/"Love Rollercoaster"
    b. 4 Seasons/"Rag Doll"
    c. Edgar Winter Group/"Frankenstein"
    d. Mac Davis/"Baby, Don't Get Hooked..."

46. Who was Burt Bacharach's writing partner?

47. Who tipped Berry Gordy off to the Jackson 5?
    a. Diana Ross
    b. Bobby Taylor (of the Vancouvers)
    c. Gladys Knight
    d. Levi Stubbs (Four Tops)

48. What group's biggest hits were penned by the likes of Randy Newman, Nilsson, Leo Sayer, and Hoyt Axton?

49. The original versions of "Come Monday", "Lola", and "Me & Julio Down by the Schoolyard" were banned by the BBC for what reasons?
    a. Use of the word "crap"
    b. Use of a current legal case over a guitar riff that Chuck Berry claimed he had ownership of
    c. They referred to "branded" products
    d. Because the artists of those tunes had supported John Lennon's efforts to become an American citizen

50. What band was named after the British unemployment-benefit card?

51. Who played mellotron/piano on Bowie's "Space Oddity", "Life on Mars" and "Changes", piano on Cat's "Morning Has Broken", and keys on *Sabbath Bloody Sabbath*?
    a. Mick Ronson
    b. Rick Wakeman
    c. Chris Stainton
    d. Jim Dickinson

52. What pop singers sang background vocals on Pink Floyd's *The Wall*?
    a. Kiki Dee and Elton John
    b. Mike Love and Donna Summer
    c. Toni Tennille and Bruce Johnston
    d. Melissa Manchester and Peter Cetera

53. CBGB is the famous NYC club where the Ramones, Patti Smith, and Talking Heads sprang from, but what do the letters "CBGB" stand for? Bonus money for cracking the code of "UMFUG".

54. Peter Frampton played on George Harrison's *All Things Must Pass*. True or False?

55. What was the nickname for the rhythm section at Muscle Shoals Sound Studios? Extra points if you can come up with the first hit they had...

56. Which famous guitar slinger graced the grooves of Stevie Wonder's *Talking Book* album?

57. Dion's follow-up to "Abraham, Martin, and John"?
    a. "Johnny B. Goode"
    b. "Both Sides Now"
    c. "Clean Up Your Own Back Yard"
    d. "Purple Haze

58. Around '68, Jackson Browne was working with the band "Soft White Underbelly" to be his backup band. Who did this group eventually become?

59. Connect the singers with their early bands

a. Rod Stewart	1. Bluesology
b. Elton John	2. Chicken Shack
c. Christine McVie	3. Stealers Wheel
d. Gerry Rafferty	4. Steampacket

60. In the song "More Than a Feeling," who does Boston see "walking away"?

61. What British group are the following veterans of? Are you ready? Ginger Baker, Long John Baldry, Eric Burdon, Robert Plant, Charlie Watts, Graham Bond, Jack Bruce, John Mayall, Jimmy Page, and Keith Richards.

62. The line, "She got down but she never got tight, but she'll make it alright" is from what song?

63. "Beside You", "Slim Slow Slider", and "Sweet Thing" can be found on what album?
    a. Doors' *Strange Days*
    b. Van Morrison's *Astral Weeks*
    c. Carly Simon's *Boys in the Trees*
    d. Jethro Tull's *Songs from the Woods*

64. When Mitch Ryder and the Detroit Wheels broke up, what group did Mitch form as a successor?
    a. Detroit Lyons
    b. Long Ryders
    c. Detroit
    d. Rock City

65. What's the commonality between T. Rex, Attila (featuring Billy Joel), and Lee Michaels?

66. What pianist(s) had the most Top Ten hits?

67. This guitarist did session work for Clarence Carter, King Curtis, Aretha Franklin, Wilson Pickett, Percy Sledge, and jazz flautist Herbie Mann before breaking into the big time as a member of an infamous jam band. Who is he?

68. Carly Simon's dad, Richard, is best known as:
    a. An Illinois senator
    b. A car polish manufacturer
    c. A book publisher
    d. A professional golfer

69. *"I was born in Pennsylvania in '48. First group was a bar band called Woody's Truck Stop. You might remember me as a member of a group I formed in Philly in '67 named after a Yardbirds song. After a few years of limited success, I left the group to go solo and had a Top 5 hit in '73 with a remake of a song first released by my former group. During the 70s, 80s, and 90s, I was a producer/engineer, and provided vocal/instrumental tracks for many famous artists."* Who am I?

70. Who did "Mama Told Me Not to Come" first?
    a. Three Dog Night
    b. Eric Burdon and the Animals
    c. Lou Rawls
    d. Stefan Gwildis

71. In what movie did Paul Simon appear as music industry weasel Tony Lacey?

72. They spelled their name as a nod to the Beatles... their leader was an oboist on Sinatra sessions... and Frank Zappa helped them land a record contract. Who are they?

73. Of the following bands who are generally considered to be "Eighties" acts, which one was actually created in the Seventies?
    a. Depeche Mode
    b. Frankie Goes to Hollywood
    c. The Cure
    d. Pet Shop Boys

74. Eric Clapton was in how many '60s bands with Stevie Winwood, One, two, or three?

75. This song's roots began with Lennon writing a tune for Timothy Leary's gubernatorial campaign in California against Reagan, one which promptly ended when Leary was sent to prison for possession of marijuana. Was it...
    a. "All You Need is Love"
    b. "Come Together"
    c. "Power to the People"
    d. "Instant Karma"

76. The LP cover's background is brown and illustrated is an over-flowing chest bounded by playthings. What is it?

77. Match the famous manager with their famous clients:

a. Albert Grossman	1. Sabbath, ELO, Small Faces
b. Don Arden	2. Zep, Bad Co., Yardbirds
c. Peter Grant	3. Dylan, Janis, Todd Rundgren

78. What '68 hit started out as an ode to a First Lady but ended up as an ode a seductive "cougar"?

79. Who sang the female part in "Gimme Shelter"? C'mon, sista – it's just a shot away.

80. What famous Rock and Soul-oriented record producer worked on the Manhattan Project contributing to the atomic bomb?

81. The first ELO song with no string section?
    a. "Don't Bring Me Down"
    b. "Telephone Line"
    c. "Ma-Ma-Ma Belle"
    d. "Showdown"

82. "He played it left hand… Jiving us we were voodoo" is a line from…
    a. Hendrix' "Voodoo Chile"
    b. Bowie's "Ziggy Stardust"
    c. "Metal Guru" by T. Rex
    d. "Telegram Sam" by T. Rex

83. They headlined the first Glastonbury Festival, opened for Wings, spawned a tune that became one of Elvis Costello's best, and appeared in *Stardust* with David Essex. They are:
   a. Sutherland Brothers and Quiver
   b. Rockpile
   c. Stealers Wheel
   d. Brinsley Schwarz

84. Henry Mancini did themes for all of the following TV shows except one. Which? *What's Happening, Ironside, Peter Gunn, Newhart, Late Night with David Letterman.*

85. Name one act that Stevie Winwood's brother, Muff, produced. Just one, that's all, I promise...

86. Complete these stanzas in Country Joe & the Fish's infamous "Feel Like I'm Fixin' to Die Rag"...
   a. ...put down your books and pick up a ___
   b. ...you know that peace can only be won when ____ _____ __ ___ __ ______ ____
   c. ...be the first one on your block to have ____ ___ _____ _____ __ _ ___

87. Who was the only group to have a legitimate hit with a cover of a Buffalo Springfield tune?
   a. The Rose Garden
   b. The Mojo Men
   c. Harpers Bizarre
   d. Prelude

88. We're going into urban mythdom, so hold on to your hiney. Here's a coupla legends for you to figure out...
    a. Who *supposedly* ate their own poop on stage?
    b. Who *supposedly* had a rib removed so they could, uh, you know...?
    c. Who *supposedly* had a cow's tongue grafted onto their own?
    d. Who *supposedly* did Angie Bowie catch David in bed with?

89. The first Belgian record to reach the top of the U.S. charts was what? *Record,* not waffle...

90. And, moving inches across Europe… The first French artist to top of the U.S. charts was who?

91. When Carlos Santana adopted a friend's "spiritual leader", who was the friend and what was the name of the spiritual leader? And, if you want some brownie points, what name was Carlos given by this certain spiritual leader?

92. What late '70s singer-songwriter had a cameo playing a wannabe folk singer whose guitar John Belushi smashes in the movie *Animal House*?
    a. Dan Fogelberg
    b. Warren Zevon
    c. Stephen Bishop
    d. Jennifer Warnes

93. Robert Thomas Velline is better known as whom?

94. Sam Phillips sold Sun Records to whom?
    a. Elvis Presley's estate
    b. RCA
    c. Shelby Singleton
    d. MCA

95. "Jubilation, she loves me again, I fall on the floor and I'm laughing", is written about which girl?
    a. Amie
    b. Cecilia
    c. Mary Lou
    d. Rosalita

96. Who are the two R&B solo stars that came out of the Impressions?

97. Randy Bachman's stop between the Guess Who and BTO was in what group?
    a. Zephyr
    b. Mashmakhan
    c. Brave Belt
    d. Sons of Champlin

98. Who produced Joni Mitchell's first album?
    a. David Crosby
    b. Steve Stills
    c. Graham Nash
    d. Bob Johnston

99. What seminal alternative band's drummer played standing up?

100. Which one(s) of these songs are not instrumentals?
    a. K-Jee
    b. Keem-O-Sabe
    c. Kaw-Liga
    d. Day-O

101. The lyrics of this classic album's title cut feature a disgraceful tramp, wandering the streets and ogling little girls with an appalling goal. What's the album?

102. Look at this passage: "Ten year old girl on a street corner help me build a mountain from a little pile of clay. This really blew my mind." That passage is built from three chart records from the mid-'60s to mid-'70s. Break it down into segments and see if you can come up with those three songs.

103. On his 1969 appearance on the *Tonight Show,* Jimi Hendrix...
    a. Appeared with new bass player Billy Cox
    b. Session drummer Ed Shaughnessy sat in for Mitch Mitchell
    c. Lost sound from his amp, unplugged, and walked off-stage
    d. Was joined by Pete Townshend
    e. A & B
    f. B & D

104. Which '70s metal act crossed over to the dark side of Disco to score a hit?

105. This group's lineage has ex-pats from the Tubes, the Babys, Jefferson Starship, and others… features a guitarist who was offered a slot in Derek & the Dominos… started out as a mostly vocal-less jazz-fusion band… even did commercials for Budweiser. Who are they?

106. Which folkie released an album first?
   a. Bob Dylan
   b. Joan Baez
   c. Buffy Sainte-Marie
   d. Tom Rush
   e. John Prine

107. What's the next line in this ABBA song? "You were humming to yourself and softly strumming your guitar..."
   a. For liberty, Fernando
   b. I could hear the distant drums
   c. They were shining there for you and me
   d. The stars were bright, Fernando

108. The Rock era would be nothing without its three deuces, a four-speed, and a 389. A three-parter about "car" songs before we set your nostril hairs on fire and drive you to Milwaukee...
   a. Why do many people think of Jan & Dean's "Dead Man's Curve" as prophetic?
   b. Fill in the blank: "Nothing can catch her, nothing can stop my ___________"
   c. In what song was the singer listening to Brenda Lee on his car radio?

109. Pete Townshend did a duet album with which Small Faces alum?
   a. Rod Stewart
   b. Ronnie Lane
   c. Steve Marriott
   d. Kenny Jones

110. Brian Wilson sang half of the lead on "Barbara Ann". What *non*-Beach Boy sang the other half?
   a. Dean Torrence
   b. Jan Berry
   c. Dino Martin
   d. Ted Templeman

111. Connie Hamzy performed with probably more artists than anyone short of Hal Blaine. What did she play?

112. Carlos Santana's recording debut was on...
   a. The first Santana album
   b. Harvey Mandel's *Cristo Redentor*
   c. *Live Adventures of Bloomfield and Kooper*
   d. Johnny Winter's *Second Winter*

113. Which "Lewis" had more Top 10 hits? Jerry Lee, Barbara, Bobby, Gary, or Ramsey?

114. The oldest artist to hit #1 on the charts was...
   a. Cher
   b. George Burns
   c. Willie Nelson
   d. Louis Armstrong

115. What held up the completion of the Allman Brothers' *Eat a Peach*?

116. Given that "Midnight Train to Georgia" was Gladys Knight & the Pips biggest single, what song would be next in the chart achievement line?
   a. "I Heard it Through the Grapevine"
   b. "Best Thing That Ever Happened to Me"
   c. "Neither One of Us"

117. Below are the first four Beatles singles to chart on (U.S.) Billboard. Put them in order.
   a. "From Me To You"
   b. "I Want To Hold Your Hand"
   c. "She Loves You"
   d. "Please, Please Me"

118. What was the name of the label (hint: it references a term for the un-nameable name of God) that Bill Cosby co-owned, issued his own "Little Ol' Man (Uptight)" single, the first two Deep Purple albums, et al?

119. 30,000 copies of what Seventies album were seized by Newark police when the records arrived at the airport? And do you know the reason they were seized?

120. What group had its origins in bands such as the Abdabs, the Screaming Abdabs, the Architectural Abdabs, Sigma 6, Leonard's Lodgers, Megadeaths, and the Tea Set?

121. Who sings lead on the Monkees "I'm a Believer"?
  a. Mickey
  b. Davey
  c. Michael
  d. Peter

122. What was the first commercial rock-and-roll recording to include a string orchestra?
  a. Etta James/"At Last"
  b. The Drifters/"There Goes My Baby"
  c. Bobby Darin/"Dream Lover"
  d. James Brown/"It's a Man's Man's Man's World"

123. I'll give you the roster and you give me the label, okey dokey?
  a. DeFranco Family, Barry White: __________
  b. Jaggerz, Sopwith Camel: __________
  c Jan & Dean, the Chipmunks: __________
  d. Partridge Family, Dawn: __________
  e. Al Green, Ann Peebles: __________
  f. Geo. McCrae, KC & Sunshine Band: ______
  g. Bill Withers, Gallery: __________

124. It was... the first time Ron Wood contributed to a Stones song; Jagger sang it with Tina Turner at *Live Aid*; it was the first album after Jimmy Miller left the producer's role. Is it...
  a. "Beast of Burden"
  b. "It's Only Rock 'n Roll"
  c. "Sweet Little T&A"
  d. "Time Waits for No One"

125. What Ray Charles song has been proclaimed by a certain state's legislature as the official song of that state?

126. The composer credits read "Page/Plant/Jones/Bonham/Ian Stewart/Mrs. Valens". What is the song and why those credits?

127. Chas Chandler, the guy who turned Slade into a hit act (at least in the U.K.), was the same guy who turned who else into a rock sensation?
   a. The Who
   b. Jimi Hendrix
   c. Cream
   d. Elton John

128. Bismillah, Beelzebub, Scaramouch, and Galileo are characters in what song?
   a. Rush's "Lakeside Park"
   b. Meatloaf's "Paradise by the Dashboard Lights"
   c. Queen's "Bohemian Rhapsody"
   d. Pink Floyd's "Astronomy Domine"

129. Springsteen refers to "Route 9" and "Route 88" in what two songs?

130. The largest crowd to attend a rock concert was...
   a. Woodstock
   b. California Jam
   c. Texas Pop
   d. Summer Jam at Watkins Glen

131. Who's the group whose first hit was thought by many to be Neil Young, gave us the phrase "purple rain", and had great success with a Beatle fellow as their producer?

132. When Mick Taylor left the Stones, he headed where?
   a. Back to Mayall's Bluesbreakers
   b. Off to form a supergroup with Jack Bruce
   c. To Ten Years After replacing Alvin Lee
   d. Off to be a solo act

133. Who was the first Jamaican-born artist to score a number one single in the United States?
   a. Carl Douglas
   b. Jimmy Cliff
   c. Bob Marley
   d. Johnny Nash

134. Dusty Springfield had hits with three Bacharach-David songs. Which one of these wasn't theirs?
   a. "Wishin' and Hopin'"
   b. "I Just Don't Know What to Do with Myself"
   c. "You Don't Have to Say You Love Me"
   d. "The Look of Love"

135. Having spent eight years in jail, they sent Dylan a copy of their autobiography. Dylan visited them in prison, and convinced of their innocence, wrote a song about them. Who is it?
   a. Squeaky Fromme
   b. Charles Manson
   c. Jim Gordon
   d. Hurricane Carter

136. Ok, so let's pretend Jim Gordon *was* the person Dylan visited in jail/prison. Who is Jim?
   a. Derek & the Dominos drummer famous for writing the coda to "Layla"
   b. Drummer on the Incredible Bongo Band's *Bongo Rock* album
   c. Drummer on much of Steely Dan's *Pretzel Logic* LP
   d. Drummer in Frank Zappa's 20-piece "Grand Wazoo" big band tour

137. Some of this artist's bigger hits were remakes of Sir Mack Rice, Chris Kenner, and Dyke & the Blazers hits. Who dat?

138. Which Yardbird went on to fame as a producer for Cat Stevens, Carly – and Paul – Simon?
   a. Jimmy Page
   b. Paul Samwell-Smith
   c. Jim McCarty
   d. Chris Dreja

139. Which member of the band appears in drag on the cover of *English Rose* by Fleetwood Mac?

140. What is the <u>name</u> of the song about "the world's largest shovel", what is the <u>location</u> in the song, who is the <u>singer</u>, where is he <u>from</u>, and what did he do <u>before</u> he became a singer?

141. What do the T-Bones, Brass Ring, Carly Simon, Sonny & Cher, and the Bob Crewe Generation have in common?

142. What's big and purple and lives in the ocean?

143. Which of the following *weren't* on Apple Records?
   a. Lon & Derek Von Eaton
   b. James Taylor
   c. Splinter
   d. Hot Chocolate
   e. John Tavener
   f. Doris Troy

144. The first *female* to join Bruce Springsteen's E-Street Band was…?
   a. Patti Scialfa
   b. Cindy Bullens
   c. Soozie Tyrell
   d. Suki Lahav

145. Deep Purple's first two U.S. hits were covers of...
   a. Neil Diamond and the Box Tops
   b. Billy Joe Royal and the Dave Clark Five
   c. Neil Diamond and Billy Joe Royal
   d. Box Tops and Crow

146. The trio Emerson, Lake and Palmer were former members of which three bands?
   a. Atomic Rooster, the Nice, Yes
   b. The Nice, King Crimson, Toe Fat
   c. King Crimson, Atomic Rooster, the Nice
   d. Toe Fat, Yes, King Crimson

147. What was the longest title of a song to reach #1 on the *Billboard* Hot 100 in the '70s?

148. What song had <u>two</u> versions on the *Saturday Night Fever* soundtrack?
   a. "More Than a Woman"
   b. "If I Can't Have You"
   c. "You Should Be Dancin'"
   d. "Jive Talkin'"

149. "I Wanna Be Your Man" was recorded by both the Rolling Stones *and* the Beatles. Which version was released first?

150. Without looking, take a stab at what #1, 2, and 3 are on *Rolling Stone*'s list of the "500 Greatest Songs of All Time". Can you get at least one right?

151. At the end of this song, the title is repeated 23 times, each being a different note and spanning four octaves. The song is:
   a. "Good Vibrations"
   b. "Fame" (Bowie, not Irene Cara)
   c. "Ain't No Sunshine"
   d. "Under Pressure"

152. What <u>scene</u> can you pull out of this abstract? Members of the Traveling Wilburys and the Butterfield Blues Band, Newport, the producer of Lynyrd Skynyrd, and a member of failed supergroup, KGB. Think "group" *and* "event".

153. Each of these—McCartney & Wings, Lionel Richie, and Petula Clark – had different hit songs but with the same title. What it that title?

154. The theme song for *That 70s Show* is called "In the Street." It was originally released around '72, but the TV version is performed by *another* '70s band. Name both.
    a. Big Star and Cheap Trick
    b. Cheap Trick and the Romantics
    c. The Stories and Dwight Twilley Band
    d. The Plimsouls and Oingo Boingo

155. What's the connection between "Born to Run" and "Paradise by the Dashboard Light"?

156. Married to Kristofferson, sang with Cocker, and a hit with a Boz tune. Who is she?

157. Who had the most Top 20 hits? Bobby Rydell, Bobby Vinton, or Bobby Darin?

158. (Purportedly,) Crosby, Stills and Nash asked which of these musicians to join their band? Can be one, all, or none.
    a. Eric Clapton
    b. Steve Winwood
    c. Neil Young
    d. George Harrison

159. Springsteen *originally* wrote "Hungry Heart" for whom?
    a. Flo & Eddie (the Turtles)
    b. The Ramones
    c. The Pointer Sisters (follow-up to "Fire")
    d. The Bangles

160. Who was the first member to leave the Supremes?

161. They popularized remakes of Dale Hawkins, Screamin' Jay Hawkins, Leadbelly, and Little Richard songs for the rock crowd. They are...?
    a. Ricky Nelson
    b. Nitty Gritty Dirt Band
    c. Creedence Clearwater Revival
    d. Del Shannon

162. Their biggest hit was credited to "Ann Orson and Carte Blanche". Who were they?
    a. Sonny & Cher
    b. Donny Hathaway & Roberta Flack
    c. Kiki Dee & Elton John
    d. Marvin Gaye & Tammi Terrell

163. Berry Gordy, the founder of Motown Records, got his start by writing songs for...
    a. Jackie Wilson
    b. Little Richard
    c. Chuck Berry
    d. Sam Cooke

164. What Classic Rock song staple is built around a guy who visits Martin Guitars' hometown of and is talked into checking up on a gal pal's friends?

165. The Rolling Stones got their name from a song by:
    a. Blind Melon Jefferson
    b. Muddy Waters
    c. Little Walter
    d. Long John Baldry

166. What show is notable for Pete Seeger's first network TV appearance since being blacklisted in the '50s, for broadcasting "music videos" for "Hey Jude" and "Revolution", and where an explosion at the end of the Who's set caused Townshend to temporarily lose his hearing ?

167. It's widely believed that five folks bought out the original investor for the Monterey Pop Festival and took over the production of the event. Which of the following were those five?
   a. Terry Melcher
   b. Murray Wilson
   c. Brian Wilson
   d. John Phillips
   e. Johnny Rivers
   f. Paul Simon
   g. Lou Adler
   h. Dick Cavett
   i. Herb Alpert

168. Staying in the 'hood, what member of the Stones introduced Hendrix at Monterey Pop?

169. "I would climb any mountain, sail across a stormy sea, if that's what it takes me, baby, to show you how much you mean to me," are lyrics to which Foreigner song?
   a. "Feels Like the First Time"
   b. "Hot Blooded"
   c. "I Want to Know What Love Is"
   d. "Dirty White Boy "

170. The LP *Vincebus Eruptum* produced what hit about the trials and troubles of teenage life in America?

171. Who did David Bowie help with her (U.K.) hit cover of "The Man Who Sold the World"?

172. On their album *Pretzel Logic*, Steely Dan does a note-for-note recreation of Duke Ellington's "East Saint Louis Toodle-Oo" and a pretty good rip off of...
    a. Charlie Parker's "Parker's Band" (heard on the chorus)
    b. Hank Williams Jr.'s "With A Gun" (chorus)
    c. King Curtis' "Knight by Night" (in the bridge)
    d. Horace Silver's "Song for My Father" (copped in the song's intro)

173. Who are Stanley Mouse, Roger Dean, Robert Crumb, Rick Griffin, and Guy Peellaert?

174. "Crazy Janey" was a character in which Springsteen song?
    a. "Incident on 57th Street"
    b. "Spirit in the Night"
    c. "Blinded by the Light"
    d. "10th Avenue Freeze-Out"

175. Where was the "total eclipse of the sun" and what racetrack did the conceited subject flit off to in Carly Simon's "You're So Vain"?

176. Bobby Fuller Four's "I Fought the Law", the theme to the *Mary Tyler Moore Show,* and Leo Sayer's hit "More Than I Can Say" were written by...
   a. Sonny Curtis
   b. Buddy Holly
   c. Norman Petty
   d. Johnny Burnette

177. What's the most direct connection between Poco and the Eagles?
   a. They both recorded Willie Nelson songs
   b. Both of their original lineups featured ex-members of Buffalo Springfield
   c. Eagles got both of their bassists from Poco
   d. Members of both co-produced the first Dan Fogelberg album

178. From the following lyrics name the song title, the artist, and the year. "I was talking to an Eskimo. He said he was hoping for a fall of snow when up popped a sea lion ready to go"?

179. What child star's picture appeared on the cover of the *Sgt. Pepper* album?
   a. Robert Blake
   b. Jerry Mathers
   c. Angela Cartwright
   d. Shirley Temple

180. Chuck Berry changed the lyric "colored boy" to "country boy" to get what song played?

181. Ry Cooder, Frank Zappa, Jack Nicholson, Leon Russell, and Neil Young all collaborated on:
   a. The Monkees' *Head* film
   b. The Rolling Stones *Gimme Shelter* movie
   c. Mothers of Invention's *Absolutely Free*
   d. The first Sopwith Camel album, *Hello Hello*

182. What's the common ground between all these names: Rick Danko, Bootsy Collins, Paul McCartney, Jack Bruce, and Brian Wilson?
   a. They were part of his backup band when Dylan was inducted into the Rock & Roll Hall of Fame
   b. They all played at *The Last Waltz* (albeit in different configurations)
   c. They've all been to rehab
   d. They all play Bass

183. What soul legend wrecked his Corvette the first time he drove it?
   a. James Brown
   b. Wilson Pickett
   c. Ray Charles
   d. Chuck Berry

184. "B.B." in B.B. King's nickname stands for what? Super, fat, extra bonus points if you can come up with how his guitar became to be called "Lucille"!
   a. Beale Street Blues Boy
   b. Blue Baby
   c. Baby Blues
   d. Boogie Boy

185. Another test for you lyric sleuths. What song describes a conversation between "Hattie" and "Matty" concerning the American bison and the allure of developing dance skills?

186. Harmonicats!
    a. What group did Magic Dick blow for?
    b. Who (usually) played harp for the Beatles?
    c. Who did Lee Oskar play harmonica with?
    d. Who played harmonica on Billy Joel's "Piano Man"?
    e. What Motown star's first hit included a harmonica break?

187. What group had the *original* hit version of "Shakin' All Over"?
    a. The Who
    b. The Guess Who
    c. Johnny Kidd and the Pirates
    d. The Tornados

188. In the various lineups of the Byrds, there were two members who shared the <u>same last name</u>. What is it? Battin, Clark, Clarke, Crosby, Hillman, McGuinn, Parsons, or White?

189. Who are the two artists to have a US #1 single with both a <u>vocal</u> tune *and* an <u>instrumental</u>?

190. What Doors song does Ray Davies of the Kinks claim is a rip-off of his "All Day and All of the Night"?

191. Jon Landau, the music critic who proclaimed, "I saw rock and roll's future and its name is Bruce Springsteen" and who wound up as Bruce's manager and sometimes co-producer, had *pre*-Bruce producer credits with which of the following? (BTW, it can be more than one...)

    a. Jackson Browne
    b. MC5
    c. J. Geils Band
    d. Holy Modal Rounders

192. Which of these songs were altered due to censorship?

    a. Van Morrison's "Brown Eyed Girl"
    b. Jethro Tull's "Locomotive Breath"
    c. The Kingston Trio's "Greenback Dollar"
    d. All of the above

193. Which of these artists is the oldest?

    a. Eric Clapton
    b. Bonnie Raitt
    c. Jimmy Buffett
    d. Boz Scaggs

194. What was the first album that Joe Walsh produced independent* of his association with the artist?

    * We put that in there 'coz some say he helped produce James Gang's *Thirds*.

195. Who's the cat that played pedal steel on Brewer & Shipley's, "One Toke Over the Line"?

196. The songs "Blue Jay Way", "Celluloid Heroes", "Heart of Gold" and "MacArthur Park" are all about:
   a. Los Angeles
   b. Movie star lust
   c. Depression
   d. Driving

197. Who were the "lefties" in the Beatles?
   a. Ringo and George
   b. Paul and Ringo
   c. John and George
   d. Paul and John

198. What TV show banned the Doors after Morrison failed to honor his commitment to alter the "Girl, we couldn't get much higher" lyrics in their performance of "Light My Fire"?
   a. *Mike Douglas*
   b. *The Tonight Show with Johnny Carson*
   c. *Ed Sullivan Show*
   d. *Hullabaloo*

199. After Clapton quit the Yardbirds, he wound up in what other band?
   a. Alexis Korner's Blues Band
   b. John Mayall's Bluesbreakers
   c. Cream
   d. Delaney and Bonnie and Friends

200. Arthur Conley references <u>five</u> artists in "Sweet Soul Music". How many can you name?

201. M.U.S.E. (Musicians United for Safe Energy) was formed by:
    a. Jackson Browne
    b. John Hall
    c. Graham Nash
    d. All of the above

202. The line-up for "Beck's Bolero" was Beck and Jimmy Page on guitar, John Paul Jones on bass, Nicky Hopkins on piano, and who on drums?
    a. John Bonham
    b. Keith Moon
    c. Cozy Powell
    d. Cozy Cole
    e. Mick Fleetwood

203. Over the course of pop music, there've been some odd instruments that played a big role in classic records. Which of the following oddball instruments/song combinations is/are incorrect?
    a. An ocarina and "Wild Thing" by the Troggs
    b. A theremin and Beach Boys' "Good Vibrations"
    c. An autoharp on Steely Dan's "My Old School"
    d. A mellotron on "Strawberry Fields" by the Beatles

204. This cover features the band standing on a pile of rubble and, in the background, a city collapsing in a cloud of smoke. What's the LP?

205. There's a certain song the Stones recorded two versions of – one that's, shall we say, *familiar*, and one that's down-right *country* and both appeared on different albums that came out the same year. What's the song? Bonus points for which was done first and what was on the flip of the hit version! Heck, I'll buy you a pony if you get the year, too.

206. *Songs of Love & Hate* and *Songs from a Blue Room* are albums from what artist?
   a. Elton John
   b. Leonard Cohen
   c. Tim Buckley
   d. Tim Hardin

207. Which famous rock star was in these groups before he hit the big time: Arnold Corns, Riot Squad, the Manish Boys and the Lower Third?
   a. Elvis Costello
   b. David Bowie
   c. Peter Gabriel
   d. Billy Joel

208. Some of these Bluesmen play guitar and some don't… You tell me which.
   a. Charlie Musselwhite – Guitar or no?
   b. Little Walter – Guitar or no?
   c. Junior Wells – Guitar or no?
   d. Buddy Guy – Guitar or no?
   e. Paul Butterfield – Guitar or no?
   f. Pinetop Perkins – Guitar or no?

209. All of the following are Grateful Dead spin-offs except which one?
   a. Ratdog
   b. The Other Ones
   c. Kingfish
   d. Skyline Quartet

210. What was the song George Harrison was accused of plagiarizing for "My Sweet Lord"?
   a. "Da Doo Ron Ron"
   b. "Sweet Talkin' Guy"
   c. "He's So Fine"
   d. "Soldier Boy"

211. In the song "Fire and Rain," James Taylor told that his woman had left when?

212. Which of these is named after a constellation?
   a. "Southern Cross" by CSN
   b. "Moondance" by Van Morrison
   c. "Midnight Special" by CCR
   d. "Song to Orion" by Kansas

213. What artist had an identical twin brother who died at birth?
   a. John Lennon
   b. Elvis Presley
   c. Bono
   d. Eric Clapton

214. Which classic album features a woman sitting in window with a grey tabby cat in front of her?

215. Put together the song and the brand/commercial it was used for...

a. I'm Free	1. Jeep
b. Rock Me Gently	2. Chase Bank
c. I Just Want to Celebrate	3. Royal Caribbean
d. Lust for Life	4. AT&T

Bonus: Name a product Richie Havens sang about.

216. These places — Baton Rouge, New Orleans, Kentucky, California, Salinas — were listed in which famous song?
   a. "Please Come to Boston"
   b. "Me and Bobby McGee"
   c. "Sweet Little Sixteen"
   d. "Truckin'"

217. What's the connection between all of the following? Ziggy Stardust... the shortest Monkee... Keith Partridge... we know him as "the Edge"... Van Halen's original singer... Annie Lennox's musical partner... song that begins "Born on a mountain top in Tennessee"... Ray's brother and fellow Kink...
   a. They're all British
   b. They're all no longer associated with those musical groups
   c. They're all "Davids"
   d. They're all members of the Rock and Roll Hall of Fame

218. Who's sold more records, worldwide – Kenny G, Eddy Arnold, Dave Clark Five, or the Drifters?

219. What famous Bluesman wrote "Little Red Rooster" that the Stones recorded, "Back Door Man" that the Doors did, and "Bring It on Home" recorded by Led Zeppelin?
   a. Muddy Waters
   b. Robert Johnson
   c. Willie Dixon
   d. Blind Willie McTell

220. What band headlined the closing of Fillmore East in '71, playing until 7:00 a.m.?
   a. The Grateful Dead
   b. The Jefferson Airplane
   c. Santana
   d. Allman Brothers

221. Warren Zevon played piano and was band leader for these musical brothers shortly before their breakup...
   a. Hudson Brothers
   b. Everly Brothers
   c. Isley Brothers
   d. Blues Brothers

222. Who had a <u>hit</u> with a Jimmy Webb song first – 5th Dimension with "Up, Up, and Away" or Glen Campbell with "By the Time I Get to Phoenix"?

223. The uniqueness of Bo Diddley's guitar is that it's...
   a. Round
   b. Made out of glass
   c. Rectangular
   d. Double-sided

224. How were George Harrison and Mick Fleetwood related at one point?
    a. They were next door neighbors
    b. Mick was married to George's sister, Jeanie
    c. George's dad was Mick's stepfather
    d. Both married to the Boyd sisters, Pattie and Jenny

225. Which Jackson Browne album was created entirely during a tour, with songs recorded on stage, on the tour bus, and in hotel rooms?
    a. *The Road and The Sky*
    b. *The Pretender*
    c. *Running on Empty*
    d. *Highway Song*

226. In 1968, Keith Moon of the Who drove his Lincoln where in Flint Michigan?
    a. Thru the front window of a Chevy dealership
    b. Into the swimming pool of a Holiday Inn
    c. Into Lake Huron
    d. Through a drive-in at a Frisch's, naked

227. Put these Springsteen LPs in chronological order: *Born to Run, Tunnel of Love, Nebraska, The River...*
    a. *Born to Run, Tunnel of Love, The River, Nebraska*
    b. *The River, Born to Run, Tunnel of Love, Nebraska*
    c. *Born to Run, The River, Nebraska, Tunnel of Love*

228. Which of the following is *not* connected to Led Zep – member or the group as a whole – in one way or another?
   a. Donovan
   b. Uncle Earl
   c. Terry Reid
   d. Memphis Minnie
   e. None of the above
   f. All of the above

229. Child of a Broadway star, raised Quaker, went to Radcliffe majoring in African Studies... Is it:
   a. Gillian Welch
   b. Bonnie Raitt
   c. Karla Bonoff
   d. Emmylou Harris

230. This artist has appeared in the movies *Talladega Nights, Spiceworld, Austin Powers* and on TV in *Frasier* and *Third Rock from the Sun*. He is...?
   a. Elvis Costello
   b. Sting
   c. David Bowie
   d. Burt Bacharach
   e. Mick Jagger

231. In *Rolling Stone*'s list of the Greatest Guitarists of All-Time, who was the highest-ranked *woman* on the list?
   a. Bonnie Raitt
   b. Joni Mitchell
   c. Michelle N'degeocello
   d. Joan Jett

232. What rocker was film star Faye Dunaway (*Bonnie and Clyde, Chinatown, Towering Inferno*, etc.) married to from '74-'79? And while we're in the 'hood of Parker and Barrow, who had a Top 10 hit with "The Ballad of Bonnie and Clyde"?

233. Fats Domino first hit the Top 10 with "Ain't That a Shame" but someone else hit #1 with the tune the same year and broadened the audience by crossing racial lines. Who was that someone?

234. Obsession the topic, now... One artist seems obsessed with the name "Caledonia" – using it as the name of his first production company, the name of his studio, his publishing company, two of his backing groups, one of his songs about a "lion", and even going as far as recording a cover of the song, "Caldonia" (but spelled "Caledonia") in 1974. Who is this obsessed person?

235. The soul group Friends of Distinction's ("Grazing in the Grass", "Love or Let Me Be Lonely") career was guided – and funded – by what sports star?
   a. O.J. Simpson
   b. Kareem Abdul-Jabbar
   c. Jim Brown
   d. Willie Mays

236. What artist won a Clio for doing the musical score on a Luden's Cough Drops TV commercial?

237. Who was Isaac Hayes' writing partner at STAX?

238. Which of these songs did *not* featured a sitar?
   a. The Stones/"Paint it Black"
   b. Box Tops/"Cry Like a Baby"
   c. Lemon Pipers/"Green Tambourine"
   d. The Byrds/"Eight Miles High"
   e. John Fred and His Playboy Band/"Judy in Disguise"

239. Which of these albums *title* songs were the longest in length of time?
   a. Yes' *Close to the Edge*
   b. Iron Butterfly's *In-a-Gadda-da-Vida*
   c. Pink Floyd's *Atom Heart Mother*
   d. Rare Earth's *Get Ready*

240. In the deal between Columbia and Atlantic Records that enabled Graham Nash to get out of his contract with Epic and David Crosby from his deal with Columbia so they could record with Crosby, Stills & Nash, who were their rights "traded" to Atlantic for?
   a. Richie Furay and Jim Messina
   b. Dewey Palmer and Al Kooper
   c. Kenny Loggins and Modern Jazz Quartet
   d. The Rascals

241. The Byrds only album with Gram Parsons was...
   a. *(Untitled)*
   b. *Sweetheart of the Rodeo*
   c. *Dr. Byrds & Mr. Hyde*
   a. *Notorious Byrd Brothers*

242. Which set of the following Dylan songs were songs where the title was not in the lyrics?
   a. "Sad-Eyed Lady of the Lowlands", "Wigwam"
   b. "Positively 4th Street", "Rainy Day Women #12 & #35"
   c. "My Back Pages", "Copper Kettle"
   d. "Rainy Day Women #12 & #35", "With God on Our Side"

243. You were waiting for this... Who are the six artists mentioned in the song "Rock and Roll Heaven"?

244. What's the commonality between Bobby Bloom's "Montego Bay", Otis Redding's "Dock of the Bay" and Billy Joel's "The Stranger"?

245. Which Hendrix song do the Traveling Wilburys refer to in "End of the Line"?
   a. "Purple Haze"
   b. "Hey Joe"
   c. "All Along the Watchtower"
   d. "Red House"
   e. "Crosstown Traffic"

246. Staying with the Jimi thing and echoing back to our *Tonight Show* question... One of the great rumors is that when Johnny Carson asked Hendrix, "How's it feel to be the world's greatest guitarist," he replied "I don't know – you'll have to ask __________." Fill in the blank with the guitarist on the other end of this folklore.

247. What famous rocker did Chrissie Hynde of the Pretenders have a child with and without the "benefit of clergy"?
   a. Joe Walsh
   b. Elvis Costello
   c. Ray Davies
   d. Jeff Beck

248. What was the live bootleg of the Velvet Underground's final performance with Lou Reed?
   a. *Live and Loaded*
   b. *Live from Max' Kansas City*
   c. *VU/UV*
   d. *Night Light, Night Heat*

249. Performers can give their kids some pretty interesting names. Which one of these is true?
   a. Keith Richards has a daughter "Dandelion"
   b. Bono named his daughter "Memphis Eve"
   c. John Mellencamp named a son "Speck Wildhorse"
   d. Frank Zappa named a son "Blue Unit"

250. Nickname time... Gimme the real name for each of the following:
   a. Skydog __________
   b. No Show Jones __________
   c. Motor City Madman __________
   d. Bocephus __________
   e. Thin White Duke __________
   f. The Ice Man __________

251. Which one of these people is inter-connected to all of the following: Billie Holiday, Aretha Franklin, Bob Dylan, and Bruce Springsteen?
    a. Clive Davis
    b. Arif Mardin
    c. John Hammond, Sr.
    d. Ahmet Ertegun

252. Who played harp on the Doors' "Roadhouse Blues" under the pseudonym of G. Puglese?
    a. Rick Danko
    b. John Sebastian
    c. Bob Dylan
    d. Arthur Lee

253. "Doin' That Crazy Thing"/"Goin' Down To Rio" was the single released when what band leader first went (or tried to go) solo?
    a. Ozzy Osbourne (when he left Sabbath)
    b. Jeff Lynne (when he left ELO)
    c. George Clinton (after Parliament/ Funkadelic)
    d. Richard Carpenter (post-Carpenters)

254. The Yardbirds were actually a replacement for another band in the movie *Blow Up*. Was it…
    a. The Who
    b. Led Zeppelin
    c. The Troggs
    d. Jimi Hendrix Experience

255. A gimme... What musical nerve center is considered home to the following '70s music venues? Vulcan Gas Company, Victory Grill, Antone's, and the Armadillo World Headquarters?

256. The intro of what Motown classic did John Sebastian and the Lovin' Spoonful ape for their intro to "Do You Believe in Magic"?

257. What do José Feliciano, Doc Watson, Ronnie Milsap, and Clarence Carter have in common?

258. This gentleman - born Henry Saint Clair Fredericks - took his stage name from dreams about Gandhi, India, and social tolerance. Who is said gentleman?

259. There are many legendary Top 40 radio stations around the world but one 50,000 watt blowtorch in Chicago - WLS - impacted many a teen's life in the Rock era because of the vast geography they covered at night. What do the call letters "WLS" actually stand for?

260. There were several solo artists in the '50s, '60s, and '70s who used the moniker "Little" in front of their name. Name three of them.

261. Who was Stevie Wonder pointing the finger at in his 1974 tune from *Fulfillingness' First Finale,* "You Haven't Done Nothin'"?

262. What 70s classic tells the tale of a man who has committed theft and is headed to the gallows to die? Hint: the opening lines are a letter to his mother.

263. Early episodes of this U.S. TV show included segments taped in the UK hosted by Brian Epstein. Which was it?
    a. *Where the Action Is*
    b. *Hullabaloo*
    c. *Shindig*
    d. (primetime edition of) *American Bandstand*

264. This artist's first three American solo releases are sometimes referred to as "Car," "Melt," and "Scratch," based on the album covers.
    a. David Bowie
    b. Eno
    c. Kate Bush
    d. Peter Gabriel
    e. Robert Fripp

265. Which of these four '70s art-rock groups released a debut album that featured songs originally done by the Beatles and the Byrds?
    a. Yes
    b. King Crimson
    c. Sparks
    d. Roxy Music

266. Who is/was Elston Gunn?

267. Who played the tremolo intro on Aretha's "Chain of Fools"?
   a. Steve Cropper
   b. Joe South
   c. Teenie Hodges
   d. Ry Cooder

268. Which of these classic early '70s album tracks has never been commercially released as a single?
   a. "Stairway to Heaven"
   b. "Free Bird"
   c. "Won't Get Fooled Again"
   d. "Layla"

269. We'll do the whole country later, but for now, match the artists with their songs about New York City (and surrounding burbs)...

a. Bobby Womack	1. New York City Rhythm
b. Steely Dan	2. Brooklyn Roads
c. Village Stompers	3. Across 100th Street
d. Neil Diamond	4. Washington Square
e. Joni Mitchell	5. Brooklyn
f. 10cc	6. Chelsea Girls
g. Tradewinds	7. Wall Street Shuffle
h. Barry Manilow	8. NY's a Lonely Town
i. Simon & Garfunkel	9. Bleecker Street
j. Velvet Underground	10. Song for Sharon

270. On a 1977 Christmas special, David Bowie and sang a duet on "Peace on Earth"/"Little Drummer Boy" with what Forties crooner?

271. For those of you who hate Bluegrass, I'm sorry, but you must oblige me one round of torture...
   a. What's the only true Bluegrass record to be a Top 10 hit in the Rock era?
   b. What Bluegrass group was Jerry Garcia in?
   c. Roy Acuff described 'em as a "bunch of long-haired West Coast boys" that came to Nashville in '71 to do a double album with Bluegrass greats. Who are they?

272. Elvis' version of "Hound Dog" was based on an adaption by whom?
   a. Cliff Richard
   b. Freddie Bell and the Bellboys
   c. Carl Perkins
   d. Lonnie Donegan
   e. Eartha Kitt

273. Was Tommy Iommi, the guitarist for Black Sabbath, ever in Jethro Tull? Oui or no?

274. There was this really sorta cheesy record in the '70s by Hurricane Smith called "Oh, Babe, What Would You Say" (#3 on the singles charts). What was "Hurricane's" relationship to Pink Floyd?
   a. Roadie
   b. Accountant
   c. Produced some of their albums
   d. Roger Waters' gardener

275. What was the name of the group Billy Gibbons was in *before* Z.Z. Top?

276. What band recorded and released "Jesus is Just Alright" first?
    a. Doobie Brothers
    b. New Riders of the Purple Sage
    c. The Byrds
    d. Clover

277. They recorded for Capitol Records... originally had the modifier "Blues" in their band's name... were lucky enough to have Paul McCartney play bass on a track (as "Paul Ramon")... appeared on the TV show *Hullabaloo* with the Supremes and Four Tops... have albums called *Rock Love* and *Number 5*. They are known as whom?

278. Which Rush album featured a whole side based on a short story by author Ayn Rand?
    a. *2112*
    b. *Fly By Night*
    c. *Moving Pictures*
    d. *Caress of Steel*
    e. *A Farewell to Kings*

279. Two-parter… 1) Who invented the Gibson "Les Paul" and 2) who, so they say, was the first rockstar guitarist to use a "Les Paul" – Eric Clapton, Keith Richards, Peter Green, or Jeff Beck?

280. During his fertile '70s stretch, Bob Seger's songwriting helped *another* artist fare better on the charts than his own songwriting did for himself. Name the artist and song.

281. What's the similarity between these songs?
- Eric Carmen/"All By Myself"
- The Toys/"Lover's Concerto"
- Mindbenders/"Groovy Kind of Love"
- Paul Simon/"American Tune"

282. What famous record company building, with its curved awnings and the tall spike emerging from the top of the building gives it the appearance of a stack of vinyl 45s on a turntable?

283. Was Frank Sinatra's version of "It Was a Very Good Year" a song written specifically for him or just a retooled folk song?

284. Gregg Allman shot himself in the foot to avoid having to go in to the military. True or False?

285. The Allman Brothers song "In Memory of Elizabeth Reed" was inspired by...
   a. Boz Scaggs' girlfriend
   b. A coed Dickey Betts met while playing a Chi Omega party at 'Ole Miss
   c. A name on a tombstone in a graveyard where Dickey Betts used to write
   d. Duane Allman's recently-departed aunt
   e. Both A and C

286. She made an uncredited vocal contribution to the Beatles' title song of *Let It Be*. Who she be?

287. Billy Joel's inspiration for "She's Always a Woman" was:
   a. Audrey Hepburn
   b. Judy Collins
   c. Christie Brinkley
   d. Gordon Lightfoot

288. Which of these things relating to Steely Dan ain't necessarily true?
   a. Becker & Fagen wrote a song for Barbra Streisand
   b. Becker & Fagen were backing musicians for Sixties pop group, Jay & the Americans
   c. Chevy Chase used to play drums with Becker & Fagen at pick-up gigs during college
   d. All of these are True
   e. All of these are False

289. Who gave Rickie Lee Jones the line, "Chuck E.'s in Love"?
   a. Prince
   b. Don Henley
   c. Tom Waits
   d. Dr. John

290. Which two of the following died in the same flat, No.12 at 9 Curzon Place, Mayfair, England?
   a. Jimi Hendrix
   b. Keith Moon
   c. Harry Nilsson
   d. Mama Cass Elliott

291. The Byrds tune referred to in "American Pie" is...

292. Which of these early Temptations songs was the *poorest* chart performer?
   a. "My Girl "
   b. "Get Ready "
   c. "Beauty's Only Skin Deep"
   d. "Ain't Too Proud to Beg "
   e. "I Wish It Would Rain "

293. What Memphis soul man produced Bill Withers debut album called *Just as I Am*?

294. Pre-lighter fluid, Jimi Hendrix backed up many R&B groups on both the chitlin circuit and in nightclubs around the country. Let's see if you can name <u>any</u> of the acts he backed...

295. The Dusty Springfield song in *Casino Royale* where Ursula Andress seduced Peter Sellers...
   a. "The Look of Love"
   b. "A Brand New Me"
   c. "I Only Want to Be with You"
   d. "All I See is You"

296. Prior to a career as a producer, Phil Spector was in a group called...
   a. The Elgins
   b. Teddy Bears
   c. The Fleetwoods
   d. The Twilights

297. When Holland-Dozier-Holland left Motown to gain greater control over their production, they...
    a. Stopped writing/production for a year
    b. Left a cryptic message to Berry Gordy in the lyrics of "Forever Came Today"
    c. Set up labels Invictus and Hot Wax
    d. All of the above

298. The origin of the name "Grand Funk Railroad" is believed to be:
    a. Three names drawn from a hat
    b. After Canada's "Grand Trunk Western Railroad"
    c. An anagram of their sound guy, Dirk Argon Landau

299. True or False time from the mother country... Badfinger was:
    a. named after the original title of a Beatles song T/F
    b. previously called the Ivy League T/F
    c. produced by Todd Rundgren and Ray Davies T/F

300. Songwriter(s) who wrote "For Your Love" by the Yardbirds, the Hollies' "Bus Stop", and "Listen, People" by Herman's Hermits...
    a. Greenway and Cook
    b. Graham Gouldman
    c. Bacharach and David
    d. Mickie Most

301. Carol Kaye is the most recorded ___ of all time with 10,000 sessions spanning four decades.
   a. Guitarist
   b. Background vocalist
   c. Bassist
   d. Percussionist

302. "Love Will Keep Us Together", "Rhinestone Cowboy", "Philadelphia Freedom", and "Before the Next Teardrop Falls" were hits in what year?
   a. 1972
   b. 1973
   c. 1975
   d. 1978

303. *Metal Machine Music* was ...
   a. A compilation on Warner Bros featuring Deep Purple, Captain Beyond, Dio, ands
   b. The original moniker Lester Bangs gave to the "Heavy Metal" genre
   c. A musical conceived by Frank Zappa that closed after one performance on Broadway
   d. Lou Reed's LP of feedback loops

304. Andy Warhol designed which of these covers?
   a. Rolling Stones/*Sticky Fingers*
   b. Rolling Stones/*Love You Live*
   c. John Cale/*Honi Soit*
   d. Diana Ross/*Silk Electric*
   e. Both of the Stones ones
   f. All of 'em
   g. None of 'em

305. This co-leader's illness led to the emergency hiring of Michael McDonald. Are they...
   a. Walter Becker of Steely Dan
   b. Donald Fagen of Steely Dan
   c. The Doobie Brothers' Tom Johnston
   d. The Doobie Brothers' Patrick Simmons

306. The rhythm section of Boz Burrell (bass) and Simon Kirke (drums) were a part of what band?
   a. UFO
   b. Trapeze
   c. Bad Company
   d. Deep Purple

307. *Forever Changes* and *Da Capo* were albums by:
   a. Fever Tree
   b. The Charlatans
   c. Quicksilver Messenger Service
   d. Love

308. For its day, what made the Dave Clark 5 unique?
   a. The drummer was leader of the group
   b. They recorded for a classical label
   c. There was no guitarist

309. Which Spanky & Our Gang single became John Lindsay's campaign song during his successful run for Mayor of New York City?
   a. "Making Every Minute Count"
   b. "Give a Damn"
   c. "Sunday Will Never Be the Same"
   d. "Like to Get to Know You"

310. Part of the LP's concept was that its lyrics were penned by 8-year-old Gerald "Little Milton" Bostock. What's the album?

311. The "B-A-N-G" in "BANG Records" came from the first names of their founders, who were who?

312. Which of these "greatest hits" packages really wasn't a greatest hits set?
   a. *Under Wheels Of Confusion*
   b. *Shaved Fish*
   c. *Naked in the Shade*
   d. *Shaking the Tree*

313. Which of the following Moody Blues LPs does not have a song that matches the album's title?
   a. *On the Threshold of a Dream*
   b. *A Question of Balance*
   c. *To Our Children's Children's Children*
   d. None of these

314. What roles did the members of the Village People play? (choose <u>all</u> that <u>fit</u>)
   a. Fireman
   b. Indian
   c. Doctor
   d. Cowboy
   e. Policeman
   f. Biker
   g. Soldier
   h. Construction worker
   i. Hairdresser

315. Whodunit? The song in question is the story of an FBI agent who is scouting a nightclub prior to a raid. There he meets a tall, beautiful woman who he later protects in an ensuing shootout. Afterward, the District Attorney congratulates him on his fine work and the agent gets the girl, so to speak. What is the song?

316. Who's the Texas group that modified their name to benefit from the British Invasion and had a hit with "She's About a Mover"?

317. Let's do "Rhythm Sections" for $100, Alex! Tell me what instrument (bass or drums) each of the following rhythm section members played and what group did they play it in?

Player	Drums or Bass	Group
Geddy Lee		
Al Jackson		
Peter Cetera		
Tom Hamilton		
Artimus Pyle		
Stu Cook		

318. What classic does a few variations of "God Rest Ye Merry Gentlemen" somewhere in the song?
    a. "Frankenstein"
    b. "Smoke on the Water"
    c. "Hocus Pocus"
    d. "In-a-Gadda-Da-Vida"

319. In "Call It Stormy Monday" what day does the singer say the eagle flies?

320. What ace session guitarist replaced Brian Wilson on the Beach Boys' 1965 tour?

321. Pre-Eagles, Glenn Frey was with which of the following?
    a. Shiloh
    b. Longbranch Pennywhistle
    c. American Flyer
    d. The Dillards

322. Off all the lineups in the Yardbirds, none ever included...
    a. Jimmy Page
    b. Chris Dreja
    c. Peter Green
    d. Keith Relf

323. When Richie Blackmore left Deep Purple, it was to form his own band named what?

324. Connect the "Marys" with the people who recorded songs about them...

a. Mary, Queen of Arkansas	1. Bruce Springsteen
b. Mary Lou	2. Steve Miller Band
c. Marianne	3. Stephen Stills
d. Mary, Mary	4. Butterfield Blues Band

325. Which of the following is true about Mister Frank Vincent Zappa?
    a. He produced a pre-Little Feat group called the Factory
    b. He produced Alice Cooper's first two LPs
    c. He produced a GTOs album that included a track featuring Rod Stewart on vocals
    d. He produced a Grand Funk Railroad LP
    e. All of these

326. *Tommy* time! 1) What instrument other than bass did Entwistle play; 2) Who's the only non-Who member who contributed a song; 3) Who did Jack Nicholson play in the movie?

327. Steve Marriott quit the Small Faces because...?
    a. They refused to add Peter Frampton
    b. Ronnie Lane and Ron Wood wanted to add Rod Stewart as a vocalist
    c. The critics had railed against *Ogden's Nut Gone Flake*
    d. The Small Faces' producer Shel Talmy had brought in Jimmy Page to overdub one of his guitar parts

328. Let me set the scene: Memphis, Tennessee... December 4, 1956... Sun Record Studios. Got it? "Million Dollar Quartet" was the name given to a legendary unplanned session that happened that day. Name the four celebrated musicians who took part in that jam.

329. What's the only <u>animal</u> act to have a hit record?

330. Virgin Records' first artist was...
   a. Gong
   b. Faust
   c. Mike Oldfield
   d. Sally Oldfield
   e. Tangerine Dream

331. What's a significant little twist regarding the Gentrys' "Keep on Dancing"?

332. What song mentions these dances: the Pony, the Chicken, the Mashed Potato, the Alligator, the Watusi, the Twist, the Fly, the Jerk, the Tango, the Yo-Yo, the Sweet Pea, the Hand jive, the Slop, the Bop, the Fish, and the Popeye – some 16 in all?

333. What artist recorded an album with the Edmonton (Canada) Symphony Orchestra?
   a. Moody Blues
   b. Elton John
   c. Procol Harum
   d. Supertramp

334. Dylan refused to appear on *The Ed Sullivan Show* after being told he couldn't perform what song?
   a. "Subterranean Homesick Blues"
   b. "Talking John Birch Society Blues"
   c. "Like a Rolling Stone"
   d. "Just Like a Woman"

335. Alan Freed was given co-writing credit on what Chuck Berry song that led to the payola scandal?

336. I accompanied Phil Spector to – and played piano at – some of the early Stones sessions, and had a British Top Ten'er with a song Mick & Keith wrote... penned hits like "He's a Rebel" and "Rubber Ball"... used Indian instruments three years before the Beatles... was the first pop star to perform at the Oscars. Who am I?

337. Sam Cooke was shot and killed in a motel where?
   a. Las Vegas
   b. Reno
   c. Los Angeles
   d. Scottsdale

338. Jimmy Page's only pre-Zeppelin single was called:
   a. "Clam Bakin'"
   b. "She Just Satisfies"
   c. "She's Justified"
   d. "Pagey's Prowess"

339. There were two...
   a. Sonny Boy Williamsons
   b. Little Walters
   c. John Lee Hookers
   d. Junior Wells'

340. Bob Dylan's first wife was Sara Lownds, the subject of his song...
   a. "Just Like a Woman"
   b. "Love Minus Zero/No Limits"
   c. "I Want You"
   d. "Sad-Eyed Lady of the Lowlands"

341. The *New York Times* once referred to Jimi Hendrix as...
    a. Jesus meets Martin Luther King
    b. A black messiah
    c. The black Elvis
    d. A rock 'n rolling religious experience

342. John Lennon and Yoko Ono were married in...
    a. Miami Beach
    b. New York City
    c. Amsterdam
    d. Gibraltar

343. The hit-making precursor to 10cc was called what and spawned what single?
    a. Pipkins/"Gimme Dat Ding"
    b. Hotlegs/"Neanderthal Man"
    c. Whistling Jack Smith/"I Was Kaiser Bill's Batman"
    d. Giorgio/"Son of My Father"

344. Ok, mystery meat time, again... He co-wrote a song with Sonny Bono that became a hit for Jackie DeShannon, became an arranger and conductor for Phil Spector, did the keyboard textures for "Paint it Black" and "Let's Spend the Night Together" and the choral arrangement for "You Can't Always Get What You Want" for the Stones, co-produced Neil Young's first album, joined Crazy Horse for a year, married Buffy Sainte-Marie, worked on film scores like *The Exorcist* and *One Flew Over the Cuckoo's Nest*. Who is this chap?

345. The songwriter who wrote "Joy to the World" is the son of the...
    a. ...lady who wrote "Heartbreak Hotel"
    b. ...lady who co-owned STAX Records
    c. ...lady who was Col. Parker's secretary

346. Who was the backing band for Lennon's "Power to the People"?

347. What was the relationship between Grand Funk Railroad and Paul McCartney?

348. Ike & Tina Turner's last hit as a duo was...
    a. "Proud Mary"
    b. "River Deep, Mountain High"
    c. "Nutbush City Limits"
    d. "Lodi"

349. How did Bobby Darin die?
    a. A heart attack on-stage at the Sands
    b. Heart failure during open heart surgery
    c. Drug overdose
    d. Lung cancer

350. Is Jim Morrison's wife, Pam, dead or alive?

351. David Bowie's *David Live* was recorded where?
    a. Madison Square Garden
    b. The Forum in L.A.
    c. Tower Theatre in Philadelphia
    d. The Bottom Line

352. What of the following is Chips Moman *not* typically associated with?
   a. Nashville
   b. American Sound Studios
   c. Memphis
   d. Muscle Shoals
   e. Ardent Studios

353. The first solo LP by any of the Rolling Stones was:
   a. Keith Richards *Talk is Cheap*
   b. Mick Jagger's *She's the Boss*
   c. Bill Wyman's *Monkey Grip*
   d. Ron Wood's *Gimme Some Neck*

354. Zeppelin's first LP on Swan Song Records was...

355. Who created the program *Pop Clips* for Nickelodeon, then sold that concept to Time Warner/Amex, who then developed it into MTV?
   a. Bob Pittman
   b. James William Guercio
   c. William McEuen
   d. Michael Nesmith

356. Pink Floyd's follow-up to *Dark Side of the Moon* was called what?

357. Kraftwerk is German for...
   a. Automation
   b. Superhighway
   c. Power plant
   d. Manufacturer of household goods

358. Name the '73 hit about a man who learns from his friend Andy that his wife had cheated on him with both Andy and someone named Seth.

359. John Lennon celebrated his 35th birthday, by...
    a. Hosting *Saturday Night Live*
    b. Appearing as a guest on *SNL*
    c. Receiving the good news of the reversal of his deportation papers
    d. Witnessing the birth of his son, Sean

360. "Rock 'n Me" and "Take the Money and Run" are from Steve Miller Band album?

361. Which of these did Brian Epstein <u>not</u> manage?
    a. Gerry & the Pacemakers
    b. Billy J. Kramer and the Dakotas
    c. The Cyrkle
    d. Peter & Gordon

362. Because Jeff Beck had an accident and Rod Stewart joined the Faces, what group had to settle forming with a guitarist from the Detroit Wheels and the singer from the Amboy Dukes?

363. The Kinks' *Percy* was a soundtrack to a film about...
    a. Percy, Ray Davies' pet hamster
    b. Their transvestite manager
    c. A penis transplant
    d. Percy "Thrills" Thrillington

364. Which member of the Dead had a project called *Rolling Thunder*?

365. Queen named two of their albums after...
    a. The monarchy's bills of legislation
    b. Marx Brothers' movies
    c. Elvis lyrics
    d. French Revolution freedom cries

366. Missing from Elton John's first touring band was...
    a. A bassist
    b. A guitarist
    c. A drummer

367. The title of Neil Young's movie, *Rust Never Sleeps*, was inspired by what band?
    a. Boomtown Rats
    b. Oingo Boingo
    c. Devo

368. Which Chicago album was the first *single*-disc set? *I, II, III, IV, V, VI, VII, VIII, IX,* or *X*?

369. What's the relationship between Herb Alpert and Sam Cooke?

370. He portrayed Franklin Von Tussle in John Waters' *Hairspray*. Who is he?

371. Joe Cocker's hit, "You Are So Beautiful" was written by whom?

372. He wrote (or co-wrote) "Evergreen" (from *A Star is Born*), "Old Fashioned Love Song", "Rainy Days and Mondays", "We've Only Just Begun", "Rainbow Connection", "(The theme from) Love Boat", and played Little Eno in *Smokey and the Bandit* and Virgil, the brainiac orangutan in *Battle for the Planet of the Apes*. He is who?

373. What record eclipsed the 7:05 (single version of) "Hey Jude" as the longest single to reach Number One?

    a. "Roundabout"
    b. "Taxi"
    c. "Layla"
    d. "American Pie"

374. Mudcrutch, Tom Petty's first band to get a record deal, was originally signed to what artist's label?

    a. Leon Russell's Shelter Records
    b. Herb Alpert's A&M Records
    c. John Denver's Windsong Records
    d. Frank Sinatra's Reprise Records

375. What massive hit had its roots as a Cuban cha-cha tune, owes a debt to Chuck Berry's "Havana Moon", and was investigated for more than two years by the FBI?

376. What's the geographic connection between April Wine, Steppenwolf, Triumph, Five Man Electrical Band, and Gino Vannelli?

377. The first member of The Band Dylan hired to play or record with him was:
   a. Rick Danko
   b. Levon Helm
   c. Robbie Robertson
   d. Garth Hudson

378. Jackson Browne's first taste of success as a songwriter came when his "These Days" was recorded by...
   a. The Eagles
   b. Petula Clark
   c. Nico
   d. Nitty Gritty Dirt Band

379. What '70s funkmeister(s) got his start as part of the JBs, James Brown's band?
   a. George Clinton
   b. Bootsy Collins
   c. Rick James
   d. The Brothers Johnson

380. Who is William George Perks?

381. Paul Simon used what gospel group for the background singers on "Loves Me Like a Rock"?
   a. Blind Boys of Alabama
   b. Edwin Hawkins Singers
   c. Dixie Hummingbirds

382. OK, let's see you if you believe the origin of the name "Herman's Hermits" came from the *Rocky and Bullwinkle Show*. You *do* or *don't* buy that?

383. Which glam guitar slinger was selected for Dylan's *Rolling Thunder Revue* tour backing band?
   a. Mick Ronson
   b. Ian Hunter
   c. Lou Reed
   d. Sylvain Sylvain

384. Why is it "Get Together" is credited sometimes to *Dino Valente* and sometimes to *Chet Powers*?
   a. The original was a folk song in the public domain and both gents wrote versions of and have copyrights to the song
   b. Dino Valente is a pen name for Chet Powers
   c. Chet Powers is a pen name for Dino Valente
   d. All of the above is rubbish. The song is always credited to "Chet Powers"

385. Which *two* of the following bands did *not* include (former) members of Jefferson Airplane?
   a. Moby Grape
   b. Quicksilver Messenger Service
   c. New Riders of the Purple Sage
   d. Hot Tuna
   e. The Youngbloods

386. The first musical guest on *Saturday Night Live*?
   a. Paul Simon
   b. George Harrison
   c. Janis Ian
   d. Steve Martin
   e. Billy Preston

387. What husband/wife team wrote the hits "Da Doo Ron Ron", "Chapel of Love", "Be My Baby", and "Leader of the Pack", among others?
    a. Barry Mann/Cynthia Weil
    b. Jeff Barry/Ellie Greenwich
    c. Gerry Goffin/Carole King
    d. Alan/Marilyn Bergman

388. Multi-talented Barry Manilow was once the producer-arranger for what famous vocalist?
    a. Frank Sinatra
    b. Paul Anka
    c. Barbra Streisand
    d. Bette Midler

389. What first name was Cher born with?
    a. Cherilyn
    b. Cherise
    c. Cheri

390. There was a string of reggae tunes popularized by rockstar-types. We know Clapton covered Marley with "I Shot the Sheriff". Who did Three Dog Night cover with "Black and White" <u>and</u> who did Blondie cover with "The Tide is High"?

391. Who played lead guitar on Edgar Winter's "Frankenstein"?
    a. Sammy Hagar
    b. Johnny Winter
    c. Rick Derringer
    d. Ronnie Montrose

392. This band's logo features the zodiac signs of its four members... two lions for the two Leos in the group, a crab for the Cancer, and two fairies for the Virgo. What group is it?

393. Who was the baseball announcer on Meatloaf's "Paradise by the Dashboard Light"?
    a. Phil Rizzuto
    b. Dizzy Dean
    c. Bob Costas
    d. Harry Caray

394. Duane Allman – along with most of the Allman Brothers – produced a record for a cat whose instrumental track Beck later sampled for the basic rhythm track on "Loser". Name the artist and the tune.

395. Who wrote Rod Stewart's 1977 hit "The First Cut Is the Deepest"? And extra points if you know who had the original hit version of this in Britain.

396. The guy who wound up as the lead singer of Player ("Baby, Come Back") sang lead on Elvin Bishop's "Fooled Around and Fell in Love? T or F

397. Who is "Janet Planet"?
    a. A Zappa character
    b. Infamous groupie and plaster caster
    c. Van Morrison's ex-wife
    d. Girl in Alice Cooper's "Ballad of Dwight Fry"

398. They wrote "Tell Me Something Good" for Rufus and "Until You Come Back to Me (That's What I'm Gonna Do)" for Aretha Franklin. They are:
   a. Holland-Dozier-Holland
   b. Luther Vandross
   c. Curtis Mayfield
   d. Stevie Wonder

399. Which of the following songs was from *Jesus Christ Superstar*?
   a. "Everything's Alright"
   b. "Love Him, Love Him, Love"
   c. "Jesus is a Soul Man"
   d. "Jesus Was a Crossmaker"

400. What '70s R&B artist wrote the Talking Heads' hit "Take Me to the River"?

401. What was the first single (45 rpm) release on Rolling Stones Records?

402. What rocker was ejected from Graceland by security guards in '76?
   a. Elvis Costello
   b. Robert Plant
   c. Gene Simmons
   d. Bruce Springsteen

403. Born in Berlin as Wulf Wolodia Grajonca, he walked across Europe to escape the Nazis (really). Raised in New York by foster parents, he moved to the west coast to become an actor, but became a rock impresario instead. Who is he?

404. Until Michael Jackson's *Thriller* came along, this was the largest-selling album of all-time...
   a. *Tapestry*
   b. *Dark Side of the Moon*
   c. *Frampton Comes Alive*
   d. *Saturday Night Fever*

405. Who recorded the first digitally-produced album in 1979?
   a. Jackson Browne
   b. Paul Simon
   c. Steely Dan
   d. Ry Cooder

406. What band took its name from a 1972 Jeff Bridges movie?
   a. Fabulous Thunderbirds
   b. Heart
   c. Bad Company
   d. Pablo Cruise

407. Which two of the Bee Gees are twins?

408. Hmm... It's said that Joe Cocker based his spastic on-stage antics on which artist?
   a. Little Richard
   b. Sammy Davis, Jr.
   c. Jerry Lee Lewis
   d. Ray Charles

409. Only one of the Beach Boys' Wilson brothers was truly a surfer. Which one?

410. Put together the real names with the stage names for these artists…

a. Henry John Deutschendorf Jr.	1. Del Shannon
b. James Newell Osterberg, Jr.	2. John Denver
c. Charles Weeden Westover	3. Iggy Pop
d. Ellen Naomi Cohen	4. Jerry Jeff Walker
e. Paul Crosby	5. Cass Elliott
f. Pauline Mathews	6. Chaka Khan
g. Arnold George Dorsey	7. Kiki Dee
h. Carole Yvette Marie Stevens	8. Engelbert Humperdinck

411. Bowie, Bing Crosby, Hendrix, Dean Martin, Levi Stubbs, Ringo, Elvis, and Jim Morrison are all:
   a. Tenors
   b. Baritones
   c. Countertenors
   d. Contraltos

412. Before she became a solo artist, Maria Muldaur was a member of what group?
   a. Jim Kweskin's Jug Band
   b. Dan Hicks and the Hot Licks
   c. The New Vaudeville Band
   d. The Mugwumps

413. Simon and Garfunkel recorded which song in 1970, using the tune of an 18th century Peruvian folk song?

414. George Martin's first Rock project outside of the Beatles was who...
    a. Curved Air
    b. Jeff Beck
    c. Seatrain
    d. The Flock
    e. America

415. Which *two* of the following were not written by Kris Kristofferson?
    a. "Me and Bobby McGee"
    b. "Viet Nam Blues"
    c. "She Left Me While I Slept"
    d. "What Made Milwaukee Famous (Has Made a Loser Out of Me) "

416. Eric Clapton played on solo projects for all four Beatles after they disbanded, but for which track on the *White Album* did he join them?

417. You already know that Roger Daltrey played the lead in the movie *Tommy*, but what other lead role did he play in a movie?
    a. Errol Flynn in *Swashbuckler*
    b. Franz Liszt in *Lisztomania*
    c. Bobby Darin in *Mack the Knife*
    d. Cliff Richard in *Ready, Steady*

418. In "Maggie May", what was Rod Stewart complaining about given that it was September?
    a. He should be back in school
    b. Maggie should be back in school
    c. He and Maggie should be back in school

419. What song was considered "too black for white radio, but too white for black radio"... cost some $22k to produce... required two dozen session musicians and background vocalists... compared a woman's love to the love that a child feels for a doll, or a puppy feels for his master... and did so miserably on the pop charts that (it's said) it caused a famous producer to shut his label down?

420. Some peg this as the beginning of "acid rock" given its purported ties to a Timothy Leary book, *The Psychedelic Experience*. It is...
   a. Beatles' "Tomorrow Never Knows"
   b. Grateful Dead's "Anthem of the Sun"
   c. Beatles' "Within You, Without You"
   d. Yardbirds' "Happenings Ten Years Time Ago"
   e. Jefferson Airplane's "White Rabbit"

421. Who is "V. Ford" and why are they credited for "No Woman, No Cry"?
   a. "V. Ford" is Bob Marley's pen name
   b. Vincent Ford was a friend of Bob's who ran a soup kitchen where Marley grew up. The royalty checks that went to Ford ensured the soup kitchen's survival.
   c. The song is <u>not</u> credited to a "V. Ford"
   d. "V. Ford" is "Victoria Ford", birth name of Marley's mother

422. Just like the lyrics of "Mama Tried", Merle Haggard really did turn 21 in prison. T/F?

423. What album cover featured a young topless lass holding a silver spaceship in her hands?

424. If you take a Temptations song that the Stones covered and couple it with a Stones song that Otis Redding covered, you get...
   a. My girl is hard to handle
   b. It's growing and it's a bitch
   c. My girl can't get no satisfaction
   d. I ain't too proud to beg 'cause, baby, I'm out of time

425. The backing track you hear on the Mamas & Papas version of "California Dreamin'" was first heard on an album by:
   a. Barry McGuire
   b. Scott McKenzie
   c. PJ Proby
   d. The Artie Kornfeld Tree

426. Van Morrison wrote (at least) two songs inspired by legendary Soul singers. One is "Jackie Wilson Said". The other?

427. An early brush with fame came when Traffic did the theme to the film...
   a. *Hole in My Shoe*
   b. *Here We Go 'Round the Mulberry Bush*
   c. *Early in the Morning*
   d. *40,000 Headmen*

428. Was Albert King left-handed or right-handed?

429. What super-selling Epic label album was marketed with the phrase "Better music through science"?
   a. Culture Club
   b. Boston
   c. ELO
   d. Argent

430. The Kinks' line-up includes a pair of brothers who are named...
   a. Ray and Guy
   b. Dave and Rennie
   c. Ray and Dave
   d. Ray and Don

431. What well-known Marvin Gaye song contains the words "Where did all the blue skies go / Poison is the wind that blows / From the north and south and east..."?
   a. "Inner City Blues"
   b. "Come Get to This"
   c. "Peace, Brother, Peace"
   d. "Mercy Mercy Me"

432. She wrote hits for Blood Sweat & Tears, 5th Dimension, Babs Streisand, Three Dog Night...
   a. Carole King
   b. Laura Nyro
   c. Carole Baker Sager
   d. Dory Previn

433. Which Bowie album did Stevie Ray Vaughan's guitar work grace?

434. "Blackie" is the preferred guitar of whom?
   a. Jimmy Page
   b. B.B. King
   c. Eric Clapton
   d. Jeff Beck

435. What folk trio had John Denver in their lineup?
   a. The Limelighters
   b. The Chad Mitchell Trio
   c. The Kingston Trio
   d. The Lettermen

436. Who is the only other person to appear on stage with the Beatles?
   a. Crane Downing
   b. Klaus Voorman
   c. Neil Aspinall
   d. Jimmy Nicol

437. "She stood alone on her balcony, she could hear the cars roll by out on 441… And, for one desperate moment there…" That's some verbiage from Tom Petty's "American Girl". Did he write it after hearing about a University of Florida co-ed who leapt to her death from the Beatty Towers dorm? Would that be yes or no?

438. When Simon and Garfunkel first began to collaborate, they were known by another name, which was also the name of a well-known cartoon duo. What was it?

439. Who was/were the first white performer(s) to play Harlem's Apollo Theatre?
   a. Bobby Darin
   b. Buddy Holly and the Crickets
   c. Bill Black Combo
   d. Tom Jones

440. Which one is (more often than not) the beardless one in Z.Z. Top?
   a. Frank Beard
   b. Billy Gibbons
   c. Dusty Hill

441. Who assisted John Lennon and Paul McCartney in writing "Yellow Submarine" and Macca returned the favor by singing background on one of their songs?
   a. Mick Jagger and Keith Richards
   b. Donovan
   c. Brian Wilson and Mike Love
   d. Peter and Gordon

442. George Harrison originally signed them to Apple, the male half produced Clapton's first solo LP, and the female half co-wrote one of the Carpenters' biggest hits. Who are we talking about?

443. What group had an LP mis-titled because when a U.S. secretary rang to get the title from their British label, no one answered, so she wrote "no answer"?

444. Which member of the Who drew the cover of their 1975 album *The Who by Numbers*?

445. Of the following, which one(s) are associated with Leiber & Stoller?
    a. Stealers Wheel/"Stuck in the Middle"
    b. Dixie Cups/"Chapel of Love"
    c. Peggy Lee/"Is That All There Is"
    d. Elvis Presley/"If I Can Dream"

446. Which one of these Southern rock bands released an album that contained a deed conferring ownership of a small plot – one square inch to be exact – of land in the band's home state?

447. Years before the Sex Pistols launched their assault on the world, this quintet shocked audiences by dressing in drag, vomiting in airports, and losing their first drummer to a drug-related drowning.
    a. New York Dolls
    b. Slade
    c. The Ramones
    d. The Misfits
    e. Stiff Little Fingers

448. Which of these British glam-rockers was forced to re-title a single in 1971 that was about to bring his band international fame when an American group called Chase charted with a song by the same name?
    a. T. Rex
    b. Gary Glitter
    c. Christie
    d. Sweet

449. The phone # "362-436" is in what rock classic?

450. Which '70s guitarist claimed to have been visited by the spirit of Hendrix and, so, based a career on his ability to mimic Hendrix's style?
   a. Ted Nugent
   b. Frank Marino
   c. Joe Perry
   d. Mick Jones

451. Which Smokey Robinson & the Miracles song does this line belong to: "Outside I'm masquerading... Inside, my hope is fading"?

452. Which two of these groups had eponymous (self-titled) albums with similarly titled songs?
   a. Rainbow
   b. Bad Company
   c. Black Sabbath
   d. Whitesnake

453. Neil Young was once in a band called the Mynah Birds with this 70s funkmeister...
   a. George Clinton
   b. Rick James
   c. Bootsy Collins
   d. Sly Stone

454. The front cover of the Rolling Stones' *Get Your Ya-Ya's Out!* features a bemused-looking pack mule and which member of the band?

455. The Doors lacked a bassist, so how were the bass parts played?

456. Exactly how is the title of Led Zeppelin's "Dyermaker" punctuated on their 1973 album *Houses of the Holy*?
   a. D'yer Maker
   b. Dyer M'aker
   c. Dy'er Ma'ker
   d. D'yer Mak'er

457. What is the stage name of Marvin Lee Aday?

458. Roberta Flack hit with "First Time Ever I Saw Your Face" after it was featured in what Clint Eastwood movie?

459. What group's debut had a richly fragrant cover?
   a. Mom's Apple Pie
   b. The Raspberries
   c. The Froot Loops
   d. The Banana Splits

460. On tour in Britain, a famous singer/guitarist was taken off the top of the bill and replaced by the Beatles, who were contracted as support for this man. He was...
   a. Bruce Chanel
   b. Frank Ifield
   c. Roy Orbison
   d. Chris Montez

461. Who gave his seat to J.P "Big Bopper" Richardson on the ill-fated plane ride that took the lives of Richardson, Ritchie Valens, and Buddy Holly?

462. Which of these Jim Croce hits wasn't written by him?
   a. "I Got a Name"
   b. "Time in a Bottle"
   c. "I'll Have to Say I Love You in a Song"
   d. "Operator

463. The Hollies' "He Ain't Heavy, He's My Brother" features who on piano... ?
   a. Keith Emerson
   b. Elton John
   c. Carole King
   d. Barry Manilow

464. On *Ed Sullivan*, the Stones were required to change the lyrics of "Let's Spend the Night Together" to...
   a. Let's spend the day together
   b. Let's spend some dough together
   c. Let's spend some time together
   d. Let's spend this night forever

465. The inspiration behind Elton John's "Philadelphia Freedom" was...
   a. Benjamin Franklin
   b. The story of the gay gentleman Tom Hanks later portrayed in *Philadelphia*
   c. The Sound of Philadelphia / Gamble & Huff recordings
   d. Billie Jean King

466. What Mellencamp classic did John McCain and John Edwards use in their Presidential campaigns?

467. The first woman elected to the Rock 'n Roll Hall of Fame?
   a. Bessie Smith
   b. Big Mama Thornton
   c. Janis Joplin
   d. Aretha Franklin

468. When Dylan hired The Hawks (who became The Band), Levon Helm – dismayed by the negative response Dylan was getting for going "electric"– opted out and moved back to Arkansas for a coupla years. The question here is: Who replaced him?
   a. Bobby Gregg
   b. Robert Zildjian
   c. Liberty DeVitto
   d. Spencer Dryden
   e. Mickey Jones

469. Whose wistful 1971 love song about California threatened to "kiss a Sunset pig"?

470. After which Eagles album did Bernie Leadon opt to leave the group?
   a. *On the Border*
   b. *One of These Nights*
   c. *Hotel California*
   d. *The Long Run*

471. Which Seventies band claimed to have mixed their own blood in with the red ink used to print a comic book about them?

472. All four of these singer-songwriters helped define the sound of Southern California in the '70s, but only one of the following gents was actually born in the state. Which one?
   a. Jackson Browne
   b. Glenn Frey
   c. David Crosby
   d. Warren Zevon

473. The first label to be entirely devoted to Rap music was:
   a. Sugar Hill
   b. Def Jam
   c. Interscope
   d. Diplomat

474. Which of these has never contained siblings?
   a. Fanny
   b. The Ramones
   c. Sly & the Family Stone
   d. The Carpenters

475. What was the quickest rise to #1 for a single, ever, on the Country charts?
   a. Tammy Wynette/"D-I-V-O-R-C-E"
   b. Johnny Cash/"A Boy Named Sue"
   c. Red Sovine/"Teddy Bear"
   d. Johnny Paycheck/"Take This Job and Shove It"

476. Name the albino sax-playing keyboardist who served as a sideman in his brother's group before launching a "shabby" band of his own in 1970.

477. What did Della wear, kids? Get out the maps – it's geography time! I'll give you the song; you give me the artist. Are you ready?

a) "San Francisco (Wear Some Flowers in Your Hair)"
b) "Indiana Wants Me"
c) " (The Lights Went Out in) Massachusetts
d) "Kentucky Woman"
e) "Honolulu Lulu"
f) "L.A. Goodbye"
g) "Detroit City"
h) "Tulsa Time"
i) "Dallas"
j) "Houston"
k) "Jackson"
l) "Memphis"
m) "Nashville Cats"
n) "Galveston"
o) "Vienna"
p) "Kansas City"
q) "London Calling"
r) "Oh, Atlanta"
s) "Alta Mira"
t) "Brooklyn Roads"
u) "Bowling Green"
v) "Doraville"
w) "El Paso"
x) "Funky Nassau"
y) "He Went to Paris"
z) "Bristol Stomp"

478. What surname did Paul McCartney's little brother Mike, who released a solo album in 1974 with songs co-written and produced by Paul, adopt in the '60s in order to avoid identification as a sibling gold digger?

479. Three of the Taylors below are siblings of James Taylor and also launched recording careers in the '70s. Name the fictitious Taylor.
   a. Livingston
   b. Alex
   c. Andrew
   d. Kate

480. It's obvious how many Jacksons were in the Jackson 5, but how many performing Osmonds were there in the '70s —both in the Osmonds as a group or as a solo act? Extra points for every one you can name.
   a. Five
   b. Six
   c. Seven
   d. Eight

481. Who wrote "Tears of a Clown"?
   a. Smokey Robinson
   b. Berry Gordy
   c. Holland-Dozier-Holland
   d. Stevie Wonder
   e. Diana Ross
   f. Eddie Kendricks
   g. Andy Kim & Jeff Barry

482. What was the name of the mystery group that would not reveal its identity which led to speculation that it was really the Beatles recording under a pseudonym?
    a. The Masked Marauders
    b. Ambrosia
    c. Klaatu
    d. Bonzo Dog Doo Dah Band

483. The one-time supergroup of John Lennon, Eric Clapton, Keith Richards and Mitch Mitchell that Lennon put together for *The Rolling Stones Rock and Roll Circus* was called what?
    a. Bad Blood
    b. Ivry
    c. The Dirty Mac
    d. Birtha

484. From which British Invasion group did Rod Argent, the namesake of Argent, hail?

485. For what product did Lou Reed allow his "Walk on the Wild Side" to be used as a jingle?
    a. Valium
    b. Honda Motorcycles
    c. Shick Razors
    d. Paco Rabanne

486. What do these songs have in common: David Bowie's "Changes", Elton John's "Bennie and the Jets", Bachman-Turner Overdrive's "You Ain't Seen Nothing Yet"?

487. Which of these about Randy Newman is true?

   a. When he was a child, his Jewish family moved from L.A. To Louisiana
   b. His uncle is Paul Newman
   c. His song "You Can Leave Your Hat On" was featured in the steamy Southern striptease club scene in *Body Heat*
   d. His biggest hit was "Short People" off of *Trouble in Paradise*

488. Which of these U.S. Top 40 hits was adapted from a British song entitled "Mom, True Love, and Apple Pie"?

   a. "Billy, Don't Be a Hero"
   b. "I'd Like to Teach the World to Sing"
   c. "Brand New Key"

489. What was the time period between the release of Lynyrd Skynyrd's eerily prophetic *Street Survivors* and the occurrence of the band's fatal plane crash?

   a. 3 days
   b. 3 weeks
   c. 3 months

490. Amazingly, the Who never had a #1 LP in the U.S., but they did achieve "AVIS" status (#2, but they try harder) a couple of times. Which of these <u>two</u> albums fit that bill?

   a. *Who Are You*
   b. *Tommy*
   c. *Who's Next*
   d. *Quadrophenia*

491. Which of these groups was really just a New York songwriting team masquerading as a trio from Australia?
   a. The Easybeats
   b. Split Enz
   c. The Strangeloves
   d. Sherbet

492. Which famous rock & roll act originally recorded "Love Hurts," which the Scottish band Nazareth remade and scored a Top 40 hit with?

493. Who collapsed from a stroke on stage at the Latin Casino in Cherry Hill, NJ on September 25, 1975, and spent the rest of his life a coma?

494. Neil Young's "Alabama" started the whole Lynyrd Skynyrd "Sweet Home Alabama" brouhaha, but which of Neil's songs did he subsequently make an allusion to the whole 'Bama business within its lyrics?
   a. "Rust Never Sleeps"
   b. "Comes a Time"
   c. "Walk On"
   d. "Rockin' in the Free World"

495. Which American musical institution did Stevie Wonder pay fond tribute to in a 1977 chart-topper?
   a. The Apollo Theatre
   b. Martin Luther King
   c. The 4th of July
   d. Duke Ellington

496. Who did ZZ Top rip off for their song "La Grange"? Was it…
   a. Muddy Waters
   b. John Lee Hooker
   c. Big Joe Turner
   d. Little Milton
   e. Taj Mahal

497. James Brown defected to what label (albeit momentarily) during a contract dispute with King Records?

498. *The Button-Down Mind of Bob Newhart* has the distinction of being what?
   a. First album of the Sixties to be certified "Gold"
   b. First comedy album to ever top the *Billboard* chart
   c. First release on Reprise Records
   d. The album that unseated the Beatles at the top of the Album charts

499. What singer took the liberty in '76 of remaking five of his own band's songs for a solo LP?
   a. Bryan Ferry
   b. Peter Gabriel
   c. Paul Weller
   d. Scott Walker

500. Who sometimes masquerades under the name of "Marvin Gardens"?

501. What English group that evolved from another English group had a 1977 American hit by redoing a 1972 classic from the repertoire of its parent band? Yo comprende?
   a. Foreigner
   b. Electric Light Orchestra
   c. Wings
   d. 10cc

502. Many believe there are two Zeppelin songs that Page adapted the guitar line from "White Summer", a song by his former band the Yardbirds, for. If so, those two songs are...
   a. "Black Mountain Side"
   b. "Over the Hills and Far Away"
   c. "Going to California "
   d. "Hey, Hey, What Can I Do? "

503. What song on the first Bad Company record did guitarist Mick Ralphs reprise from his tenure with his former band?
   a. "Can't Get Enough"
   b. "Silver, Blue, and Gold"
   c. "Ready for Love"
   d. "Burning Sky"

504. The first Clash album released in the U.S.?
   a. *Give 'Em Enough Rope*
   b. *The Clash*
   c. *London Calling*
   d. *Rebels*

505. Figure out the Monkees song from this story line: Dude's been drafted and getting ready to leave for Vietnam where he knows he may die.

506. They were one of the most productive Disco groups. The bass line of one of their songs was the foundation for "Another One Bites the Dust" and the guitar hook from the same song provided the groove in "Rappers Delight". Because of their success, they were handed the keys by their label to produce <u>any</u> act they wanted. Who were they?

507. Tony Visconti, who produced many of Bowie's biggest '70s albums, also worked on albums by:
    a. The Strawbs
    b. Gentle Giant
    c. T. Rex
    d. Roy Harper
    e. All of 'em
    f. A & C only

508. Which '70s musician won a Grammy for Best Male R&B *Vocal* only two years after taking home a pair of Grammys for his *instrumental* work?
    a. Grover Washington, Jr.
    b. George Benson
    c. Bobby Womack
    d. Isaac Hayes

509. The husband/wife duo of Jimmy Bracken and Vivian Carter owned what label that helped launch the careers of John Lee Hooker, the Staple Singers, Jerry Butler, and the Beatles?

510. *"I was born in 1947, went to the University of Illinois where I got my start booking bands. When I left for LA I took the son of a band director and a guy who had previously turned to stone with me. I wound up managing folks as diverse as Neil Diamond and Morrissey. I say I'm a giant of a man. Who am I?"*

511. What Top Ten hit employs the oldest lyrics in all of history? Hint: Sixties, Solomon, !!!.

512. Players like Mac Gayden, Wayne Moss, Kenny Buttrey, and Norbert Putnam made up one of Nashville's more famous session groups (much like Memphis had Booker T & the MGs) and their work can be heard on albums like *Nashville Skyline* and *Blonde on Blonde,* Elvis and Roy Orbison sessions. As a "band" these cats recorded under two formations. Name one.

513. Which of these didn't appear at Woodstock?
    a. Keef Hartley
    b. The Incredible String Band
    c. Bert Sommer
    d. Jethro Tull

514. Two of Ray Charles big hits were originally recorded by:
    a. Don Gibson and Buck Owens
    b. Kitty Wells and Buck Owens
    c. Eddy Arnold and Don Gibson
    d. Hank Williams and Kitty Wells

515. Lyrics from which track on the Knack's debut LP had to be rewritten before it could be released as a single due to its blatant vulgarity?

516. His resume includes entries like: had a group called "Grin"; became a member of the E-Street Band; his first album contained a tribute to Keith Richard; he was a guitar slinger on Neil Young's *After the Goldrush*. Who is he?

517. Which of these R&B groups were non-existent in the '50s, '60s, and '70s?
   a. Three Degrees
   b. Four Tops
   c. Five Satins
   d. Six Teens
   e. DC-8

518. Willie Mitchell, famed Memphis-based R&B producer, stepped out of that genre to produce one significant "white" act. Who?
   a. Jesse Winchester
   b. The Amazing Rhythm Aces
   c. Danny O'Keefe
   d. The Band

519. After a gig on the roof an L.A. apartment building, this artist was signed to a Mercury label deal...
   a. The Runaways
   b. City Boy
   c. Rush
   d. Sir Douglas Quintet

520. Gamble & Huff used the "shower you with love and affection, look out, it's comin' in your direction" lyrics in two different songs. Name 'em.

521. What 70s prog-rock group reinvented Mussorgsky's "Pictures at an Exhibition"?

522. David Gates (of Bread) was the first to produce Captain Beefheart. True or False?

523. Like a phoenix out of the ashes, Johnny Rotten arose from the demise of the Sex Pistols on Christmas Day, 1978, with what new group?
    a. The Clash
    b. Public Image Ltd.
    c. Gang of Four
    d. Big Audio Dynamite

524. The Quarrymen are to the Beatles as...
    a. Stories is to Hot Chocolate
    b. Chad Allen & the Expressions are to the Guess Who
    c. Pud is to the Doobie Brothers
    d. A and B
    e. B and C

525. Which Supertramp album features one of Winston Churchill's speeches?
    a. *Even in the Quietest Moments*
    b. *Crime of the Century*
    c. *Breakfast in America*
    a. *Indelibly Stamped*

526. Fable or Fact?
    a. The inspiration behind "Midnight Train to Georgia" was Farrah Fawcett. T or F
    b. Quincy Jones holds the title as the Male with the most Grammy wins. T or F
    c. Sonny Bono's tombstone reads "And the beat goes on...". T or F

527. Figure out who this is: Rockabilly's Billy Lee Riley played harp on his Harold Dorman cover; did the U.S. version of the U.K.'s *Danger Man* theme; discovered what he calls the "Black Mamas & Papas"; published Jim Webb's early hits; had a hit with a Willie Dixon cover...

528. They were the first to have a hit with Bob Dylan-penned, Pete Seeger-penned, and John Denver-penned songs. Who are they?

529. Ok, packaging... What two LPs do you remember being packaged in brown paper bags? And what two album covers include text written in Braille? And what LP came with a pair of panties?

530. If one is to believe Tony Joe White in the song "Polk Salad Annie", polk salad looks like:
    a. Shredded zucchini
    b. A turnip green
    c. Begonias
    d. Cauliflower leaves

531. What classic sax player did the break on Foreigner's "Urgent"?

532. Identify the artist who did the original recording of the following tunes...

a. Go Now	Moody Blues *or* Bessie Banks
b. Hanky Panky	The Raindrops *or* The Shondells
c. Somethin' Stupid	Carson & Gaile *or* Frank & Nancy Sinatra
d. Rock Around the Clock	Sonny Dae & the Knights *or* Bill Haley & the Comets
e. Little Bit O' Soul	Ohio Express *or* The Little Darlings
f. Wild Thing	The Troggs *or* The Wild Ones
g. Close to You	Richard Chamberlain *or* The Carpenters

533. Tom Waits has been known to be disapproving of cover versions of one of his songs, going as far as saying he was "not that particularly crazy about [the Eagles'] rendition of it. I thought their version was a little antiseptic." What's the song?

534. Double trouble: Buffalo Springfield got their name from a ________ (animal, veggie, mineral, place, thing, etc.) and their song "For What It's Worth" ("Stop, hey, what's that sound") got its title from ________ (animal, situation, whatever)?

535. "Disco Lady" by Johnnie Taylor was...
    a. Considered to be the first disco record
    b. The first single to go "Platinum"
    c. Columbia's biggest hit of the Seventies
    d. His debut on Epic when he left STAX

536. Pun-a-riffic, here we go... Tequila must've put a bad taste in their mouth, as they became hummingbird worshipers. Who are they?

537. Which two artists contributed two songs each to the soundtrack of *Easy Rider*?
    a. Electric Prunes
    b. Steppenwolf
    c. Smith
    d. Roger McGuinn

538. Which Beatle funded the making of *Monty Python's Life of Brian* movie?

539. What's the connection between the Alan Parsons Project and *Abbey Road, Dark Side of the Moon, Year of the Cat*, and the Chicago Bulls?

540. This song uses a circus theme as a metaphor for dealing with the difficulties and wrong choices of life. It is...
    a. Peggy Lee/"Is That All There Is"
    b. Three Dog Night/"The Show Must Go On"
    c. Bruce Springsteen/"Wild Billy's Circus Story"
    d. Cymarron/"Rings"

541. Rod Temperton, who wrote the title track and several others on Jacko Wacko's *Thriller*, came out of what '70s funk/disco band?
   a. Tavares
   b. Heatwave
   c. Rufus
   d. SOS Band

542. Put the artist (or film) with the songs the Beatles covered:

a. Shirelles	1. "Act Naturally"
b. Cookies	2. "Boys"
c. Dr. Feelgood & the Interns	3. "Mr. Moonlight"
d. The Donays	4. "Devil in Her Heart"
e. Buck Owens	5. "Chains"
f. The Top Notes	6. "Money"
g. Carl Perkins	7. "Honey Don't"
h. Barrett Strong	8. "Twist & Shout"
i. *The Music Man*	9. "Till There Was You"

543. Which of these artists isn't for real?
   a. Insect Trust
   b. The Hurley Girlies
   c. Ultimate Spinach
   d. Weasel Spagnola

544. Cannonball Adderley did an instrumental version of the Buckinghams' "Mercy, Mercy, Mercy" *or* did the Buckinghams do a lyrical version of Cannonball's version of the song?

545. Pre-ABBA, "Björn & Benny" released a single in America on what label?
   a. Polydor
   b. Playboy
   c. EMI/Capitol
   d. Casablanca

546. Arthur Lee was guitarist and singer for...
   a. The Grass Roots
   b. Love
   c. Neither
   d. Both

547. Let's play colors! Fill in the color for these songs::
   a. ____Velvet
   b. ____Manalishi
   c. ____River
   d. (The Angels Wanna Wear My) ____Shoes
   e. ____is ____
   f. Old ____ Shoe
   g. ____Betty

548. What female rocker helped John Mellencamp gain traction with her version of "I Need a Lover"?

549. Who's the oldest J-boy of the Jackson 5 – Michael, Marlon, Jackie, Tito, or Jermaine?

550. Some labels had "sisters" (ok, *brother*) labels. Hook these together...

a. Bell	1. Checker
b. Decca	2. Amy
c. Chess	3. Brunswick
d. Liberty	4. Smash
e. Mercury	5. Imperial
f. STAX	6. Volt
g. London	7. Parrot

551. There were some single-name artists back in the day who charted with singles. Which of these didn't exist?
   a. Keith
   b. Kitten
   c. Latimore
   d. Cugini

552. Keepin' it all in the family... Put these brothers/ sisters together with their respective bands/groups:

a. Alvin & Ric Lee	1. The Stooges
b. Jimmy, Jack & Donna Hall	2. Tin Machine
c. Ron & Scott Asheton	3. Wet Willie
d. Hunt & Tony Sales	4. The Valentinos
e. Bobby & Cecil Womack	5. Ten Years After

553. Who wrote these? "Your Good Thing is About to End", "When Something is Wrong with My Baby", and "B-A-B-Y"?
   a. Steve Cropper
   b. Isaac Hayes & David Porter
   c. Eddie Floyd
   d. Holland-Dozier-Holland

554. Which of these Dylan-as-sideman is T or F?
   a. Played harmonica on Harry Belafonte's "The Midnight Special" T/F
   b. Plays harmonica on Priscilla and Booker T. Jones' "Crippled Crow" T/F
   c. Plays guitar, lends background vocals on Noel Harrison's "A Young Girl" T/F
   d. Calls himself "Bob Landy" (get it?) and plays piano on "Downtown Blues" with the Blues Project T/F

555. Before his solo career took off, Robert Palmer toiled in a band featuring he and Elkie Brooks on lead vocals. That group was...
   a. The Alan Bown Set
   b. Wiggy Bits
   c. Vinegar Joe
   d. Amen Corner

556. Otis Redding's manager was instrumental in creating the record label credited for establishing Southern Rock as a genre. Name the guy, the label, or both if you can.

557. Who's the odd man out when it comes to Sun Records or Sun Recording Studios?
    a. Howlin' Wolf
    b. Roy Orbison
    c. Bill Black
    d. Carl Perkins
    e. Hound Dog Taylor
    f. Little Junior Parker
    g. Rufus Thomas

558. One of the following is an imposter when it comes to having an album entitled "______ *at the Fillmore*" [either East *or* West]...
    a. Allman Brothers
    b. Virgil Fox
    c. Kaleidoscope
    d. Buffalo Bob
    e. King Curtis
    f. Chuck Berry

559. Only one of these mustered a Top 15 album...
    a. James Gang
    b. Frijid Pink
    c. Uriah Heep
    d. Cashman & West

560. Early in his career, Allen Toussaint wrote under what pseudonym?

561. Janis Joplin and Pigpen of the Grateful Dead shared the same "drink of choice". What was that drink?

562. What's the only Top Ten pop hit that used the word "et cetera" in its lyrics?

563. Buddy Holly's last single released before his death was...
   a. "Peggy Sue"
   b. "True Love Ways"
   c. "It Doesn't Matter Anymore"
   d. "Rave On"

564. What '60s rocker was (supposedly) pegged to take Orbison's place in the Wilburys but he ran off and killed himself?

565. Which of these never appeared on your TV screen?
   a. Doobie Brothers on *What's Happening*
   b. Dr. John on *Chico and the Man*
   c. Buffalo Springfield on *Mannix*
   d. Phil Spector on *I Dream of Jeanie*

566. In Harry Chapin's "Taxi", the falsetto part was sung by his...
   a. Drummer
   b. Bassist
   c. Cellist
   d. Lead Guitarist

567. Look at this sentence: "*I got worries thinking about our fortune all across the nation.*" That sentence is built from three chart records from the mid-'60s to mid-'70s. Break it down into segments and see if you can come up with those three songs.

568. This smash was based on the French tune "Le Moribond" by Jacques Brel with lyrics and melody modified to honor a friend who had died of leukemia. Was it...
   a. Bobby Goldsboro's "Honey"
   b. Terry Jacks' "Seasons in the Sun"
   c. Mark Dinning's "Teen Angel"
   d. Ray Peterson's "Tell Laura I Love Her"
   e. Austin Roberts' "Rocky"

569. What soundtrack has these tunes? "Hello, Texas"... "Nine Tonight"... "Times Like These"?

570. Which band included a mate who left the group to have a Country & Western hit?
   a. Paul Revere and the Raiders
   b. The Buckinghams
   c. The Grassroots
   d. Gary Puckett and the Union Gap

571. How long does the sustaining end note on "A Day in the Life" last? Give or take five seconds...

572. What was the first CD to be pressed in America? In the U.K.?

573. What was the first CD to sell more than one million copies?
   a. Eagles/*Greatest Hits*
   b. Bruce Springsteen/*Born in the USA*
   c. Dire Straits/*Brothers in Arms*
   d. Bob Seger/*Night Moves*

574. What Sixties nugget was inspired by a Mutual of New York sign?

575. How much did Elvis weigh when he died? C'mon, take a stab. Just be within 10 pounds.

576. How much did Sam Phillips sell Elvis' contract to RCA for?

577. What LP features the NYC skyline made out of breakfast dishes?

578. Who gave Jimmy Page the Les Paul that he used to record Led Zeppelin *II*?

579. Bee Gee Robin Gibb wrote the lyrics "I've Gotta Get a Message to You" with whom in mind?
    a. Percy Sledge
    b. James Brown
    c. The Righteous Brothers
    d. Solomon Burke

580. What music icon to-be was the producer of Leslie Gore's hits, "It's My Party", "Judy's Turn to Cry", and "You Don't Own Me".

581. In the day, Coca-Cola would use popular acts to record commercials for them. Who was the first?
    a. The Troggs
    b. Jay & the Americans
    c. The Fortunes
    d. We Five

582. Cat Stevens used a one for his piano on "Sad Lisa"... Zep used it to process Plant's vocals in "What Is and What Should Never Be"... the Beatles also one to process George Harrison's voice on "Blue Jay Way" on. What is it?

a. A harmonizer
b. A Moog oscillator
c. A Leslie speaker
d. A wah-wah pedal

583. What band took the name for one of their biggest LPs from the lyrics of Dr. John's "Right Place, Wrong Time"?

584. His real name is James Wesley Voight, he's the uncle of Angelia Jolie, and he's responsible for writing hits for the Troggs, Merilee Rush, Evie Sands/Vanilla Fudge, the Hollies and others. He goes by what stage name?

585. Who was the youngest 60s/70s artist to hit #1 on the singles charts? Stevie Wonder, Donny Osmond, or Michael Jackson?

586. The chords and structure of which Tommy James and the Shondells' single, "Mirage", were actually the chords to which one of his previous hits?

a. "Crimson and Clover"
b. "Hanky Panky"
c. "I Think We're Alone Now"
d. "Do Something to Me"

587. Paul Simon took the title of what from the name of a chicken-and-egg dish he saw on a Chinese restaurant's menu?

588. What classic gig happened Thanksgiving Day, 1976, at the Winterland in San Francisco?

589. Who is the only non-Beatle to receiving billing as an artist alongside the Beatles (separate from receiving credit as a session musician on album packaging) on an official Beatles record release?

590. Who are the only Mother and son to both have a number one hit on the *Billboard* Hot 100?

591. Which of these did not record a J.J. Cale tune?
   a. Lynyrd Skynyrd
   b. Kansas
   c. Sergio Mendes
   d. America
   e. José Feliciano
   f. Poco

592. Many jazz cats are heard on Steely Dan's tunes, including the man who's possibly the most-recorded jazz string acoustic bass player ever. Who would that be?
   a. Ray Brown
   b. Ron Carter
   c. Stanley Clarke
   d. Wilton Felder
   e. Elliott Randall

593. Freda Payne's "Band of Gold" is credited to "Ron Dunbar & Edith Wayne". Who, why?

a. "Ron Dunbar & Edith Wayne" were really (former Motown writers) Holland-Dozier-Holland who were embroiled in a lawsuit with their former employers and had to use pseudonyms

b. "Ron Dunbar & Edith Wayne" were the alter-egos for Ashford & Simpson when they did songwriting for Invictus

c. "Ron Dunbar & Edith Wayne" were just two ordinary songwriters who happened to pen a hit record

d. "Ron Dunbar & Edith Wayne" were really staff writer Ronald Wayne and Holland-Dozier-Holland masquerading as "Edith Wayne" because they were embroiled in a lawsuit with their former employers and had to use pseudonyms.

594. Let's see how you know-it-all Yanks fare on this one. Put these '76 U.K. #1s together with the correct artist:

a. "Save Your Kisses for Me"	1. The Real Thing
b. "You to Me Are Everything"	2. Tina Charles
c. "I Love to Love"	3. Brotherhood of Man
d. "Mississippi"	4. Johnny Mathis
e. "When a Child is Born"	5. Pussycat

595. Janis Joplin's "Mercedes Benz" was the very first "a capella" record to hit #1. True or False?

596. What's the next line in this Hall & Oates song... "Sorry Charlie for the imposition"?
   a. One less toothbrush hanging in the stand
   b. I think I've got it, got the strength to carry on
   c. I need a drink and a quick decision
   d. Pretty bodies help dissolve the memories

597. Linda Lawrence is/was...
   a. The girl who was the inspiration for Jan & Dean's hit, "Linda"
   b. The girl who birthed Brian Jones' child
   c. Donovan's girlfriend/wife
   d. The girl Elvis dated right before he died
   e. A & B
   f. B&C
   g. C&D

598. Female singer... a capella... 250-year old hymn... million-seller. The answer is what?

599. What's the connection between Jim Croce, Otis Redding, Rick Nelson, and John Denver?

600. What did "MC" in the MC5's name stand for? (I said "5", not "Hammer").

601. What Southern Rock band had a Top 20 re-do of Classics IV's "Spooky"?

602. Two-parter... Of the *New Musical Express'* year-end "Best Albums of 1977", a) which one of the following failed to chart *at all* on *Billboard's* American album charts; b) which one charted the highest on the American charts?

   a. *Heroes* - David Bowie
   b. *New Boots & Panties* - Ian Dury
   c. *My Aim is True* - Elvis Costello
   d. *Never Mind the Bollocks* - Sex Pistols
   e. *Marquee Moon* – Television
   f. *Exodus* - Bob Marley & the Wailers
   g. *The Clash* - The Clash
   h. *Lust for Life* - Iggy Pop
   i. *Leave Home* - The Ramones

603. Name two prominent labels that featured a butterfly in their logo (and, no, "Butterfly Records" doesn't count!)

604. Peter Green, Jeremy Spencer, Danny Kirwan, Bob Weston, Bob Welch, Rick Vito, Dave Mason, Billy Burnette, Lindsey Buckingham... What's their connection to each other?

605. According to the Eagles, what city is… "Where the old world shadows hang heavy in the air"?

606. In the movie *Pretty in Pink*, Duckie (played by Jon Cryer) lip-syncs to what classic Rhythm & Blues tune? (Note: it's in the movie, but not on the soundtrack)

607. What was the nearby lake where Deep Purple recorded "Smoke on the Water" and who did they rent their mobile recording studio from?

608. Who said "Rock and Roll is phony and false. Sung, written, and played for the most part by cretinous goons"?

609. Although they're usually believed to be Australian, the Bee Gees are actually:
   a. Welsh
   b. Irish
   c. English
   d. Scottish

610. Only one of these acts has scored more than one U.S. Top 10 single in the '70s. Which one?
   a. Neil Young
   b. Santana
   c. Pink Floyd
   d. Led Zeppelin

611. What's Brian Eno's full name?
   a. Brian Henry Eno
   b. Brian Benjamin Disraeli Eno
   c. Brian David Lloyd George Eno
   d. Brian Peter George St. John le Baptiste de la Salle Eno
   e. Brian Miguel DeChamps Eno

612. The lead singer of The Archies was the same person who produced Barry Manilow. T or F?

613. Which offense does Charlie Brown *not* commit in The Coasters' hit of the same name?
   a. Shooting craps in the gymnasium
   b. Smoking in the boys' room
   c. Spitball-throwing
   d. Addressing his English teacher as "Daddy-O"

614. The first British male to have a Number One single in the U.S. was...
   a. Mr. Acker Bilk
   b. Donovan
   c. Tom Jones
   d. Matt Monro

615. An urban myth, but still a good one: Glen Matlock was booted from what influential band for admitting he liked the Beatles?
   a. The Clash
   b. Velvet Underground
   c. Funkadelic
   d. Sex Pistols

616. Who played *acoustic* guitar alongside Jimi on "All Along the Watchtower"?

617. Math time! Let's say you're Truman Capote and we're doing a "(quasi-) six degrees of separation" thing 'tween you (being Capote) and Eric Clapton – a line that includes Shuggie Otis, the Brothers Johnson, Quincy Jones, and Johnny Otis. How would you lay out that line of relationships?

618. Which family had three generations of artists who had Number One records?
   a. The Nelsons
   b. The Reddings
   c. The Boones

619. Was Dog a doughnut?

620. Who holds the record for most Hot 100 entries without a #1 song? Is it...
   a. Creedence Clearwater Revival
   b. James Brown
   c. The Ventures
   d. Neil Diamond

621. What label got in a heap o' trouble by using the Superman logo for their logo?

622. What do these folks have in common? John Barry & Orchestra, Matt Monro, Shirley Bassey, Paul McCartney & Wings, Lulu, Carly Simon, Tom Jones, Nancy Sinatra, Louis Armstrong?

623. Pre-Fleetwood'ing, Buckingham/Nicks recorded their own duet LP that included one song the Mac'ers would cover on their first album with Lindsey and Stevie in the lineup. Was it...
   a. "Never Let Me Down Again"
   b. "Crystal"
   c. "Crying in the Night"
   d. "Frozen Love"

624. Despite hits with lots of other people's songs like Roy Orbison, Warren Zevon, Smokey Robinson, Neil Young, et al, did Linda Ronstadt ever record anything *she* wrote?

625. Elton John had a huge hit with "Song for Guy" in the U.K. (#4 over there, but a bomb at #110 in the U.S.). What was it about?
   a. The French writer, Guy de Maupassant
   b. Guy Whittingham, a British footballer
   c. Elton's messenger, Guy, who had died in a traffic accident the day he wrote the song
   d. The original title was "Song for (a) Guy" and was to quietly celebrate Elton's "coming out"
   e. Bernie Taupin, who EJ called "Guy"

626. What's the Stiff Records slogan?

627. What Brit rockers had to change their name from "Traffic" after the Winwood-led version hit it big?
   a. The Move
   b. Soft Machine
   c. Yes
   d. Status Quo

628. In the song "Rock and Roll" on Led Zep *IV*, what <u>three</u> of the following '50s songs are referenced?
   a. "The Stroll"
   b. "The Book of Love"
   c. "Reet Petite"
   d. "Walking in the Moonlight"
   e. "Ready, Steady"

629. Who am I? *While I have Portuguese roots, many consider me a true Southerner because of where I grew up. After doing the Folies Bergères in Vegas, I moved to L.A. to study Philosophy at UCLA. Eventually, I started writing songs, and thanks to a wicked little storyline that produced a hit record, my career took off. My first album even knocked 'Sgt. Pepper' out of first place on the chart! After that, my American hit successes waned, however after having enough germs to catch pneumonia, my career rebounded a bit with a #1 in Britain. My successes at the altar are short-lived, too. My first marriage was to the guy who owned Harrah's casino, but we were only married three months. I then wed a girl named Bill, but we were only married for 11 months. I've gotten out of the business and pretty much stick to myself under my real name of Streeter, now.* Again, who am I?

630. *Bonanza* + Beatle = ________?

631. What band named itself because they were formed a decade after Elvis' initial success?

632. What/who, in God's name, is Nanker Phelge?
   a. The name Rod Stewart uses for his "willy"
   b. A collective pseudonym for several Rolling Stones group compositions
   c. Helen Reddy's Indonesian nanny who left her employ to become Don Henley's live-in
   d. A little-known, British chap and the very last artist Clive Davis signed at Columbia
   e. Blues legend Son House's real name

633. A certain prominent '50s group was incorporated, giving each member equal shares of stock which was bought back when they left. However, many of its ex-members decided to reform *their* version of the group and tour under the band's name creating a real cluster you-know-what. Who was that group? Hint: Their leader was one of BMI's top five songwriters/air play in its first 50 years.

634. What Motown act's name was taken from a combination of Della Reese and Detroit's Van Dyke Street?

635. Who recorded "Born Under a Bad Sign" first?
    a. Cream
    b. Freddie King
    c. Albert King
    d. King Curtis

636. Who was the only person to drum live for the Who before Kenney Jones took over after Keith Moon died?
    a. John "Rabbit" Bundrick
    b. Horton "Chucky" Tannerton
    c. Cozy Powell
    d. Scott Halpin

637. The story line is "*two lovers in a car that's stranded on the railroad tracks... dude pulls the girlfriend from the car, but she freaks because she left her class ring behind, and when she runs back to get it, she gets run over by the train...*" (sigh). What's the song, Romeo?

638. Which of these bands (or albums) did not feature "twin lead guitars"?
   a. Allman Brothers
   b. Wishbone Ash
   c. Lou Reed's *Rock 'n Roll Animals* album
   d. Thin Lizzy
   e. Derek & the Dominos
   f. A&B
   g. C&E
   h. All of the above

639. CTI Records – regarded as a Jazz label – had one Top 10 singles hit. What was it? Who was it by?

640. What Brit band had to change their name because there was a naming conflict with an American group?
   a. Roxy Music
   b. King Crimson
   c. Supertramp
   d. Steeleye Span

641. We all know that Steppenwolf was named after a Hermann Hesse novel and Steely Dan was named after a dildo in a William Burroughs novel. What other band got the inspiration for its name from Mr. Burroughs?
   a. Spandau Ballet
   b. Soft Machine
   c. Strawberry Alarm Clock
   d. Fotheringay

642. The phrase, "You shook me all night long" was first introduced to the *Rock* audience by...
   a. Led Zeppelin
   b. Jeff Beck
   c. AC/DC
   d. Love Sculpture

643. Which two of these facts are correct about Billy Joel's "Only the Good Die Young"?
   a. Was originally written as a reggae tune
   b. Was banned by several archdioceses
   c. Edited out of his SNL performance
   d. Came out of a "birds and bees" conversation with his mom, and he turned it around from pro-Catholic/anti-lust to pro-lust/anti-Catholic

644. Leslie West of Mountain did the original guitar parts on the Who's "Behind Blue Eyes" and "Won't Get Fooled Again" and we just don't know it. T/F?

645. And while we're doing a Mountain thing, I'll give you a choice of two Felix Pappalardi questions to deal with. 1) Which Cream song(s) did he write? 2) What Cream album(s) did he produce? Go for it.

646. What's the name of Willie Nelson's guitar?

647. George Thorogood's version of "Move It On Over" is a cover, original, or a tune in the public domain?

648. Mark Knopfler of Dire Straits played the solo on which of these other artists' tunes?

   a. Pink Floyd/"Welcome to the Machine"
   b. Steely Dan/"Time Out of Mind"
   c. Hot Chocolate/"You Sexy Thing"
   d. Donna Summer/"Hot Stuff"

649. "Ain't No Mountain High Enough", "Ain't Nothing Like the Real Thing", "Your Precious Love", and "You're All I Need to Get By" were written by whom?

   a. Goffin & King
   b. The Addrisi Brothers
   c. Ashford & Simpson
   d. Holland-Dozier-Holland

650. What was the first Genesis album to feature Phil Collins as lead singer?

   a. *And Then There Were Three*
   b. *A Trick of the Tail*
   c. *The Lamb Lies Down on Broadway*
   d. *Wind & Wuthering*

651. Who was the first woman to have a UK #1 single with a self-written song?

   a. Kate Bush with "Wuthering Heights"
   b. Charo with "Dance a Little Bit Closer"
   c. Cher with "Dark Lady"
   d. Mary Hopkin's "Those Were the Days"

652. Which song has more vocal overdubs? 10cc's "I'm Not in Love" or Queen's "Bohemian Rhapsody"?

653. What's the Top 40 hit that tells the unsettling story of three guys trapped in a collapsed mine, and two of whom resort to cannibalism against the third? Extra points if you can name the songwriter and his solo hit eight years later.

654. In spite of being labeled Elton John's lyricist, Bernie Taupin actually co-wrote with other folks. Which <u>three</u> of these might they be?
   a. Roger Daltrey
   b. Alice Cooper
   c. Heart
   d. Brian Wilson
   e. Rod Stewart

655. Extending our stay on Elton's campgrounds, let me ask you this: In "Levon", who is Levon's dad?
   a. Spencer Day
   b. Jesus
   c. Alvin Tostig
   d. Paul Faraar

656. He's better known as the leader of a great funk band, but started out as a drummer for the Ramsey Lewis Trio, Muddy Waters, Buddy Guy, and Etta James. Who is this man?

657. Who is the only member of Pink Floyd to appear on every Floyd album?

658. What iconic '70s song did Will Ferrell and Christopher Walken base their *Saturday Night Live* "more cowbell" skit on?

659. Identify the novelty songs by these clues...
   a. Uke + an update of a 1929 hit

      ____

   b. Driven crazy by a mangy mutt + a flip side in reverse

      ____

   c. Youngster King meets up with untamed and fanatical chap

      ____

   d. Sheik and Clyde go to see Fatima

      ____

660. What song was inspired by the comic strip *Peanuts*, written/produced by the guy who wrote "Abraham, Martin, and John" and the guy who produced "Stay" by Maurice Williams & the Zodiacs?

661. Can you spare me another Beatles question for a moment? "Martha My Dear" was written about whom? "Dear Prudence" about whom? And "Hey Jude" was written about/for whom?

662. a) What 1967 Mamas & Papas Top 5 hit was autobiographical; b) name one of the *non*-Mamas & Papas music people they reference in the song.

663. Identify these phunky phrases with the songs they're from...
   a. Goo goo ga joob ______________________
   b. Coo coo ca-choo ______________________

664. What was the first album to debut at #1?
   a. Led Zeppelin *IV (Zoso)*
   b. Elton John's *Captain Fantastic and the Brown Dirt Cowboy*
   c. Rolling Stones' *Sticky Fingers*
   d. Bob Dylan's *Blood on the Tracks*
   e. Beatles' *Sgt. Peppers...*

665. What band took its name from a flatbed truck and fire engine, made by a company whose founder was Ransom Eli Olds?

666. What folk anthem was written as a rebuttal to Irving Berlin's "God Bless America"?
   a. "This Land is Your Land"
   b. "Blowin' in the Wind"
   c. "If I Had a Hammer"
   d. "Greenback Dollar"

667. In the late '70s, an ad showing two women bare-shouldered with the line "It was only our first time" created an "I didn't know they were lesbians"-type reaction. Who were the women?

668. The trademark sound of what instrument can be heard on "Wooly Bully", "Crocodile Rock", and "Double Shot of My Baby's Love"?
   a. Jews harp
   b. Farfisa
   c. Moog
   d. Hurdy gurdy
   e. Hammered dulcimer

669. Were the Walker Brothers ("The Sun Ain't Gonna Shine Anymore") brothers, men named Walker, or neither?

670. Actor Cuba Gooding Jr.'s father was in what '60s/'70s soul group?
    a. Chi-Lites
    b. Main Ingredient
    c. O'Jays
    d. The Impressions

671. We know that Neil Bogart founded Casablanca Records to ride the wave of Disco with Donna Summer, the Village People, Meco, Santa Esmerelda and others. What other wave did he ride at another record company in the Sixties?

672. What's the only Top Ten song* that was a palindrome (read the same forward or backward, character for character without regard for punctuation) for both the artist *and* the song title?
*at least in the U.S.

673. (Paul Revere &) the Raiders only Number One was an update of what previous semi-hit?
    a. Marvin Rainwater's "The Pale Faced Indian"
    b. Don Fardon's "Indian Reservation (The Lament of the Cherokee Reservation Indian)"
    c. Joe South's "Birds of a Feather"
    d. Bobby Sherman's "Mr. Sun, Mr. Moon"

674. There is a two-way tie for the shortest title of a song to make it to number one on the *Billboard* Hot 100 in the '70s. Both were Motown Records tracks. What were they?

675. After Elvis, who had the most Number One singles from 1955 thru 1964?
   a. Ricky Nelson
   b. Pat Boone
   c. Bobby Vinton
   d. Bobby Rydell

676. Inspiration for Melanie's "Lay Down (Candles in the Rain)" apparently came from what situation?

677. Hendrix' tune "Spanish Castle Magic" is about...
   a. An LSD-based experience Jimi had on the coast of Spain
   b. A rock club in Des Moines, Washington that Jimi used to frequent
   c. An anagram he based on a painting one his groupies, a "Miss Alpaca" did: "Miss Alpaca's Etching"
   d. Nothing in particular – it's just Jimi being freaky with his lyrics

678. The first million-selling Country song to cross over to both the Pop *and* R&B charts was...
   a. "Heartbreak Hotel"
   b. "Blue Suede Shoes"
   c. "Hound Dog"
   d. "Rock Around the Clock"

679. Led Zeppelin's 1972 concert in Singapore was cancelled by government officials for what reason?
   a. Plant had spoken out against their capital punishment laws in *Melody Maker*
   b. The band's hair was too long
   c. The government was afraid of a riot because seating was "festival style"
   d. Bonham had fathered a child out of wedlock on a previous trip to Singapore and had refused to provide for it

680. Chicago's "Make Me Smile" and "Colour My World" came from what ballet?

681. What song starts with this producer-to-singer exchange on the squawk box?

   Producer: *"7A"* (referring to the take of the song)
   Singer: *"What number is this, Chip?"*
   Producer and others (annoyed): *"7A!"*
   Singer: *"Okay. I mean, don't get excited, man. Just 'cause I'm short, I know."*

682. The first <u>double</u> album was...
   a. Mr. Dylan's *Blonde on Blonde*
   b. Mothers of Invention's *Freak Out!*
   c. Aphrodite's Child's *666*
   d. James Brown's *Live at the Apollo, Vol. II*
   e. Cream's *Wheels of Fire*
   f. Benny Goodman's *Live at Carnegie Hall*
   g. Deep Purple's *Live in Japan*

683. Why did Columbia have to change the album cover of the first Moby Grape album?

684. While we're in the changing room, why did Lloyd Price have to recut "Stagger Lee"?

685. Little Richard kicked off his career on what label?
   a. RCA
   b. Specialty
   c. Arhoolie
   d. Peacock

686. Who penned "Reason to Believe" (Rod Stewart recorded it, among others) and "If I Were a Carpenter" (Bobby Darin, et al)?
   a. Harry Chapin
   b. Gary Wright
   c. Ian Matthews
   d. Tim Hardin
   e. Tim Moore
   f. Nick Drake

687. Before her singing career, Roberta Flack was ...
   a. A waitress
   b. In law school
   c. A teacher
   d. The Entertainment reporter for *The Washington Post*

688. Which of these did *not* spend time in prison? Ike Turner, James Brown, Johnny Cash, Gary Glitter, Chuck Berry, or Sid Vicious.

689. What record labels did Frank Zappa form (with manager Herb Cohen)? Can be more than one...
    a. Straight
    b. Bearsville
    c. Skin Graft
    d. Bizarre
    e. Fantasy
    f. Tender Loin

690. The Young Rascals "Good Lovin'" was originally recorded by whom? And if you can tell me what similarity it has to "Paperback Writer" and "Monday, Monday", I'll give you an extra brownie."
    a. The Hully Gullies
    b. The Olympics
    c. The Orlons

691. After Simon & Garfunkel's debut LP, *Wednesday Morning, 3 A.M.*, proved to be a dud, Paul moved to England to pursue a solo career and there he met Bruce Woodley (songwriting member of the Seekers and the uncredited co-writer of S&G's "Cloudy"), and together they co-wrote what hit?
    a. "Red Rubber Ball" (Cyrkle)
    b. "Lovin' Things" (Grassroots)
    c. "Georgy Girl" (Seekers)
    d. "You've Got Your Troubles" (Fortunes)

692. What Temptations song uses the word "leeching" in the lyrics?

693. Which of these Elton John studio albums didn't spawn a single?
    a. *Rock of the Westies*
    b. *Blue Moves*
    c. *Tumbleweed Connection*
    d. *A Single Man*

694. Right before her LPs *Writer* and *Tapestry*, name the two groups Carole King toiled in/worked with...

695. What artist(s) took out their frustration of being rejected by Columbia Records in one of their hits?
    a. Sugarloaf
    b. Looking Glass
    c. Alan O'Day
    d. Pacific Gas & Electric

696. The Funk Brothers – Motown's session group – sometimes moonlighted outside the label's watchful eye. One of the more prominent of those recordings was...
    a. Major Lance/"Monkey Time"
    b. Tyrone Davis/"Can I Change My Mind"
    c. Jackie Wilson/"(Your Love Keeps Lifting Me) Higher and Higher"
    d. The Manhattans/"Kiss and Say Goodbye"

697. What '70s pop hit wound up as the theme to TV's *Golden Girls* sitcom?

698. Bon Scott was the first, second, or third lead singer of AC/DC?

699. Owsley Stanley was...
   a. The guy who supplied the Grateful Dead most of their LSD
   b. The Grateful Dead's sound guy
   c. The guy who created the Dead's lightning bolt skull logo
   d. All of the above
   e. A and B
   f. B and C
   g. None of the above

700. In the Standells "Dirty Water", one finds the lead singer down by the banks of the River Charles with what three kinds of reprobates?

701. What band commissioned *Playboy* artist Alberto Vargas to do the cover of their '79 LP?
   a. Little Feat/*Down on the Farm*
   b. Foreigner/*Head Games*
   c. Nick Lowe/*Labour of Lust*
   d. The Cars/*Candy-O*

702. In Aaron Neville's "Tell It Like It Is", what's the next line after "Baby, my time is too expensive"?

703. Why did the Purple People Eater come down to Earth?

704. I know you've been waiting all day for me to throw some "sequels" your way, so I'll keep it simple. What was the "sequel" to Buddy Holly's "Peggy Sue"?

705. Who backed up Johnny Nash on "I Can See Clearly Now"?
   a. The Wailers
   b. Toots and the Maytals
   c. Dave and Ansell Collins
   d. Jimmy Cliff's band

706. What song was originally called "Revolution" but changed because the Beatles came out with a song of the same name first?
   a. "Something in the Air"
   b. "In the Year 2525"
   c. "Spirit in the Sky"
   d. "A Whiter Shade of Pale"

707. Who was the first Australian rock and roll act to have an *international* pop hit?
   a. The Seekers
   b. The Easybeats
   c. Midnight Oil
   d. The Rooftop Singers

708. The prolific Jackie DeShannon wrote a bunch 'o tunes. The test is to see is you can tell us which three of these Top 40 hits she wrote!
   a. Her own "Put a Little Love in Your Heart"
   b. Marianne Faithfull's "Come and Stay With Me"
   c. Kim Carnes' "Bette Davis Eyes"
   d. Her own "Needles and Pins"
   e. Elvis 's "Kentucky Rain"

709. In the version we all hear(d) on the radio, what line was bleeped out in Johnny Cash's "A Boy Named Sue"?

710. What live music TV show was Wolfman Jack the announcer on from '73-'81?
   a. *In Concert*
   b. *Midnight Special*
   c. *Sound Stage*
   d. *Hollywolf & Vine*

711. What's (probably) the only album to feature a toilet on the album jacket?

712. Who gave Chubby Checker his stage name?
   a. Dick Clark
   b. Dick Clark's wife
   c. Dick Clark's daughter
   d. Bob Horn

713. What artist was the first to cover Joni Mitchell?
   a. Judy Collins
   b. Tom Rush
   c. Al Kooper
   d. Murray McLauchlan
   e. The Walker Brothers?

714. Which of these records had the fewest unique words in their lyrics?
   a. Silver Convention's "Fly Robin Fly"
   b. The Beatles' "Her Majesty"
   c. Iron Butterfly's "In-A-Gadda-Da-Vida"
   d. (folk song) "Hava Nagila"

715. I bet you thought we'd never get around to pelting you with one-hit wonders, did you? Who did these one-and-dones?

a. "Born to Be Alive"
b. "Israelites"
c. "My Boy Lollipop"
d. "You, I"
e. "The Pied Piper"
f. "Ballad of the Green Berets"
g. "Reflections of My Life"
h. "Oh, Happy Day"
i. "Beautiful Sunday"
j. "How Do You Do? "
k. "I'm Easy"
l. "Gallant Men"
m. "The Men in My Little Girl's Life"
n. "One Tin Soldier"
o. "Lay a Little Lovin' On Me"
p. "Rubber Duckie"
q. "For the Good Times"
r. "Thunder Island"
s. "Chirpy Chirpy Cheep Cheep"
t. "Desiderata"
u. "Day by Day"
v. "Good Time Charlie's Got the Blues"
w. "Hot Child in the City"
x. "Pop Muzik"
y. "Reach Out of the Darkness"
z. "Precious and Few"

Bonus points for our extreme trivia fans:
What artist did 28 <u>localized</u> versions of his song about "high school"?

716. Who is the "first name only" artist who scored hits with songs from *The Prime of Miss Jean Brodie* and *Hair*?

717. What song came about after Bob Crewe (wrote many 4 Seasons classics) and Kenny Nolan ("I Like Dreamin'") made first-hand observations in New Orleans, Louisiana?

718. David Johansen, lead singer of '70s glammers New York Dolls, reinvented himself in a parallel pseudonymic life in the '80s as whom?

719. Who wrote "Mr. Bojangles"?
    a. John Prine
    b. Jerry Jeff Walker
    c. David Bromberg
    d. Jeff Hanna (Nitty Gritty Dirt Band)
    e. Mickey Newbury

720. Which *two* of the following were <u>not</u> a multi-racial group in their *first* incarnation?
    a. Traffic
    b. Little Feat
    c. Three Dog Night
    d. Allman Brothers

721. What song paid homage to '50s TV star Duncan Renaldo?
    a. "Cisco Kid"
    b. "Hot Rod Lincoln"
    c. "Pancho and Lefty"
    d. "Corazon"

722. Noted author/professor Wilson Bryan Key made a claim in his book *Subliminal Seduction* that the chant in what song was momentarily changed to the phrase "who got sucked off"?
   a. "Running Bear"
   b. "Hooked on a Feeling"
   c. "Papa-Oom-Mow-Mow"
   d. "Who Do You Love? "

723. Let's see how well you can count. Pick out the correct original configuration for the following:
   a. Rush: Trio | Quartet | Quintet
   b. Ramones: Trio | Quartet | Quintet
   c. The Kinks: Trio | Quartet | Quintet
   d. The Dells: Trio | Quartet | Quintet
   e. The Band: Trio | Quartet | Quintet
   f. Sex Pistols: Trio | Quartet | Quintet

724. Who owns Hank Williams' Martin D-28 guitar?

725. What pop star wrote the theme to Johnny Carson's *Tonight Show,* "My Way" for Sinatra, Tom Jones' "She's a Lady", the last single release for Buddy Holly, and #1 hits of his own in the '60s and '70s?

726. Did Jazz greats Miles Davis or John Coltrane ever play on a "rock-oriented" album?

727. What song was written as an after-effect of Brenda Ann Spencer's 1979 attempted massacre at an elementary school in San Diego, California?

728. What's Georgio Moroder's place in music?

729. What groups spawned these solo artists?
   a. Jeffrey Osborne____________________
   b. Ben E. King ____________________
   c. Sam Cooke____________________
   d. Marvin Gaye____________________
   e. Lionel Richie____________________
   f. Minnie Riperton ____________________

730. Which British Invasion act was the *first* to appear on *The Ed Sullivan Show*?
   a. Billy J. Kramer
   b. Freddie & the Dreamers
   c. The Beatles
   d. Gerry & the Pacemakers
   e. Chad & Jeremy

731. After appearances at Monterey and Woodstock, a band that was named after a song about an alcoholic who had desperately turned to drinking Sterno acquired worldwide fame with a lineup consisting of guys nicknamed Fito, Big Bear, and Blind Owl. Who are they?

732. David Geffen co-founded what iconic record label in 1970?

733. Take a look at these song titles: "Shame","M.T.A.", "Dancing in the Moonlight", and the phrase ""Elvis has left the building". What theme might I be going for if I played those four tunes back-to-back?

734. Which of these items are true about the Police? Could be none, one, two, three, or all four.
   a. They were once a quartet
   b. They went blonde as part of their role in a commercial for Wrigley's gum
   c. The name and image of the band was Stewart Copeland's before there were any real members
   d. There are three different incarnations of the band

735. Who wrote "The Twist" and invented the dance?

736. Which '60s/'70s album stayed in the #1 slot on the album charts for more than a year - longer than any other album in chart history?
   a. *West Side Story*
   b. *Rumours*
   c. *Blue Hawaii*
   d. *Saturday Night Fever*
   e. *Dark Side of the Moon*

737. A Hendrix/Santana-influenced guitar solo, an album with a pair of "3's", and an updated cover of a tune they released nine years earlier that was inspired by the Impressions... Who is the group and what is da song?

738. If I said to you, a la *Jeopardy*, "3:35 or 3:34 a.m.", what song title would you answer me with?

739. Who is the "Mr. Hughes" who "hid in Dylan's shoes" in Rick Nelson's "Garden Party"?

740. How many people were on the ship that set sail from San Francisco Bay in Blues Image's "Ride Captain Ride"?

741. What U.S. president was lionized by both Chicago and Danny O'Keefe in separate mid-70s songs?

742. What song was based on a true life experience by Justin Hayward of the Moody Blues?
   a. Moody Blues/"Legend of a Mind"
   b. Queen/"You're My Best Friend"
   c. 10cc/"Dreadlock Holiday"
   d. Bonnie Tyler/"It's a Heartache"

743. Which Temptation sang lead on "My Girl"?
   a. Dennis Edwards
   b. David Ruffin
   c. Jimmy Ruffin
   d. Eddie Kendricks
   e. Melvin Franklin

744. Which '50s/'60s group was begun by Neil Sedaka only for the group *and* Sedaka to achieve success after Neil split to go solo?
   a. The Ad-Libs
   b. The Tokens
   c. The Happenings
   d. Jay & the Americans

745. Name one of the gospel groups Elvis employed as his background singers, either on stage *or* in the studio.

746. What Grateful Dead album did Lowell George (Little Feat) produce?
   a. *Terrapin Station*
   b. *From the Mars Hotel*
   c. *Shakedown Street*

747. A little more label grillin'...
   a. What label's slogan was "The Sound of Young America"?____________
   b. What label featured a pair of snapping fingers? ____________
   c. What TV music show host co-owned their own R&B record label? ____________
   d. What fuchsia-colored label had its first British #1 with a song produced by Mick Jagger and written by Jagger/Richards?

      ____
   e. The Nashville label that was the outlet for Dolly Parton's first album, as well as home for Roy Orbison, Ray Stevens, and Kris Kristofferson. ____________

748. The dates on the "Date Due" card on the back jacket are significant moments in the history of rock and roll. Identify at least *four* of these...
   a. February 3, 1959______________________
   b. February 9, 1964______________________
   c. June 16, 1967 ______________________
   d. August 15, 1969 ______________________
   e. December 8, 1980 ______________________
   f. July 3, 1971 ______________________
   g. August 16, 1977______________________

749. Gimme an F! Gimme the songs that belong to the following lyrics that begins with the letter "F"...

  a. Fear is the lock and laughter the key to your heart______________________________
  b. For what is a man, what has he got? If not himself, then he has naught. To say the things he truly feels, and not the words of one who kneels. ______________________
  c. Freedom, well, that's just some people talking. Your prison is walking through this world all alone. ____________________
  d. Feel the thrill of totting up a balanced book, a thousand ciphers neatly in a row. When gazing at a chart that shows the profits up, their little cup of joy should over flow. ______________________________
  e. Feel no sorrow, feel no shame, come tomorrow feel no pain. _________________
  f. Fools, said I, you do not know, silence like a cancer grows. ________________________

750. Which Doors song is featured in the film *Apocalypse Now*?

(psst – There's bonus material awaiting you right around the corner…)

[Extra Little Treat]

WELL, THIS IS WHERE WE'RE *supposed* to stop, but we're already planning for a revised (and larger) edition and thought we'd give you a little taste. There's plenty of room for your involvement, too – if you have any interesting Q&A, send 'em our way to "garyworld@ gmail.com" and look for your name to get a little ink when the new edition comes out.

751. Which Fleetwood Mac song did both the Dixie Chicks and the Smashing Pumpkins cover?

752. What orchestral-sounding, -based, -genre, whateveryouwannacallem group did John Lennon once refer to as "The Sons of Beatles"? Let me clue you in – it *ain't* Zak, Dhani, Julian, and Sean.

753. What future Crosby, Stills, and Nash track did the Hollies first take a crack at?

754. My grandma Addie used to eat Vicks Vapo-Rub before she went to bed which I thought was flipped out, but what's the most outlandish thing that Keith Richards claims *he* ever snorted?

755. Tell me it's not true! One of these couples was in a Creedence Clearwater Revival cover band before they became famous in their own configuration. Which pair was it, pray tell?
   a. Frank Black + Kim Deal of the Pixies
   b. Kurt Cobain + Krist Novoselic of Nirvana
   c. Anthony Kiedis + Flea of Red Hot Chili Peppers

756. The year was 1964 and Jimmy Page was one hot session cat. Which of the following British Invasion nuggets did he *not* play guitar on?
   a. The Who/"Can't Explain"
   b. Them/"Gloria"
   c. Nashville Teens/Tobacco Road
   d. Rolling Stones/"Heart of Stone"
   e. The Kinks/"You Really Got Me"

757. What gigantic troupe was made up of musicians given the pet names of the Master of Space and Time, the Gentle Giant, the Ruby-Lipped Essence of Lubbock Texas, the Stellar Gypsy, and the Price is Right, among others?

758. Who won every dang Grammy for Best Vocal Performance from 1967 thru 1974? Was it...
   a. Diana Ross
   b. Aretha Franklin
   c. Tina Turner
   d. Roberta Flack

759. The ice cream vendor in Chicago's "Saturday in the Park" was singing what kind of songs?

760. An Elvis two-fer...
   a. What crooner did EP sing alongside in a '50s TV special where Elvis and Mr. X did each other's songs?
   b. What contemporary vixen beat out Presley for the most #1 hits by a *solo* performer?

761. Besides Sinatra, two of his fellow Rat Pack'ers had a #1 in the '60s/70s. Who were they and what were the songs?

762. Only *two* of these items about Woodstock are <u>true</u>. Which ones?
   a. All the songs on the Woodstock soundtrack weren't actually recorded at Woodstock.
   b. Joni Mitchell tried to get to the festival to perform but got waylaid by traffic and never made it to the site.
   c. One of the guys who bankrolled the fest was the guy who co-wrote "Dead Man's Curve" for Jan & Dean and "The Rain, the Park, and Other Things" for The Cowsills.
   d. All told, all the participating artists were paid a total of $320,600.

763. Not known for standard issue anything, Frank Zappa gave his kids some interesting names. Of these five, which is the fake? Moon Unit, Ahmet Emuukha Rodan, Pilot Inspektor Lee, Ian Donald Calvin Euclid Zappa, or Diva Thin Muffin Pigeen?

764. What R&B staple did Cassius Clay (Muhammad Ali) cover and release as his first (and only) single?

765. What song did the Orange County Sheriff order The Association not to play at Disneyland because of its alleged references to mar-a-ja-wanna?

766. The wife of what famous philanderer said, she "wasn't some little woman 'standing by my man' like Tammy Wynette"?

767. Besides the Twist, what's another dance Chubby Checker popularized?

768. What Lennon song came about as a reflection of his, Yoko, and Eric Clapton's efforts to beat drug addiction?

769. What's the connection between Bruce Springsteen and the Partridge Family?
    a. The guy who played Reuben Kincaid, the band's manager, is Springsteen's uncle
    b. The guy who was Springsteen's manager is the same guy who wrote five of the Partridge's songs, including their hit "Doesn't Somebody Want to Be Wanted"
    c. Two members of the E Street Band - Max Weinberg and Garry Tallent - played on several of the later Partridge Family tracks
    d. Springsteen sent some of his earlier stuff to the Partridge Family for review and David Cassidy and company actually demo'ed "Blinded by the Light".

770. 'nuther crack at nonsense lyrics… What songs go with:

   a. Gliddy glub gloopy, Nibby nabby noopy, La la la lo lo ______________________
   b. Lincoln, Lincoln bo Bincoln Bonana fanna fo Fincoln ______________________
   c. Doo doo doo down doo be do down down ______________________
   d. Bon c'est bon, bon bon c'est bon, bon ______________________
   e. Yip yip yip yip yip yip yip yip Mum mum mum mum mum mum ______________
   f. Doo lang do lang doo lang doo lang ______________________

771. True or False… Michael Jackson owned the rights to the entire Beatles song catalogue.

772. What song takes place in Rosedale, Mississippi, at the intersection of Highway 8 and Highway 1?

773. What famous rocker was the sperm donor for the two kids Melissa Ethridge had with Julie Cypher?

774. In the '70s, a well-known rockin' chick punched out Elvis Costello when he called James Brown a "jive-ass [n-word]" and Ray Charles a "blind ignorant [n-word]". The lady with the fist was…

   a. Bonnie Tyler
   b. Bonnie Raitt
   c. Bonnie Bramlett

775. What tune says, "If you want a hit, you have to make it fit, so they cut it down to three-o-five."?

776. As we've learned, groups name themselves after everything from a dildo in a William Burroughs novel to an unemployment form. I dare not insult you with the Leonard Skinner gym teacher question, but let's see if you can handle these bad boys...

   a. What '60s folk-rock group named themselves after a line in a Mississippi John Hurt song? ______________________
   b. A well-known British band's agent used to change the band's name after every gig because they were having trouble getting repeat bookings. One time, they were named after an 18th-century agriculturist and the name stuck with 'em because a club manager liked their act well enough to invite them to return. Who was this band?

      ____
   c. What band was named after the rare breed of a Siamese cat that belonged to a friend of their manager. Tip: The name is Latin for "Beyond these things".______________
   d. What group's moniker was inspired by an Australian Aboriginal custom of sleeping with a dog for warmth on a cold night in the Outback?______________________

777. What later-to-be Grammy-winning group was the house band for Boz Scaggs' *Silk Degrees*?

778. The writer said, "I had the TIME magazine there, with that girl looking up from a dead student lying on the ground with the blood and the whole deal. I just wrote it. It just came out right there on the porch. It was really like the folk process at work. You know, that was really like music as news." Who's the writer and what's the song?

779. Who was the first black male singer to record five consecutive multi-platinum albums?
   a. Al Green
   b. Teddy Pendergrass
   c. Marvin Gaye
   d. Barry White
   e. Freddie Jackson

■ ■ ■

Answers

1. [b] Dave Dee, Dozy, Beaky, Mick, and Tich (the group's name is a combination of their nicknames). Not that we Yanks know much about 'em, but their biggest record in the Isles was "The Legend of Xanadu" (a #1 in '68) for those of you keeping score.

2. [b] "Taxi". The other songs were doin' other nasties in the backseats of their cars.

3. [c] Botticelli ("…Got to hurry on back to my hotel room, where I've got me a date with Botticelli's niece. She promised that she'd be right there with me when I paint my masterpiece…").

4. [c] and [d] Satchmo and the 5th Dimension hit the top of the pops, although it's interesting that four songs from *Hair* made it to the top five: "Aquarius", then the Cowsills (#2), Three Dog Night (#4), and Oliver's version of "Good Morning Starshine" which peaked at #3.

5. [a] "The Battle of Evermore". Fairport Convention'er Sandy was the only person to ever

do a guest vocal on a Zeppelin studio record. BTW, she also made a brief cameo on Lou Reizner's version of the Who's *Tommy*.

6. The four symbols represent (from left to right) Jimmy Page, John Paul Jones, John Bonham, and Robert Plant. Every symbol was designed by its respective member and supposedly has some personal meaning to each. While the cheap drunks in the crowd will tell you that Bonham's symbol is the same as the Ballantine Beer logo, it's supposed to represent the trinity of the father, mother, and child. Back to the Sandy Denny inclusion – there's also a fifth (and smaller) symbol chosen by her which serves as an asterisk and shaped like three triangles touching at their points.

7. [d] Vivian Liberto, Cash's first wife. She met Cash at a roller rink in San Antone while he was doing basic training for the Air Force. Bonnie Owens? She was married to Buck and to Merle Haggard.

8. Cynthia. They met in lettering class at art school, married in '62 and split in '68 when John went on with Yoko. Cyn could've walked away with half of Lennon's assets, but settled for £100,000, plus £2,400 a year, custody of Julian, and their Kenwood estate.

9. David Crosby. He also penned "Almost Cut My Hair" on the LP.

10. [b] Phil Spector. "On Broadway" peaked @ #8 in '63. Fifteen years later, George Benson's version bettered the original, hitting #7 on the charts.

11. Uh, true. August 3, '74 at the Wollman Ice Rink Theatre in Central Park, NY for the Schaefer Music Festival. Brewer & Shipley was the opener.

12. Don McLean. The story behind the song belongs to Lori Lieberman who wrote a poem about her experience seeing McLean. However, Charles Fox and Norman Gimbel actually wrote the lyrics and melody. The story goes that Flack heard Lori's version on an in-flight channel and told her producer that she wanted to record the tune.

13. [b] "Blue Moon of Kentucky". Bill Black, Elvis' bassist, came up with the idea to renovate Bill Monroe's Bluegrass tune from a slow waltz into an upbeat, blues-flavored song.

14. *Happening '68* (later turned into a weekday version called *It's Happening*).

15. [d] Minnie Riperton – the same Minnie who sang background vocals for Etta James, Fontella Bass, Ramsey Lewis, Bo Diddley, Chuck Berry, and Muddy Waters records... the same Minnie who is Maya Randolph's (*Saturday Night Live*) mom (and the same Maya who Minnie's "Lovin' You" was written about). BTW, Wikipedia says the greatest range and is eight octaves and belongs to Brazilian Georgia Brown. Sweet.

16. David Gilmour. Actually, the Floyd was a five-piece band for awhile if you count Gilmour as

being a temp when Syd would lose his wheels. And, when Syd permanently lost his wheels, David was the full-time replacement.

17. [a] Steely Dan's "Everything You Did" ("turn up the Eagles, the neighbors are listening") and the Eagles' "Hotel California" ("They stab it with their steely knives but they just can't kill the beast").

18. That was the Altamont gig where spectator Meredith Hunter was stabbed and killed by Hells Angels. Supposedly, he tried to get onstage with other fans, so an Angel grabbed his head, punched him, and chased him into the crowd. After that, the story goes that his girlfriend tried to intervene when Hunter whipped out a pistol and, well, the Angels retaliated by pulling out a 50-pound can of Whup Ass and fatally stabbed him (five times).

19. Gene Simmons. Despite the lift that Ace Frehley should've gotten from his hit single "New York Groove", Chaim Witz (Gene's real name) beat his mates on the album chart, peaking at #22.

20. George Harrison, "My Sweet Lord". John actually beat him to the singles game with "Give Peace a Chance", "Cold Turkey", and "Instant Karma", but Georgie boy rang up a #1 first.

21. Roger McGuinn, although David Crosby and Gene Clark were allowed to sing background vocals. Everyone else you hear was a hired gun (Leon Russell, Hal Blaine, and Larry Knechtel - aka the Wrecking Crew). The Byrds manager got a hold of an acetate of Dylan and Ramblin' Jack Elliott demo'ing the song and the race was on. Five days

after Dylan recorded his, the Byrds did theirs, but Dylan got his out first via *Bringing It All Back Home* on March 22, '65 with the Byrds version coming out on April 12.

22. [a] and [b] are True; [c] and [d] are False – the album hit #1 in the U.K. and only #6 in the U.S.; and the covers they did were a cover of the Nerves' "Hanging on the Telephone" and Buddy Holly's "I'm Gonna Love You, Too".

23. [b] Bill Haley and the Saddlemen. Mostly Country & Western stuff like "Susan Van Dusan" and "My Palomino and I".

24. Iggy Pop ("*He's outrageous, he screams and he bawls*"). The line "*He's so simple minded, he can't drive his module*" would later serve as inspiration to Simple Minds for their name.

25. "We Love You". The tune was a slick response to the Stones never-ending legal hassles following Mick and Keith's drug bust in February 1967, managing to be both a sincere "thank you" to their fan base and a cutting attack on the establishment. The song opens with the sound of footsteps and a jail door slamming shut. Ouch.

26. [a:3] Kristofferson in a Scorcese flick that most people wouldn't consider a "Scorcese" flick; [b:5] Darin even got an Academy Award nom for it; [c:4] Rick Nelson *and* John Wayne, really? [d:2] Tom the bug eater; [e:1] Keith Richards was so livid about the scenes where his girlfriend Anita Pallenberg and Jagger were knockin' boots that he refused to play when the Stones recorded "Memo

from Turner" for the soundtrack, so Ry Cooder filled in (quite admirably).

27. [d] Columbia Records, but Columbia didn't do anything with them other than a few demos.

28. Under the pseudonym of Dr. West's Medicine Show and Junk Band, Norm recorded the "The Eggplant That Ate Chicago" which peaked around 50 on the charts.

29. [a] The Supremes were previously known as the Primettes and were formed as a sister act to the Primes with Paul Williams and Eddie Kendricks who later founded the Temptations; [b] Marvin recorded with Tammi Terrell, Mary Wells, Kim Weston, and Diana Ross; [c] Paul Peterson of *The Donna Reed Show*, Soupy Sales, Diahann Carroll, and Irene Ryan (Granny from *The Beverly Hillbillies*); [d] Mary Wells.

30. [a] Bon Jovi's (2nd) cuz, Tony Bongiovi who also produced Ozzy, Meco (the theme from *Star Wars*), Gloria Gaynor, Aerosmith, Scorpions, and the Ramones. He was the guy who turned an old NYC power station in to the Power Station recording studios which the band Power Station ("Some Like it Hot") named themselves after.

31. [d] John Martyn. Shortly after he broke the color barrier of the reggae-based label, they signed Jethro Tull, Traffic, and Free and grew into one of the leading progressive rock labels of the era.

32. Dennis Edmonton is the real name of one "Mars Bonfire" who wrote "Born to Be Wild". He was in

the original line-up of the Sparrows (with drummer brother Jerry) who went on to become Steppenwolf. Given the frequency with which "Born to Be Wild" shows up in movies (close to 50, now), and TV commercials, the boy's got some serious mailbox money coming in.

33. Paul McCartney. Okay, let's see you come up with the answers to those variations: There's Wings, there's Paul and Stevie Wonder, and...

34. In order: A fight in the House of Representatives over a section of the civil rights bill... death of Lenny Bruce... a planned Martin Luther King-led march in Cicero, Illinois... the Richard Speck murders... federal regulations on anti-Vietnam protests. All of the events were from August 3, 1966. If you're in the ballpark on any of 'em, give yourself some points, ok?

35. Fred Neil. Fred's one of the most heralded folkies ever, yet most people have never heard of him. In his early days, he penned songs for Roy Orbison ("Candy Man") and Buddy Holly. Later on, Dylan and John Sebastian played harmonica for him; he did session work for Paul Anka and Bobby Darin; and James Taylor, Joni Mitchell, Jimmy Buffett and dozens of others cite him as one of their inspirations. Stephen Stills sat at his feet and learned about the 12-string guitar. Nilsson actually proposed "I Guess the Lord Must Be in New York City" for *Midnight Cowboy* but the movie's director, John Schlesinger, choose "Everybody's Talkin'" instead.

36. [a] Charles Mingus (her LP *Mingus* paid homage and was Mingus' final sessions), Larry Klein (started out as a session bassist, wound up producing most of Joni's albums from '82 on, then marrying her), and Jaco Pastorius (the cat who helped her jazzy expansions on *Hejira, Don Juan's Reckless Daughter, Mingus* , and *Shadows and Light*).

37. There are three that we know of: 1) Donovan's daughter, Iona Skye, was married to Adam Horovitz of the Beasties; 2) both Donovan and the Beasties had records produced by Rick Rubin; 3) the Beastie Boys paid homage to Donovan on *Paul's Boutique* by not only mentioning "Hurdy Gurdy Man" in the lyrics but also sampling the (drum) break for "Car Thief". *Paul's Boutique* is a wonderful head game for anyone who likes to pick out influences 'coz the Beasties sample 105 different tunes — stuff from Zeppelin, AWB, Pink Floyd, Jean Knight, Sly, Commodores, Sweet, Mountain, Alice Cooper, Black Oak, Tower of Power, Johnny Cash, Hendrix, Eagles, on and on.

38. [d] Savoy Brown. The three Savoys that left were Dave Peverett ("Lonesome Dave", guitar/vocal), Tony Stevens (bass), and Roger Earl (drums). Their first album was produced by Dave Edmunds which had the cover of Willie Dixon's "I Just Want to Make Love to You" you probably know. And Toe Fat? There really is such a thing and it was a pre-cursor to Uriah Heep.

39. Jorge Santana; Malo; "Suavecito". "Suavecito" was written by Malo's timbale player who originally

wrote it as a poem for a chick in his Algebra class. The song has been called "The Chicano National Anthem" (José, can you see?).

40. Jim Morrison, Brian Jones, Kurt Cobain, Robert Johnson, Alan Wilson (Canned Heat), Pete Ham (Badfinger), Ron "Pigpen" McKernan (Grateful Dead), a cat from Spanky & Our Gang, someone from Uriah Heep, the guitarist from Big Star, my grandmother's third cousin, yadda...

41. Jerry Lee Lewis but, get this – Dr. Nick later wound up as Lewis' road manager for a short time. How much ink did the good doc use on 'scrips? More than 10,000 doses of sedatives, amphetamines, and narcotics – all in Elvis' name – in the eight months leading up to Presley's death.

42. [d] "Remember the Days of the Old Schoolyard". Did you know that Yusuf was deported back to the UK after he tried to enter to the States in '04 for a meeting with... drum roll, please... Dolly Parton! Really. She had recorded "Peace Train" earlier and wanted to do another of his tunes and they were just gonna chat about things, you know?

43. Bill Bruford. King Crimson *and* Yes *and* Genesis (but just on tour). He was also offered the skins gig in the Firm with Jimmy Page and Paul Rodgers, but declined.

44. [a] Carole King, the Shirelles – the group the Beatles said was their favorite – were the first "black all-female" group to have a #1 record. Some claim that Billy Joel played on "Leader of the

Pack" but I can't find any solid evidence so we'll leave this out there with the urban myth fairies.

45. [a] Ohio Players/"Love Rollercoaster". Yes, the same one with the urban myth about the scream in the middle of the song belonging to the chick covered in honey on the cover being stabbed to death in the recording studio after interrupting the band's session.

46. Hal David. "Raindrops Keep Fallin' on My Head", "I Say a Little Prayer", "Walk on By", "What the World Needs Now is Love", and dozens of others came from the pen of Hal as the music came from Burt's keys. Hal wrote with a number of different folks in the Forties and early Fifties (for songs by Sarah Vaughn, Percy Faith, et al), but things really changed in 1956 when he and Burt met in the Brill Building. They teamed up for co-writes on stuff for the Four Aces, Perry Como, Jack Jones, Merv Griffin, Marty Robbins, et al, and really hit high gear in 1962 when they did "Only Love Can Break a Heart" and "The Man Who Shot Liberty Valance" for Gene Pitney. After that, they never looked back – Dionne Warwick, Dusty Springfield, the 5th Dimension, Tom Jones, etc.

47. If you said [b] Bobby Taylor *or* [c] Gladys Knight, you get the credit. Gladys Knight first saw 'em at the Apollo in '67 but Gordy said Motown already had one "child act" (Stevie Wonder). When the J5 opened for Bobby Taylor and the Vancouvers at a Chicago gig in '68, he was blown away, brought 'em to Detroit where they slept on the floor of his

apartment and, then, the next day, auditioned for Motown by singing their version of James Brown's "I Got the Feelin'" (they had to videotape the performance for Gordy because he was in LA).

48. Three Dog Night who initially went by the moniker "Redwood" and even did some early recordings in '67 with Brian Wilson.

49. [c] Because the songs had "advertising" references. "Come Monday" for "Hush Puppies on" (changed to "hiking boots on"); "Lola" for "Coca-Cola" (changed to "Cherry Cola"); "Me & Julio..." for "*Newsweek*". Happened to "Kodachrome", too.

50. UB40 (Get it? [U]nemployment [b]enefit, form #40). Came out of a bloke sayin', "Well, you're on the dole, why not call yourselves UB40?". Their lucky break came when Chryssie Hynde heard 'em and asked them to open for the Pretenders.

51. [b] Rick Wakeman (Strawbs, Yes...), who bought his first Mini-Moog from Jack Wild, the little twerp in *H.R. Pufnstuff* because Wild didn't think it worked because it only played one note at a time. Mick Ronson did play piano on a Bowie-related project – Lou Reed's *Transformer* where his fingers can be heard twiddlin' away on "Perfect Day". Chris Stainton is an everybody's man, having started out in Joe Cocker's Grease Man, graduating to Clapton and, then, session work for the Who, B.B. King, Leon Russell, the Alarm, Bryan Ferry, et al. Jim Dickinson? He's the guy who played piano on "Wild Horses", produced Big Star's *Third*, Willy DeVille, the Replacements'

Pleased to Meet Me, many of the early Ry Cooder elpees, and whose loins brought forth two-thirds of the North Mississippi All-Stars.

52. [c] Toni Tennille (Captain & Tennille) and Bruce Johnston (Beach Boys). Toni is also considered the only female member of the Beach Boys since she sang with them in the '70s when her husband was playing keyboards with the band. Bruce isn't given the due he deserves, but let me try: Co-produced (with Terry Melcher) the Rip Chords' "Hey Little Cobra", took Glen Campbell's place in the Beach Boys (Glen had taken Brian Wilson's place on tour), was the designated Beach Boy to go to London and play *Pet Sounds* for Lennon/McCartney, and wrote "I Write the Songs" that Manilow turned into a smash.

53. Country, Blue Grass, and Blues. But, I see some hands out there that say, "What about OMFUG?", the cryptic letters below "CBGB". Well, it means Other Music For Uplifting Gormandizers (gormandizer means "ravenous eater" but in this case, it's music, not food). CBGB's also hosted the first non-European concert by the Police in '78.

54. True. And, during that *All Things Must Pass* gig, Peter got further enamored* to that talk box thang he became so famous for when he saw Pete Drake use it with his pedal steel guitar on (Pete also did the steel on "Lay Lady Lay"). Oh, and the engineers among you are curious as to how that works, huh? Go to YouTube.com, type in "Pete Drake Forever" and you'll see. The lazy man's

answer is a microphone, an amp, and a plastic tube in your mouth. *Stevie Wonder ued it first on *Music of My Mind* and that's where Frampton first heard it.

55. Some funky stuff came out of that former casket factory perched and ready to deliver to the graveyard next door and it was done by the Swampers. There's a great story about the time Paul Simon heard the Staples Singers' "I'll Take You There" and wanted to go record with whoever the band was. When he got to the studio, he was introduced to the band (who were all-white – he was expecting all-black) and thought they were the office staff. Once he embraced the notion, along came "Kodachrome", "Loves Me Like a Rock", and "Still Crazy After All These Years". And, yes, they're the same Swampers mentioned in "Sweet Home Alabama". The bonus points? Sam Cooke's nephew, R.B. Greaves' "Take a Letter, Maria".

56. Jeff Beck. *Talking Book* was a giant step in Motown crossing over to the "white" market and gaining a hip factor. And Stevie's fortune of having opened for the Stones on their world tour in advance of this LP didn't hurt, either. Beck, by the way, repaid Stevie's kindness by doing a version of "'Cause We've Ended as Lovers" on *Blow by Blow*.

57. [d] "Purple Haze". Yes, the Hendrix one – the one Jimi said he wrote after a dream where he was walking underneath the ocean and Jesus saved him. One of the early manuscripts even has the title "Purple Haze, Jesus Saves."

58. Blue Oyster Cult. After Soft White Underbelly, they became Oaxaca, then to the Stalk-Forrest Group, then St. Cecilia, onward to the Santos Sisters, and, finally, Blue Oyster Cult.

59. [a:4] Rod Stewart – Steampacket (Steampacket was a rarity in the rock lineup world, having *three vocalists* - Julie Driscoll, Rode Stewart, and Long John Baldry); [b:1] Elton John – Bluesology; [c:2] Christine McVie – Chicken Shack (where she did the lead on "I'd Rather Go Blind", a Top 10 U.K. hit); [d:3] Gerry Rafferty – Stealers Wheel.

60. Marianne. Took Tom Scholz five years to write the darn thing. Was inspired by the Left Banke's "Walk Away Renee".

61. Alexis Korner's Blues Incorporated. As you can imagine, it was a fairly loosey-goosey group, but those who wanted to get immersed in the Blues came to see Alexis. Zeppelin historians will tell you that Page found Plant jamming - and working on a record - with Korner and history turned a corner. The tables turned a few years later when Alexis formed C.C.S. (Collective Consciousness Society) and did a cover of "Whole Lotta Love" which was a Brit hit and the theme song to the Beeb's *Top of the Pops* for a number of years.

62. Bruce Springsteen's "Blinded by the Light", Springsteen's only Number 1 single as a songwriter on the Hot 100, courtesy of Manfred Mann's Earth Band. And, to clear things up for the Bossdom crowd, the Earth Band's version says

"revved up like a deuce" and Bruce's original says "cut loose like a deuce".

63. [b] *Astral Weeks*. In a 2006 interview, music critic Greil Marcus said that Martin Scorsese told him the first half of his movie *Taxi Driver* was based on *Astral Weeks*. For some reason, I just can't picture Van Morrison wearing a Mohawk as a return favor, though, can you?

64. [c] Detroit. Mitch and John Badanjek (drums) were the only hold-overs from the Detroit Wheels. The other member of any note was Steve "The Deacon" Hunter, who went on to be a guitar wiz for Alice Cooper, Peter Gabriel, and Lou Reed. Detroit released one album and had some minor success with a cover of Lou Reed's "Rock and Roll", then Mitch quit because his voice gave out.

65. They were all essentially a two-person operation (guitarist/vocalist with a drummer; keyboards/vocalist with a drummer). T. Rex is cool, Lee Michaels was bearable, but, OMG, what was Billy Joel thinking? Some critics rate the (one and only) Attila album as one of the worst records of all-time. It was Billy and drummer friend, Jon Small, who broke away from the Hassles trying to do the psychedelic thang. Billy ran off with Jon's wife, Elizabeth, who became his wife and manager, wrote "Just the Way You Are" for her, then ex-wife and ex-manager, and, then, her brother embezzled most of Billy's savings, then Small came back later to produce Joel's концерт

video and the "Live at Shea" vid. Sounds like a 12-Step program for being a rock star.

66. Henry Mancini? Nope, only one ("[Love Theme from] Romeo and Juliet"). Floyd Cramer? Nope – just three. It was Ferrante & Teicher who nailed the Top Ten four times – for the theme from *The Apartment*, *Exodus* (6.5 mil seller), the title song from *Midnight Cowboy*, and "Tonight" from *West Side Story*. Heck, see a movie goin' up the charts, do a cover of the theme, and bam! If you think those gimmicks like plucking the piano strings that Chick Corea pulls out of his bag of wow, think again. As banal as we like to think of F&T, they were clearly years ahead of the avant-garde pianists of our day. In fact, their first albums (on Columbia) were based on "prepared" pianos – pianos where the duo would wedge in pieces of glass, wood, chains, whatever they could imagine as a cool sound alteration.

67. Duane Allman. His first studio acclaim was the lead part on Wilson Pickett's "Hey Jude", which got Clapton – and Atlantic Records – attention. So much that Atlantic Records bought out his session gig contract after hearing his part over the phone.

68. [c] Book publisher (Simon of "Simon & Shuster"). He and Carly's mom (Andrea Louise) even had Jackie Robinson and his wife as boarders during the summer of '55.

69. Todd Rundgren. Interesting to note that on the day he shot and killed John Lennon, Mark David Chapman left an 8-track tape of *The Ballad of Todd*

Rundgren, among other objects, in his hotel room on the dresser.

70. [b] Eric Burdon and the Animals on *Eric is Here*, the album was Eric's transition out of the original Animals lineup and basically featured him, a drummer, and an orchestra.

71. *Annie Hall*. He came between the characters played by Woody Allen and Diane Keaton in this Oscar-winning film.

72. Little Feat, Jimmy Page's favorite American band (or, at least, that's what he told Cameron Crowe in an interview).

73. [c] The Cure. They're older than dirt, those boys, with origins dating to '76, their first album (*Three Imaginary Boys*), and their frontman, Robert Smith, being the only constant, not to mention one of the rare breeds who's been portrayed on 'South Park' (he takes on "Mecha-Streisand", but not in the way Barry or Neil did, trust me).

74. Two — Powerhouse and Blind Faith. Powerhouse was Clapton, Paul Jones (Manfred Mann, on harmonica), Jack Bruce (another Manfred Mann'er at the time on bass), Stevie Winwood (vocals from the Spencer Davis Group), Ben Palmer (on piano), and Pete York (drums, from the Spencer Davis Group). They only recorded three tracks – all featured on *What's Shakin''*, an Elektra Records sampler.

75. [b] "Come Together". The same song that got Johnny boy in a heap 'o trouble with Chuck

Berry's music publisher, Morris Levy, because a line resembled a line of Berry's "You Can't Catch Me" (the Beatles' "Here come ol' flattop, he come groovin' up slowly" vs. Berry's "Here come up flattop, he was groovin' up with me"). The two settled out of court on the promise that Lennon would record other songs owned by Levy, which he did for his *Rock 'n' Roll* album. Chuck Berry pointed his finger at Brian Wilson for pinching the melody on "Sweet Little Sixteen" for "Surfin' USA". Brian Wilson's daddy, Murray, flinched and gave Berry the copyright to the tune, but failed to inform the members of sons' band who didn't learn about the deal for some 25 years.

76. Aerosmith's *Toys in the Attic*. It's the band's biggest-selling LP - more than 8,000,000 copies in America, alone. Steven Tyler maintains his original idea for the cover was a teddy bear sitting in the attic with its wrist cut and stuffing spread across the floor, however it appears that the label's Good Taste department had the upper hand.

77. [a:3; b:1; c:2] Whether you use the descriptors of artful, cunning, or unholy, these guys' backstories are worth seeking out for your next Halloween party. For example: Don Arden. In his role as Black Sabbath's manager and Sharon Osbourne's (Ozzy's wife) dad, he got so tee'd off when she took over Ozzy's management that when she went to visit her papa, he turned his dogs on her and she lost the child she was pregnant with. When Albert Grossman signed Big Brother & the Holding Company, he told them he wouldn't

tolerate any intravenous drug use, and the band signed off on that promise. When he discovered that Joplin was injecting drugs anyway, he didn't get in her face but instead took out insurance guaranteeing him $100,000 in the event she died in an accident. And, when she had her "accidental" overdose, he got that $100k.

78. Simon and Garfunkel's "Mrs. Robinson", which came out of a tune fragment Paul Simon was working on about the past with the intent on "Mrs. Roosevelt" but Mike Nichols, *The Graduate's* producer had him change it to "Robinson". Movie buff detour: Despite the perception that Anne Bancroft and Dustin Hoffman were years apart, there was only seven years separating the two.

79. Merry Clayton, however she wasn't the first choice - Bonnie Bramlett was, but she couldn't do it. Merry's also the chick in the background on "Sweet Home Alabama". Her little brother, Sam, is the Clayton in Little Feat.

80. Tom Dowd (Atlantic Records — Cream, Allman Brothers Band, J. Geils Band, Sonny & Cher, Dusty Springfield, the Drifters, Otis Redding, etc.). Because his work on the bomb was secret, Columbia University wouldn't recognize it so he said to heck with physics and followed his bliss with music. The props he gets are numerous - everything from talking Atlantic into releasing "What'd I Say" into a two-part single to urging the label to get an 8-track recorder, making them the first to record multiple tracks.

81. [a] "Don't Bring Me Down" because of budget constraints on their typically-used cellos. And, ELO devotees, that ain't "Bruce" Jeff Lynne is singing – it's a made up word pronounced "Grroosss", quite possibly a reference to the Bavarian greeting *Grüß Gott* that he might have heard while recording the track in Munich.

82. [b] His Royal HIGHness, "Ziggy Stardust". "Ziggy" was a clothes store in London; "Stardust" from Mercury artist the Legendary Stardust Cowboy. Some think the "Played it left hand" and "voodoo" reference is towards Hendrix but Bowie was just borrowing little personas from here and there to give Ziggy his own. Had there been endless groove space, we would've gotten "All the Young Dudes" and "Rebel, Rebel" on the *Ziggy* album because they were also written as part of the Stardust plot Bowie was crafting for a hoped-for stage/TV play.

83. [d] Brinsley Schwarz, the Brit band that had Nick Lowe ("Cruel to Be Kind") and Ian Gomm ("Hold On") and whose song "(What's So Funny 'Bout) Peace, Love, and Understanding" Elvis Costello turned into one of his most loved. And, yes, there *was* someone named Brinsley Schwarz in the band.

84. *Ironside* – which was done by Quincy Jones. You question me on Letterman? Sure, I tricked you with a bit of ambiguity by not saying "<u>the</u> theme for", but look up who did the theme for David's "Viewer Mail" and you'll see for yourself!

85. Ok, here's the Muff-a-lottas... he produced (in no particular order) Dire Straits (the first album), Sparks, Bay City Rollers, Patto, Sutherland Brothers and Quiver, Russ Ballard, Noel Redding, Kevin Ayers, Mott the Hoople, Jimmy Cliff, et al. Muff is Stevie's older bro and did those fantastic bass lines on the Spencer Davis Group stuff.

86. Well, we know you've seen Woodstock more than once and should have this period piece memorized, so let's see: [a] "pick up a gun"; [b] "when we've blown 'em all to Kingdom Come"; [c] "to have your boy come home in a box". The song does a pretty good fleece job of "Muskrat Ramble" – a tune Louis Armstrong recorded in 1926 and reprised by Woody Herman and others.

87. [b] Mojo Men, who earlier recorded for San Fran's Autumn Records where they were produced by one "Sylvester Stewart" p/k/a "Sly Stone".

88. [a] would be Mister Zappa, supposedly in a gross-out contest with Captain Beefheart onstage at NYC's Garrick Theatre in '67. Frank said, uh-uh, didn't happen in his autobio, but did leave us this tidbit to prevent our doing the same: "The closest I ever came to eating shit anywhere was at a Holiday Inn buffet at Fayetteville, North Carolina"? [b] Prince supposedly had a rib taken out so he could do what dogs can do to themselves (capiche?) *SPIN's* December '09 issue wants us to know that a) The Sign formerly known as whoever has never commented on this and, b) SPIN's doctor-on-call said that having a rib removed

would actually make "doing oneself" *more* difficult. [c] Gene Simmons, however a graft of this type ain't medically achievable since Gene-o's antibodies would reject the cud-lickin' device as foreign. [d] Jagger. Angie claims it's true that they were in the same bed together, albeit passed out and not, as she says, "flagrante".

89. "Dominique" by the Singing Nun or, more officially, Soeur Sourire (Sister Smile) or, for her birth parents, Jeanine Deckers. Yes, a real, honest-to-goodness nun (Dominican Fichermont Convent in Belgium). No relation to Sally Field of Virgin Atlantic's famous Flying Nun convent.

90. "Love is Blue" by Paul Mauriat. 1968. Paul didn't write the tune, however. It was written by Andre Popp (lyrics by Pierre Cour) and first performed in French by Vicky Leandros as the Luxembourgian entry in the Eurovision Song Contest 1967 (she finished fourth). Jeff Beck even did a version, arranged by future Zep man, John Paul Jones.

91. It was John McLaughlin - of the Mahavishnu Orchestra - who turned Carlos onto Sri Chinmoy. It was Sri who gave Santana the name "Devadip" ("The lamp, light and eye of God."). Santana and McLaughlin became pals and even recorded an album together, *Love, Devotion, Surrender*. Chinmoy's followers claim he has written 1,500 books, 115,000 poems and 20,000 songs, and created 200,000 paintings. And we thought Willie Nelson and Ryan Adams were prolific!

92. [c] Stephen Bishop. Bish also appeared in another John Landis movie - *Blues Brothers* - as the "charming trooper" in the mall chase scene. He wrote the theme to *Tootsie* as well as "Separate Lives," from the *White Nights*, a song that stemmed from his personal breakup with Karen Allen (the chick in *Raiders of the Lost Ark*).

93. Bobby Vee ("Rubber Ball", "Come Back When You Grow Up", "Take Good Care of My Baby"...). How else do you know Mr. Vee? He was given the unwelcome job of filling in for Buddy Holly the day after "the music died" at Holly's would-be next tour stop in Moorhead, Minnesota.

94. [c] Shelby Singleton bought all of Sun's assets through his "SSS International" corporation. Shelby also produced "Ahab the Arab", "Harper Valley P.T.A.", among others. He still owns Sun.

95. [b] "Cecilia", the same song Paulie Walnuts had as his ringtone (albeit a techno version) in the last episode of *The Sopranos.*

96. Jerry Butler and Curtis Mayfield who met each other while singing in the same Windy City church choir. Otis Redding had a hit with "I've Been Loving You Too Long" that he co-wrote with Butler and Butler had a hit with "He Will Break Your Heart" written for him by Curtis.

97. [c] Brave Belt. Zephyr featured Tommy Bolin, later of Deep Purple (he took Richie Blackmore's place) and the James Gang; Sons of Champlin featured Bill Champlin, later of Chicago; Mashmakhan didn't spawn anyone that notable, but did have a

tune called "As Years Go By" that sold a million copies worldwide.

98. [a] David Crosby. Rarely thought of in this way, but *Song to a Seagull* was a concept album, but one that's just split into two halves: "I Came to the City" and "Out of the City and Down to the Seaside". Bob Johnston? He made the leap of faith from producing Patti Page to Dylan*, Leonard Cohen, Johnny Cash, and Simon & Garfunkel. Despite all the great output he gave Columbia, he never got a royalty. * He's the one Dylan says "Is it rolling, Bob?" to on *Nashville Skyline*.

99. Maureen Tucker of the Velvet Underground. She was recruited for the Velvets while doing a keypunch operator gig with IBM. The rhythm thing, you know.

100. [c] Hank Williams' song "Kaw-Liga (which was released posthumously and stayed at #1 for 14 weeks on the C&W charts), and [d] "Day-O" (The Banana Boat Song), a Jamaican folk song adapted by Irving Burgie (who also wrote "Jamaica Farewell"), popularized by Harry Belafonte and, for you Simpsons' fans, parodied as "Gay-O" in the episode "There's Something About Marrying". "K-Jee" was by The Nite-Liters (done by MFSB on *Saturday Night Fever*) and "Keem-O-Sabe" was a '69 Top 20 hit instrumental by Electric Indian, a studio band put together with help from Len Barry ("1-2-3") and made up of Philly musicians (some who went on to be part of MFSB) including a young Daryl Hall on keyboards.

101. *Aqualung* by Jethro Tull. The album was recorded the same time/place that Zeppelin was mixing LZ4 and Tull got the bigger of the two studios!

102. "10 year old girl on the street corner" from the Stones' "(Doo Doo Doo) Heartbreaker"; "Help me build a mountain from a little pile of clay" is from Tom Jones' "She's a Lady"; "This really blew my mind from Eric Burdon & War's "Spill the Wine".

103. [a] & [b]: Appeared with his new bassist Billy Cox; session drummer Ed Shaughnessy sat in for Mitch Mitchell. Cox had been in the King Kasuals with Jimi when they were stationed at Ft. Campbell and, allegedly, Billy got the first call to be the Experience's bassist but passed on the chance.

104. KISS with "I Was Made for Lovin' You" – a song that Paul Stanley (co-) wrote to prove how easily someone could score a Disco hit. Peter Criss is nowhere to be found on the track. Like most of the KISS stuff of that era, Anton Fig – the drummer on *Late Night with David Letterman* – beat da beat.

105. Journey. Neil Schon, who joined Santana at age 15 and who passed on an invitation to join Derek & the Dominos is the thread that runs through the band's 35+ year history. After leaving Santana, Neil and Gregg Rolie formed the group with Ross Valory and Tickner from Frumious Bandersnatch and Prairie Prince from the Tubes. Originally, they were called the Golden Gate Rhythm Section with intent on being the Bay Area version of a Muscle Shoals, Nashville or Memphis session group. That idea was eventually tossed and they became a

jazz-fusion band produced by Roy Halee who twisted the knobs for Simon & Garfunkel. After a couple of unsuccessful albums, they went more mainstream, eventually evolving into the sound they're known for. Along the way, they've had some 19-odd folks in their line-up, (including Randy Jackson*, the judge on *American Idol*) and splintered into Bad English, the Storm, and others, but always coming back for another go at fame and glory. * Randy got his start playing bass for Billy Cobham and worked his way up the food chain to a couple of Dylan albums, several of Bruce's LPs, Rundgren, and Billy Joel. He was also head of A&R for Columbia for eight years and the same at MCA for four.

106. [b] Joan Baez (1960*), then Tom Rush and Dylan in '62, Buffy Sainte-Marie in '64. The *Joan Baez* album was 13 traditional folk songs (like "House of the Rising Sun") and done in four days time at a hotel in New York City. I didn't know this until now, but Joan used to date Steve Jobs, the Apple kingpin. Hmm... *The first wholly-Joan album. There was another – *Folksingers 'Round Harvard Square* – which she and others were on in '59.

107. [b] "I could hear the distant drums." The Swedish version differs from the American version in that the narrator attempts to console the heartbroken Fernando, who's lost the love of his life where in the American version, it's two old war vets reminiscing, presumably about the Mexican revolution.

108. [a] In '66 (two years after the song was a hit), when Jan Berry (the "Jan" half of the duo) crashed his 'vette into a parked truck on Whittier Drive in L.A.

– just a short distance from the *real* Dead Man's Curve – many considered the crash prophetic. Jan suffered brain damage and partial paralysis but never gave up, finally learning new motor skills, even singing and producing again. The most renowned victim of Dead Man's Curve was Mel Blanc (voice of Bugs Bunny, Porky Pig, Daffy Duck, et al) who broke almost everything in his body and was in a coma for a few weeks. [b] That prime number, good 'ol "409" by the Beach Boys and co-written* by Brian Wilson and Gary Usher (co-wrote "In My Room", created studio groups like the Hondells and Sagittarius, produced *Younger Than Yesterday, Notorious Byrd Brothers,* and *Sweetheart of the Rodeo* for the Byrds and also wrote "In My Room"). [c] "Radar Love" by Golden Earring. *The credits now list Mike Love 'coz he sued to get his name included in the '90s.

109. You might say this is a trick question because Kenney Jones became a member of the Who later in his life, but the real answer here is [b] Ronnie Lane and the "duet" album was *Rough Mix.*

110. [a] Dean Torrence. Dean ain't credited on the LP but you can hear Carl say, "*Thanks, Dean*" at the end. Dino Martin was Dean's son and a third of Dino, Desi, and Billy; Jan was the other half of Dean in Jan & Dean (duh); Ted Templeman was a member of Harpers Bizarre ("Feelin' Groovy") and produced classic albums for the Doobies, Van Morrison, Little Feat, and Van Halen.

111. I'm gonna burn in hell, I just know it. Connie Hamzy is "Sweet Connie", the groupie made

famous by Grand Funk in "We're an American Band". What did she play? C'mon... *who* did she play? Zeppelin, Eagles, Van Hagar, Neil Diamond, KISS, the Stones, Rick Springfield, Three Dog Night, Keith Moon, Allmans, ZZ Top, Bad Company, even Doc Severinsen. And who is Hal Blaine? Well, if I have to tell you, he's probably the greatest session drummer of all-time, having played on "A Taste of Honey", "Up Up & Away", "Bridge Over Troubled Water", "Good Vibrations", "Monday Monday", "This Diamond Ring", "Mr. Tambourine Man", "Strangers in the Night", "Close to You", "The Way We Were", "Thank God I'm a Country Boy" - 39 #1 hits in all.

112. [c] *The Live Adventures of Mike Bloomfield and Al Kooper*. Carlos appears on "Sonny Boy Williamson", a tune written by Jack Bruce of Cream and Paul Jones, Manfred Mann's vocalist.

113. Gary (Lewis [Jerry's kid] and the Playboys) with seven Top Ten'ers. His first hit - "This Diamond Ring", written by Al Kooper (BS&T, Dylan, et al) - came from the hands of session players that included Leon Russell and Tommy Allsup, the guy who lost the coin toss that put Ritchie Valens on the plane with Buddy Holly. One of the eventual Playboys was Carl Radle who went on to a slot in Derek & the Dominos.

114. [d] Louis Armstrong hit #1 in 1964 with "Hello, Dolly!" at age 62, although George Burns was the oldest to have a record on the charts (at age 84 in

1980) and Cher is the oldest *woman* to top the Hot 100 is Cher (with "Believe" in 1999 at age 53).

115. Duane's death. The urban myth is that he was killed by a peach truck and that's why you see a peach truck on the cover, but ain't the case. He was actually killed by a *flatbed* truck and the artwork was a tribute to something he quipped in an interview. To the question "What are you doing to help the revolution?" Duane replied, "There ain't no revolution, it's *evo*lution, but every time I'm in Georgia, I eat a peach for peace." By the way, James Flournoy Holmes, the guy who did the cover, also did Dr. John's *Right Place, Wrong Time,* the first Marshall Tucker, and Charlie Daniels' *Fire on the Mountain.*

116. [a] "I Heard It Through the Grapevine" and [d] "Neither One of Us" - both reached #2. If I were asking you a chicken vs. egg question on whether the Pips or Marvin Gaye's version of "Grapevine" was done first, you'd probably say Gladys and the Pips, but you'd be wrong. Norman Whitfield produced both and Marvin actually recorded it first, but Marvin didn't like how the producer was forcing him to sing in an upper register like he had David Ruffin do on "Ain't Too Proud to Beg", plus Motown didn't believe in it, thought it would be silly to release another version after Gladys had a hit with it, and shelved it. Time on the shelf was a couple of years when Whitfield finally got Gordy to put it on Marvin's *In the Groove* LP. At that point, radio guys fell in love with it, and Gordy's hand was forced.

117. They're already in order! a, b, c, d! [August 3, 1963] "From Me to You" (charted at #116), [January 18, 1964] "I Want To Hold Your Hand" (#1)... [January 25, 1964] "She Loves You" (#1)... [February 1, 1964] "Please, Please Me" (#3).

118. Tetragrammaton Records. It was also the home of the very first record recognized as having the "F-bomb" on it – comedian Murray Roman's *You Can't Beat People Up and Have Them Say I Love You*, an album produced by David Briggs who produced most of Neil Young's hit albums.

119. John & Yoko's *Two Virgins* because they were on the cover naked as jaybirds. The LP came about as the end result of an all-night experimental recording session at John's home studio. The title came from John and Yoko's sense that they were like "two innocents, lost in a world gone mad", and (hold your ears, kids) because the two consummated their relationship for the first time once the album was completed. The LP was released on Tetragrammaton because Capitol thought it was a wee bit risky. See how neatly we tied these last two questions together? Sigh...

120. Pink Floyd. Seems like one night the Tea Set was on the same bill as someone else calling themselves the same thing, so Syd the Kid coined a quick name change to the Pink Floyd Sound, a little nod to two old Blues cats Floyd Council and Pink Anderson who he read about on a Blind Boy Fuller album. They continued on as both the Tea Set and the Pink Floyd Sound until the better

appellation won out, dropping "Sound" first and, eventually, "The".

121. [a] Mickey Dolenz. He also sang lead on "Last Train to Clarksville", wrote the UK Top 5 hit "Randy Scouse Git"*, and auditioned for the part of "Fonzie" but lost out to Henry Winkler. Jump that shark, babe. *The song was renamed "Alternate Title" by the label because "Randy Scouse Git" means something close to "horny Liverpudlian jerk".

122. [b] The Drifters' "There Goes My Baby". It was the Drifters sessions that Leiber/Stoller's understudy, Phil Spector, picked up on the trick of using strings and sophisticated production techniques to enhance the power of R&B tracks.

123. Here we go...

    a. The DeFranco* Family, Barry White were on 20th Century Records, and...

    b. Jaggerz, Sopwith Camel: Kama Sutra

    c. Jan & Dean, the Chipmunks: Liberty, a label started by Si Waronker, the dad of Lenny Waronker who produced Randy Newman, Rickie Lee Jones, Gordon Lightfoot, and James Taylor. "Si" is short for "Simon" who, along with other Liberty Records execs (Alvin Bennett and Theodore Keep), were the names of the three little creatures in the Chipmunks.

    d. Partridge Family, Dawn: Bell

    e. Al Green, Ann Peebles: Hi

f. George McCrae, KC & the Sunshine Band: TK Records

g. Bill Withers, Gallery: Sussex

*Tony DeFranco is now a real estate agent in SoCal – matter of fact, he was Sotheby's #1 producer in 2008

124. [b] "It's Only Rock 'n Roll"… *and* the lovely Mr. Bowie sang background vocals.

125. "Georgia on My Mind". Please, please don't tell me you missed that one. Later on, it was the theme song for *Designing Women* and also sampled for Field Mob's 2005 single, "Georgia", featuring Jamie Foxx and (do I dare call him Lewd?) Ludacris. And if you live in Ohio, you know that "Hang On Sloopy" is the official "rock" song of your good state (*and* your Ohio STATE University), don't you?

126. Led Zeppelin's "Boogie with Stu". The lyrics are taken from Ritchie Valens' "Ooh My Head." And, since Valens was dead, his mother was given a composer credit so she would benefit from the royalties. But, since no good deed goes unpunished, Mama V's peeps sued for the rights to the *whole* song.

127. [b] Jimi Hendrix. *Pre*-Jimi, Chas was the bass player in the Animals (that great riff that kicks off "We Gotta Get Out of This Place" is his). After the breakup of the Animals, he decided to switch gears and became a manager. First Hendrix, then Slade, then Nick Drake. He also produced Jimi's first two albums.

128. [c] Queen's "Bohemian Rhapsody". Bismillah is an Arabic phrase meaning "in the name of God", by the way.

129. "Highway 9" makes reference to U.S. Route 9 in New Jersey in "Born to Run", and "Route 88," in "Spirit in the Night."According to original E Street drummer Vini Lopez, Bruce's mythical "Greasy Lake" was partially inspired by Lake Carasaljo at the intersection of those roads.

130. [b] Summer Jam at Watkins Glen, where 600,000 people saw the Grateful Dead, Allman Brothers, and The Band. Only 150,000 of those paid the $10 admission - the other 450 thou got in for free.

131. America — Dewey Bunnell, Dan Peek, Gerry Beckley (Peek split after *Harbor* to become a Contemporary Christian recording artist). Many thought "Horse With No Name" (original title: "Desert Song") was Neil Young and America's never shied away from the fact that he was an influence. However, they didn't think some radio stations would ban the song because the idiots thought "horse" was a drug reference. The phrase "purple rain" was from "Ventura Highway" and preceded Prince's use by nearly a decade. George Martin came in for *Holiday* ("Tin Man"), *Hearts* ("Sister Golden Hair" [with an intro inspired by "My Sweet Lord"), *Hideaway*, and *Harbor*.

132. The plans were to [b] form a supergroup with vocalist Jack Bruce. He felt he'd had enough of the Stones, not to mention probably being a bit peeved that he didn't get credit for the co-writes on "Till

the Next Goodbye" and "Time Waits for No One" with Jagger but he didn't use that as an excuse.

133. [a] Carl Douglas with "Kung Fu Fighting". The follow-up was "Dance the Kung Fu" – a record I'm sure you *all* have in your collection. ;-)

134. [c] "You Don't Have to Say You Love Me", Dusty's only British #1. Its origins weren't in New York but in Italy where Dusty fell in love with a song she heard at the San Remo Festival, called "Lo che non vivo (senza te)" (it means "I, who can't live without you"). She asked a couple of her writer friends – Vicki Wickham and Simon Napier-Bell – to turn it into English and so it went. *Napier-Bell sound familiar? He was the Yardbirds manager and (forgivably) also Wham!'s.

135. [d] Rubin "Hurricane" Carter. Dylan's – and Muhammad Ali's – efforts to get Carter out didn't work, but he eventually won his release about 13 years later. Dylan co-wrote "Hurricane" with Jacques Levy, as well as "Isis" and four other tracks on *Desire*. Levy's first taste of songwriting success came when he co-wrote "Chestnut Mare" with the Byrds' Roger McGuinn as a song for an ill-fated off-Broadway musical centered around Ibsen's *Peer Gynt*.

136. Any of the answers will do as they're all correct. Mr. Gordon, a diagnosed schizophrenic, off'ed his mum in 1983 and was sentenced to sixteen years-to-life in prison. You can also hear his licks on "Classical Gas", *Pet Sounds, Low Spark of High-*

Heeled Boys, early Everly Brothers stuff, and *Mad Dogs and Englishmen*.

137. Wilson Pickett. The Sir Mack Rice cover was "Mustang Sally" (Wilson was in the Falcons with Mack and Eddie "Knock on Wood" Floyd), the Chris Kenner cover was "Land of 1,000 Dances", and the Dyke & the Blazers cover was "Funky Broadway". Outside the studio, Mr. Pickett was indeed wicked, getting hauled off for carrying a loaded shotgun in his car, arrested for yelling death threats while driving his car on the mayor's lawn in Englewood NJ, assaulting his grrrlfriend, striking an 86-year old pedestrian while doing the DUI nasty, among other assorted bad thangs.

138. [b] Paul Samwell-Smith. He produced Cat's *Tea for the Tillerman* and *Teaser and the Firecat*, Carly's *Anticipation*, Paul Simon's *There Goes Rhymin' Simon* and others. As a Yardbird, Paul played bass. In the movie world, he produced the music for the cult flick *Harold and Maude*.

139. Mick Fleetwood. *English Rose* is the one with "Albatross" and "Black Magic Woman".

140. "Paradise" is a tune about a strip mining operation in (Western) Kentucky (down by the Green River in Muhlenberg County, birthplace of the Everly Brothers), written and recorded by Chicagoan and former mailman, John Prine, on his first album after he was discovered by Kris Kristofferson.

141. They all had hits with songs that either became commercials or were song-length versions of music that was originally a commercial. The T-

Bones "No Matter What Shape (Your Stomach's In)" was based on an Alka-Seltzer ad (and the T-Bones grew up to be Hamilton, Joe Frank, and Reynolds ["Don't Pull Your Love']) ... the Brass Ring's "Disadvantages of You" was a long-play on a Benson & Hedges commercial ... Carly Simon's "Anticipation" – which she wrote in anticipation of a date with Cat Stevens – wound up working for Heinz ketchup ... Sonny & Cher had a Top 40 hit with their take on Budweiser's "When You Say Bud" with "When You Say Love", and the Bob Crewe Generation's "Music to Watch Girls By" was a Diet Pepsi commercial stretched out.

142. Moby Grape (ok, ok, stop – it was a bad joke).

143. [c] Splinter (although Splinter did wind up on George's Dark Horse label and had a minor hit with "Costafine Town"). Hot Chocolate found their way on to Apple after they recorded a reggae version of "Give Peace a Chance" that curried the favor of Lennon. John Tavener? Classical guy – did a cantata based on Jonah and the Whale which the Apple corps evidently thought would make them appear legit.

144. [d] "Suki" Lahav landed the first femme fatale slot in the Boss' band thanks to her husband who was engineering some Springsteen sessions when Bruce was looking for a violinist. She sang vocals on "4th of July, Asbury Park (Sandy)" from *The Wild, The Innocent and The E Street Shuffle* and played violin on the "Jungleland" from *Born to Run*. She was only in the band for about a year

(mid '74-early '75) when she and her husband returned to Israel.

145. [c] Neil Diamond ("Kentucky Woman") and Billy Joe Royal ("Hush"). The lead singer was Rod Evans who, after three Purple albums, was replaced by Ian Gillian, the man most people recognize as the lead singer of the band. In 1980, Rod led a rogue version of Deep Purple on tour but after a few riots claiming "foul", the *real* Deep Purple filed suit, awarded nearly ¾ of a million dollars, and Rod lost all future royalties of the three albums he really was with the band.

146. [c] King Crimson (Greg Lake), Atomic Rooster (Carl Palmer), and the Nice (Keith Emerson). For those of you who don't play Nice, the group was put together by (Stones producer) Andrew Loog Oldham as a backup for P.P. Arnold. Their name came from the Small Faces song "Here Come the Nice".

147. B.J. Thomas' "Hey Won't You Play Another Somebody Done Somebody Wrong Song", however the longest title of a song to hit #1 *ever* was that 41-word medley thing by Stars on 45 in 1981 ["Medley: Intro "Venus"/Sugar Sugar/No Reply/I'll Be Back/Drive My Car/Do You Want to Know a Secret/We Can Work It Out/I Should Have Known Better/Nowhere Man/You're Going to Lose That Girl/Stars on 45"].

148. [a] "More Than a Woman" - one version each from Tavares and the Brothers Gibb. And while

"Jive Talkin'" was on the soundtrack, it was *not* in the movie.

149. The Stones' version of the Lennon/McCartney song came out first, mostly because Andrew Loog Oldham begged John and Paul for a tune. In England, it as an "A" side; in the States, the flip to "Not Fade Away". Ringo sang the Beatles' version (and George Martin played organ!).

150. #1: "Like a Rolling Stone"; #2: "Satisfaction"; #3: "Imagine". "La Bamba" by Ritchie Valens is the only non-English language song; the bulk of the tunes are from the '50s, '60s, '70s with two songs from the '40s – "Rollin' Stone" by Muddy Waters and Hank Williams' "I'm So Lonesome I Could Cry" – and only three songs from the 21st century: Eminem's "Lose Yourself" and "Stan", plus "Hey Ya!" by OutKast.

151. [b] David Bowie's "Fame" (but Bill Withers does say "I know" 26 times in "Ain't No Sunshine" – it's just not at the *end,* though).

152. It was Dylan and his backup band when Bob went "electric" at the Newport Folk Festival in July of '65. The "Lynyrd Skynyrd" reference is to their producer, Al Kooper (who played organ at Newport and, coincidentally, played organ on Skynyrd's "Free Bird" under the guise of Roosevelt Gook); the "Wilburys", of course, to Dylan; the "Butterfield" reference to Mike Bloomfield, Sam Lay, and Jerome Arnold (guitar, drums, bass); and the "failed supergroup" reference is to Barry Goldberg (keyboards) who

was in a "failed" supergroup called KGB with Bloomfield and Ray Kennedy as the front guys and Ric Grech (Traffic [he co-wrote "Rock and Roll Stew" w/ Jim Gordon], Blind Faith) and Carmine Appice, (Beck, Bogart, & Appice, Vanilla Fudge Cactus) as the rhythm section. Never heard of Ray Kennedy? Interesting cat. For one thing, he co-wrote "Sail On Sailor" with Brian Wilson, but when you see all his connections – from Otis Redding to Gene Krupa to Aerosmith to Sly Stone – you might freak. Go seek it out (and be forgiving of the spelling) at raymondlouiskennedy.com

153. "My Love". Florence Henderson serenaded the bride and groom with the Petula Clark version on the *Tonight Show* when Tiny Tim married Miss Vickie. Kenny Rogers sang the backup on Lionel's version and Paul wrote his for the lovely Linda. All three hit #1.

154. [a] Big Star and Cheap Trick and, ironically enough, Alex Chilton (co-writer from Big Star) is paid $70 in royalties every time the show runs.

155. Both recordings included E-Street Band members pianist Roy Bittan and drummer Max Weinberg.

156. Rita Coolidge, who Stephen Stills referred to by the nickname "the Raven" in "Sit Yourself Down".

157. Bobby Vinton (15), but that's according to *Billboard,* and we shouldn't be too picky since Rydell and Darin both had 14 Top 20s and possibly more on another chart service.

158. All of 'em! Neil Young (who was asked fourth) was the first to accept.

159. [b] When the Boss met Joey Ramone, Joey asked Bruce to write a song for his band. Springsteen wrote "Hungry Heart" that night but decided to keep it on the advice of producer/manager Jon Landau.

160. Florence Ballard in 1967. She just wasn't diggin' on Diana Ross gettin' all the light. Not they would miss her. After all, the most we ever heard from her was the "Need you, need you" echo before the last verse of "Baby Love". In *Dreamgirls*, the Effie White character (the one played by both Jennifers [Hudson and Holliday]) is said to be modeled after Ballard.

161. [c] Creedence Clearwater Revival. How did CCR come up with that name? Well, it was a toss-up between that and Muddy Rabbit, Gossamer Wump, or Creedence Nuball and the Ruby. They finally wound up taking the elements from "Creedence" Nuball, a friend of Tom Fogerty's; "clear water", from a commercial for Olympia Beer; and "revival", which spoke to the four members' new commitment to the group.

162. [c] the pseudonym "Ann Orson and Carte Blanche" ("a horse and a cart, Blanche!") belonged to Kiki Dee and Elton John, writers of "Don't Go Breaking My Heart". Elton evidently loves a good pen name. He was "Nancy Treadlight" on Sting's version of "Come Down in Time" from *Two Rooms*, "Redget Buntovan" on an album by the group

"Blue", "Tripe" on a Kiki Dee track, and "Rockaday Johnnie" on Jackson Browne's "Redneck Friend".

163. [a] Jackie Wilson. Gordy wrote/co-wrote four songs for Jackie, including "Reet Petite" and "Lonely Teardrops". Jackie also called in a return favor from Gordy and got his cousin's (Robert Johnson [not the Blues one]) group – the Contours – signed to Motown.

164. "The Weight" (The Band). Despite all the Biblical subtext, Nazareth refers to the home of Martin Guitars (check the liner notes on The Band's box set) and the characters are people Levon Helm grew up knowing in the Turkey Scratch, Arkansas metropolitan area.

165. [b] Muddy Waters. The song was credited under his real name, McKinley Morganfield, and based on Mississippi Blues singer/guitarist Robert Petway's song "Catfish Blues" (Muddy added a beat and some changes to make it his own). "Rollin' Stone" was the first single ever released on Chess Records and, if you can find it, there's a version of the song he did with *Humble Pie at the Fillmore*, it's worth gettin'.

166. *The Smothers Brothers Comedy Hour.* First, about the Pete Seeger part: it was contentious because he chose to sing the anti-war song, "Waist Deep in the Big Muddy". CBS viewed it as an insult to LBJ and his policy on Vietnam, so they censored it the first time through but let it go play in a subsequent appearance. Regarding the Who incident (the one I

missed when I ran away from home), it seems like Keith Moon was drunk on brandy and secretly added some extra flash powder to the effects. When it went off at the end of "My Generation", his cymbal exploded with some shrapnel getting in his leg, Pete lost his hearing and his hair was seared, and Bette Davis was so freaked, that she fainted into Mickey Rooney's arms.

167. [a, d, e, f, g] Terry Melcher, John Phillips, Johnny Rivers, Paul Simon, Lou Adler. All the revenue went to charity, so all the artists did their gigs for free, except Ravi Shankar, who got $3,000 for his four-hour-long performance. Om...

168. Brian Jones (the only Stone in attendance). Legend has it that this is where Hendrix – in trying to top Pete Townshend's guitar-breaking antics – started his antics of kneeling over his guitar, poured lighter fluid over it, setting it on fire, then smashin' it. Monterey Pop was indeed monumental but there were a number of acts who were asked to appear, but couldn't or didn't. Among them Donovan (couldn't get in the States because of a drug bust), the Kinks (had pissed off the musicians union), Cream because their manager wanted to make a bigger splash, and Dionne Warwick who had a scheduling conflict with a previous commitment at the Fairmont in San Fran and thought that cancelling her hotel gig for a rock festival would mar her image. Uh, yeah.

169. [a] "Feels Like the First Time". Sorry, I don't have anything cute or cuddly to say about this song.

170. "Summertime Blues" by Blue Cheer, who was rumored to have been named after a brand of LSD that was promoted by renowned hallucinogenic chemist and former Grateful Dead patron, Owsley Stanley (whose name will pop up, again, in our little Q&A. I promise).

171. Lulu. Bowie produced both that and Lulu's version of "Watch That Man", as well as doing vocals and sax on the sessions. There were rumors that Lulu and David got it on, if you know what I mean. Lulu says yes; Bowie ain't sayin'. Lulu had quite a knack for getting good help. Duane Allman helped her out on her *New Routes* album and for a brief period she was married to Maurice Gibb.

172. [d] Horace Silver's "Song for My Father" (listen to the bass riff on the intro). And if that's not enough bootlegging for you, the opening horn riff was "rented" by Stevie Wonder for "Don't You Worry 'Bout a Thing".

173. Album or poster artists. Mouse and Griffin did most of the San Francisco concert posters, Roger Dean did the Yes/Gentle Giant/Asia covers, Robert Crumb did *Cheap Thrills*, and Guy Peellaert did *Diamond Dogs* and *It's Only Rock 'n Roll*. RCA had to recall *Diamond Dogs* because Guy painted some genitalia on dem dawgs and that just wouldn't have been proper, now, would it?

174. [b] "Spirit in the Night". Springsteen's version came about after Clive Davis whined that there weren't any tunes with commercial appeal on *Greetings from Asbury Park*, so Bruce quickly wrote

"Spirit..." and "Blinded by the Light". Since the LP was basically done and the other band mates nowhere to be found, Bruce did the recording with Vini Lopez on drums, Clarence Clemons on sax, and all the other instruments by himself.

175. Nova Scotia and Saratoga. Dick Ebersol (the guy who headed up NBC Sports), was the highest bidder – $50,000 – at a charity auction in which the prize was Carly revealing who was the focus of "You're So Vain". For what amounts to a good year's salary for most of us, Ebersol was given a private performance of the song at Carly's home. After a lunch of peanut butter and jelly sandwiches and a little vodka on the rocks, Simon whispered the subject to Ebersol with the condition that he wouldn't reveal the answer to anyone. But, alas, Ebersol revealed that he was allowed by Simon to divulge *one* clue about the person's name and that is: The letter 'E' is in the person's name. So, hey, I guess Britney Jean Spears is still a valid option.

176. [a] Sonny Curtis. In 1956, he, Buddy Holly, and Don Guess went to Nashville, where they recorded for Decca as "The Three Tunes" and where Sonny made history as the first rocker to record with a Fender Stratocaster. Sonny later became a member of the Crickets with Buddy Holly, but his hit-writing potential was championed by other artists starting with the Everly Brothers who did "Walk Right Back", Bobby Vee, and others.

177. [c] The Eagles got both of their bassists – Randy Meisner and Timothy B. Schmidt – from Poco.

178. "Junior's Farm", which was recorded by Paul McCartney and Wings in Nashville, Tennessee in '74, while the band was staying at Curly Putman Jr.'s farm. Who, in God's name is Curly Putnam? He wrote "Green, Green Grass of Home" and half of "D-I-V-O-R-C-E", "My Elusive Dreams", and "He Stopped Loving Her Today".

179. [d] Shirley Temple – and she was on there *three* times! Two as a photo on the front row (one slightly obscured) and once as a cloth doll that Jann Haworth (wife of Peter Blake, the album's designer) created where Shirley's wearing a sweater that reads "Welcome the Rolling Stones". The collage on the cover depicts more than 70 famous folk (writers, musicians, movie stars, a couple of sports figures [Johnny Weissmuller and Sonny Liston], and even the Indian gurus that Harrison insisted on). Lennon asked for Jesus and Hitler, but he was voted out.

180. "…or else it wouldn't get played on the radio," said Berry about "Johnny B. Goode". The song was part autobiographical and partly drawn from the personality of Johnnie Johnson, Berry's pianist. Johnson had been drinking too much, and Chuck thought, "Johnnie be good." The "e" at the end of "Goode" might have come from "Goode Avenue", the St. Louis street where Berry was born.

181. [a] The Monkees' *Head* film. Nicholson was the one really large and in charge, as his choice of music

and dialogue approximates the flow of the movie itself, and it was all compiled by him, as well as co-writing the script. Neil and Leon contributed to the soundtrack as well as Dewey Martin (Buffalo Springfield), Carole King, Danny Kortchmar, and Russ Titleman (producer of Winwood's "Higher Love", *Unplugged* and *Journeyman* for Clapton).

182. [d] All play bass

183. [c] Ray Charles! Ha! In the late sixties, Ray Charles bought himself a Corvette, made his son sit in the passenger seat, and as he took the 'vette for a short spin, he promptly hit a tree.

184. [a] Beale Street Blues Boy. Maybe they should've called him Beale Street *Birthin'* Boy, given that he's fathered 15 children! "Lucille" came into B.B.'s life quite by accident – literally. One night he was playing a gig in a joint being heated by a barrel of kerosene. Two men got in a fight, knocked over the barrel, the joint started burnin' to the floor when B.B. remembered he'd left his guitar inside. He rescued it and found out that the men had been fighting over a woman named "Lucille" so he named his guitar that to remind him never a) enter a burning building, and b) fight over a woman.

185. "Wooly Bully" by Sam the Sham & the Pharaohs, which to those of you who know your Texas rock roots, was first recorded in '62 as "Hully Gully Now" by Big Bo and the Arrows. "Wooly Bully" never hit #1 but it was the only record that *didn't* hit #1 to be named *Billboard*'s "Number One

Record of the Year" (1965), an honor that remained for 35 years until Faith Hill did it with "Breathe".

186. Thar' they blow… [a] Richard "Magic Dick" Salwitz blew out his face for J. Geils; [b] Lennon was the usual harpist for the Fabs. The urban legend is that John learned how to play from Delbert McClinton when the Beatles were touring with Bruce Chanel (Delbert was Bruce's harpist), then used what he learned on "Love Me Do", but experts will tell you that while John and Delbert did, in fact, meet, John already knew how to play harmonica; [c] Lee Oskar played with WAR and is responsible for co-starting the band with Eric Burdon; [d] Billy Joel played piano <u>and</u> harp on "Piano Man"; [e] Stevie Wonder's "Fingertips, pt. 2*" has a seriously good harmonica break in it. * The first live, non-studio recording to reach number-one.

187. [c] Johnny Kidd and the Pirates. Their Brit version came first, then the Guess Who, then the Who. The drummer on the Kidd version – Clem Cattini – went on to play in the Tornados and on 45 different U.K. #1 singles, ranging from the Kinks "You Really Got Me" to Edison Lighthouse's "Love Grows (Where My Rosemary Goes)" to Donovan's "Hurdy Gurdy Man" (which, btw, does *not* use a hurdy gurdy on the recording). Rumor has it that Clem was on Page's short list for the drum slot in Zeppelin that went to Bonham.

188. Parsons. Gram and Gene, completely unrelated. You already know about Gram but Gene, too, was in the Flying Burrito Brothers. For guitar techies, Gene's fame is drawn from creating the B-Bender

(StringBender) for the Telecaster which makes it possible for a guitarist to mechanically bend the B-string up a whole tone to C-sharp, effecting a pedal steel sound. The Eagles' "Peaceful Easy Feeling" was the first *hit* record to employ the device, but you can hear it on *Who Are You, In Through the Out Door, Minute by Minute*, Arlo Guthrie, the Byrds (of course), Randy Newman, Ronstadt, Nick Lowe, even Helen Reddy and Eddie Rabbitt albums.

189. Herb Alpert (the vocal – "This Guy's in Love with You" – in 1968; the instrumental – "Rise" – in 1979) and Barry White (the instrumental – "Love's Theme" by Love Unlimited Orchestra; and the vocal – "Can't Get Enough of Your Love Babe" – both in the year of our Lord, 1974).

190. "Hello, I Love You" (hum 'em and you'll see). Robbie Krieger says they ripped the vibe off of "Sunshine of Your Love" but not "All Day and All of the Night". There are other great infringements out there, too, like the Flaming Lips having to give up half their rights on "Fight Test" to Cat Stevens because it sounded too much like "Father and Son". Cat and Joe Satriani have accused Coldplay of "borrowing" one of their songs for their "Viva La Vida" (Cat's from his song "Foreigner Suite" and Satriani with "If I Could Fly").

191. Sort of a trick question, sorry. Pre-Bruce, Landau [b] produced an album by the MC5 (*Back in the USA*), however he also [c] *started* production on J. Geils' first record but it was scrapped (you can

have points for either if that'll make you feel better). And, yes, he did produce Jackson Browne's *Pretender* album, but it was *after* he hooked up with Springsteen. Score it like you want, drop it like it's hot.

192. [d] All of 'em. What's wrong with "Greenback Dollar"? "I don't give a damn about a greenback dollar", that's what. But the song's author - Hoyt Axton - was known for pissing in the Cheerios of the censors. Think about it - "The Pusher", "Joy to the World", "No-No Song"...

193. [d] Boz Scaggs. Born June of '44 (Clapton 3/45; Raitt 11/49; Buffett 12/46).

194. Dan Fogelberg's *Souvenirs* (1974). *Outside* of the producer role, Joe's charms also can be heard on Randy Newman's *Little Criminals*, Andy Gibb's *Love is Thicker than Water*, and REO Speedwagon's *Ridin' the Storm Out*, among others (even Lionel Richie's debut LP, for crying out loud).

195. Jerry Garcia. He also played pedal steel on CSN&Y's "Teach Your Children". BTW, Jerry Garcia is the most recorded guitarist in history. The data's not exactly unconditional, but it does make sense: "*With more than 2,200 Grateful Dead concerts, and 1,000 Jerry Garcia Band concerts captured on tape – as well as numerous studio sessions – there are about 15,000 hours of his guitar work preserved for the ages.*" That from *Guitar Player* magazine (quoting Henry Kaiser, Oct. '07). And, he did it all with just nine fingers! That's right - 'ol

Jer had half of his right middle finger lopped off when in a wood-chopping axe-i-dent at age four.

196. [a] Los Angeles. Blue Jay Way is a real street in the Hollywood Hills overlooking Sunset Boulevard.

197. Paul and Ringo, as are/were Bach, Glen Campbell, Isaac Hayes, Judy Garland, both of the Everlys, Albert King, Robert Plant, Chuck Mangione, David Byrne, George Michael, Vicki Carr (oops – I've now gone too far).

198. [c] *Ed Sullivan Show*. They agreed to change "higher" to "better" with the show's producer just to shut 'em up but reneged on the deal once they went live. Mr. Ed was furrrrrrrious, refused the shake the band's hands after the performance and they were never invited back. Out-of-wedlock children weren't an issue with Ed, though, as he let Diana Ross and the Supremes do "Love Child" without changing anything.

199. [b] John Mayall's Bluesbreakers. Mayall was like a midwife with all the careers he nurtured: Clapton – and Jack Bruce – left for Cream; Peter Green (who replaced Clapton), Mick Fleetwood, and John McVie to Fleetwood Mac; Mick Taylor to the Stones; Jon Mark and Johnny Almond to Mark-Almond; Harvey Mandel, Walter Trout, and Larry Taylor to Canned Heat; Andy Fraser to Free; Aynsley Dunbar to Frank Zappa.

200. Otis Redding, Sam & Dave, Lou Rawls, James Brown, and Wilson Pickett. Spotlight on the jaw, ya'll... Arthur and Otis Redding took Sam Cooke's

"Yeah, Man" and just re-wrote it to become "Sweet Soul Music". Simple as that.

201. [d] All of them. They started it up shortly after the Three Mile Island nuclear accident and then followed with a series of five No Nukes gigs. If John Hall's name fails you, he's the guy who wrote "Half Moon" for Janis Joplin (*Pearl*) and was leader of Orleans ("Dance with Me" and "Still the One"). His anti-nuclear tree-hugging paid off – now, he's a congressman from New York. Kinda funny that both Bush and McCain tried to use his "Still the One" as their campaign songs and had to be told "no mas" on both occasions.

202. [b] Keith Moon (the Who). Beck is credited for writing the track, but Pagey claims he wrote it, instead, and even integrated parts of the song in Zeppelin's "How Many More Times" as an in-joke.

203. [a: an ocarina on "Wild Thing"] [b: a theremin on "Good Vibrations"] and [d: a mellotron on "Strawberry Fields"]. Steely Dan is inventive, but no tricks were turned on "My Old School", sorry. There is, however, an interesting story behind the Beatles' employment of the mellotron. Seems like Mike Pinder of the Moody Blues was moonlighting at Streetly Electronics, the manufacturer or the mellotron, and he introduced the instrument to John Lennon and Paul McCartney of the Beatles who then used it on "Strawberry Fields Forever". I'm sure that's why L. Ron Hubbard and King Hussein went out and bought one for themselves.

204. KISS' *Destroyer*. The one with "Detroit Rock City", "Beth", and "Shout It Out Loud". It was KISS' first with Bob Ezrin, who had produced all of Alice Cooper's hits. Ezrin even pulled in Dick Wagner, Alice's guitarist, to play some of the lead parts.

205. The two songs are the familiar "Honky Tonk Women" (from *Through the Past Darkly*) and the country "Country Honk" which they recorded first for *Let it Bleed*. Other than the style, the difference is purely geographic. One lists Memphis; the other Jackson. The flip on "Honky Tonk Women" was "You Can't Always Get What You Want". And who played drums on "You Can't Always..."? No, not Charlie – it was Jimmy Miller, their producer, who also did the cowbell part of "Honky Tonk Women". 1969 was the release date for both.

206. [b] Leonard Cohen. Future long-haired country rocker Charlie Daniels played bass, fiddle, and guitar on both of 'em.

207. [b] David Bowie. The Arnold Corns group was a stepping stone towards Ziggyland, as it featured Mick Ronson, Mick Woodmansey, and Trevor Bolder, all Spiders-in-waiting. The name of the band was inspired by Pink Floyd's "Arnold Layne". Hey, you know how Bowie got that weird-lookin' eye? When he was 15, he got in a fight over a girl and the guy who punched him, hit his eye with his ringer finger and left David's pupil permanently dilated.

208. Musselwhite? No guitar, although he was supposedly the inspiration for Dan Ackroyd's Blues Brother persona and he also played on "Suicide Blonde" by INXS; Little Walter, yes; Junior Wells, no; Buddy Guy, yes; Paul Butterfield, no; Pinetop Perkins, well… hmm… he *did* start out on the guitar but he screwed up the tendons in his arm in a fight with a choirgirl and switched to piano where he reached infamy as the keyboardist for Muddy Waters.

209. [d] Skyline Quartet. Most of the musically conscious are aware of Kingfish and Ratdog, but the Other Ones was started by Bob Weir, Phil Lesh, and Mickey Hart, along with Bruce Hornsby. The lineup changed from time to time and, finally, in 2003, they changed their name to the Dead. The Other Ones took their name from "That's It for the Other One", from 1967's *Anthem of the Sun*. What a long strange trip…

210. [c] "He's So Fine". "My Sweet Lord's" original artist target wasn't George, but Billy Preston (who did release "MSL" as a single). George and Billy came up with the idea for the song while they were in Stockholm in '69. When they got back to London, George engineered the sessions and played guitar, but Billy was the principal musician and Alan White of Yes played drums. Most of the copyright infringement fingers get pointed toward Harrison for ripping off "He's So Fine", but In the course of its opinion, the court seems to imply that the infringement was really Preston's fault because he was the lead musician on the recording. The

decision was unique in that the court acknowledged that Harrison may have unconsciously copied the tune, saying "*His subconscious knew it already had worked in a song his conscious did not remember... That is, under the law, infringement of copyright, and is no less so even though subconsciously accomplished.*" Freud must've rolled over in his grave on that one. To further exasperate the process, check out what George said in a '93 interview with Paul Cashmere: "*The whole story of "My Sweet Lord" is based upon this fellow, Allan Klein, who managed the Beatles from about 1968 or '69, through until 1973. When they issued a complaint about "My Sweet Lord", he was my business manager. He was the one who put out "My Sweet Lord" and collected 20 percent commission on the record. And he was the one who got the lawyers to defend me, and did an interview in Playboy where he talked about how the song was nothing like the other song. Later, when the judge in court told me to settle with them, because he didn't think I'd consciously stolen their song, they were doing a settlement deal with me when they suddenly stopped the settlement. Some time elapsed, and I found out that this guy Klein had gone around the back door. In the meantime, we'd fired him. He went round the back door and bought the rights to the one song, "He's So Fine," in order to continue a lawsuit against me.*" Now I clearly understand why the Who's "Who Are You" and Lennon's "Steel and Glass" ("*Your teeth are clean, but your mind is capped, you leave your smell like an alley cat*") gives Klein the down-the-road.

211. Yesterday morning. And some of the references in the song are real. On *VH1's Story Tellers*, JT said that the song was about Suzanne Schnerr, a friend who died suddenly while he was away from home. JT went on to say he had been in a deep depression after the failure of his band the Flying Machine to gel and the line "sweet dreams and Flying Machines in pieces on the ground" was about that rather than an airplane crash.

212. [a] "Southern Cross" ("Song to Orion" by Kansas would be a good guess, but it's a fake... no such song). And while it's credited to Crosby, Stills, and Nash, Stills is by his lonesome on the recording with Graham and David nowhere to be found. Timothy B. Schmidt of the Eagles, Joe Lala and Joe Vitale of Joe Walsh's group, Michael Finnigan who played on Jimi's *Electric Ladyland* and assorted others did the playin'.

213. [b] Elvis Presley. His name? Jesse Garon Presley.

214. *Tapestry*. On the credits, it lists James Taylor as playing the "granfalloon" which, as best as I can tell, isn't an instrument, but some fictional religion Vonnegut created in <u>Cat's Cradle</u> and means a group of people who outwardly choose or claim to have a shared identity or purpose, but whose mutual association is actually meaningless. Huh?

215. [a:2] The Stones' "I'm Free" used in the Chase Freedom Card spot and, in the UK, for a Renault ad, was a remix of the original; [b:1] Andy Kim's '70s hit pluggin' away for Jeep; [c:4] the Rare Earth hit used in the "Brewery" ad for AT&T; [d:3] Hard

to believe a song about heroin addiction would wind up as the soundtrack for a Royal Caribbean vacation, but Iggy likes the money and you like the cruise! BONUS: Richie loaned his pipes for NBC ("We're NBC, Just Watch Us Now"), Amtrak, McDonalds, Budweiser, and the Cotton Association of America ("the fabric of our lives").

216. [b] "Me & Bobby McGee", first recorded by Roger Miller and, later, Janis Joplin just a few days before she died. Her version became the second posthumous #1 single in rock music history. The first being Otis Redding's "Dock of the Bay". Another? Jim Croce's "Time in a Bottle".

217. [c] They're all "Davids".

218. In order: Drifters (200-499 million records - same range as ABBA, The Stones, Elton, Pink Floyd), Dave Clark Five (100-199 million - same level as Bowie, Deep Purple, Eagles, Sinatra), Eddy Arnold (75-99 million - same level as Van Halen, Eminem, Earth Wind & Fire), then Kenny G-unit (50-74 million - same level as Ray Conniff, NKOTB, the Police, KISS, and Miz Streisand). Topping the list are the Beatles and Elvis (1+ billion each), then Jacko and Bing Crosby (500 mil to 1 bil each).

219. [c] Willie Dixon, author of "Hoochie Coochie Man", "Wang Dang Doodle", "Spoonful", "I Just Wanna Make Love to You", and countless others. A conscientious objector who spent 10 months in the slammer during WW2, he rose to fame doing a little of everything at Chess/Checker Records where he worked with folks like Chuck Berry,

Muddy Waters, Howlin' Wolf, Bo Diddley, Little Walter, Sonny Boy Williamson, Koko Taylor, Little Milton, and others.

220. [d] Allman Brothers, the headliner on the Fillmore East's closing, June 27, 1971, appearing alongside the J. Geils Band, Albert King, Edgar Winter's White Trash, Mountain, the Beach Boys, and Country Joe McDonald.

221. [b] Everly Brothers. After the Everlys, he recorded/toured with Manfred Mann, and even landed a song ("She Quit Me") on *Midnight Cowboy* before he hit his stride as his own man.

222. Same year (1967) but "Up, Up, and Away" was released in May while "By the Time I Get to Phoenix" was released in November. The actual *first* appearances of a Jim Webb tune was in 1965 on singles by Brenda Holloway, the Contessas, and his own "I Can't Quit", but the big bang from getting on the *Merry Christmas, The Supremes* album with "My Christmas Tree" (you see, he had a songwriting contract with Jobete, Motown's publishing arm).

223. [c] Rectangular. Bo came up with the design after he found jumping around on stage with a regular-shaped guitar was bad news for his groin.

224. [d] They were married to the Boyd sisters, Jenny and Pattie. You undoubtedly know Pattie's story with Clapton and Harrison (and the girl behind "Layla", "Wonderful Tonight", "Bell Bottom Blues", and "Something"), but Jenny was the inspiration behind Donovan's "Jennifer Juniper".

225. [c] *Running on Empty,* Jackson's fifth - and still best-selling - album. It's a rarity when it comes to live albums because none of the tracks had appeared on previous albums.

226. [b] Into the swimming pool of a Holiday Inn, part of Keith's 21st birthday celebration. He also had a penchant for other whackouts, like throwing furniture out of hotel windows and blowing up toilets with cherry bombs. It's been estimated that his destruction of toilets and plumbing ran close to half-a-mil and got him banned for life from the Sheraton, Hilton, and Holiday Inn chains. Must've been that all-you-can-drink breakfast of champagne and Courvoisier.

227. [c] *Born to Run, The River, Nebraska, Tunnel of Love.* If you're looking for a Born to Run twist, I can give you two: 1) the very first pressings have "Meeting Across the River" listed as "The Heist"; 2) the original album cover has a sepia tint and the title printed in a graffiti style font (which some believe is the actual scribble of Ralph Steadman [Fear & Loathing, Rolling Stone, et al]).

228. [e] None of the above (meaning *all of the above* are connected). John Paul Jones produced Uncle Earl and arranged some Donovan hits; when the Yardbirds disbanded, Page wanted Reid to fill the vocalist spot for a proposed new group, the New Yardbirds, which wound up as Led Zeppelin; Memphis Minnie wrote the original "When the Levee Breaks" (heard on Led Zeppelin's fourth album [*Zoso*].

229. [b] Bonnie Raitt. Her dad, John Raitt, is best known for his leads in *Carousel* and *Oklahoma* on Broadway.

230. [a] Elvis (taken from "Presley") Costello (from his paternal g-mommy's maiden name). He's been in some 70+ TV episodes or movies – even played the Earl of Manchester in that (expletive deleted) Firesign Theatre-driven movie *Americathon* and a public defender in Q-Tip's flick, *Prison Song*. Think he would appear at the opening of the beer cave at Piggly Wiggly if we paid him enough?

231. [b] Joni Mitchell. I'm not a musician and don't play one on TV, but suffice it to say that Joni's modus operandi is like no other. Nearly every song she writes is in an "open" (non-standard) tuning and she's written songs in some 50 different tunings. Remember A&M artist Shawn Phillips? He claims to have given Joni guitar lessons when she was a waitress in Saskatoon, as well as teaching George Harrison how to play the sitar. No proof – just passin' it along...

232. Faye was married to Peter Wolf (J. Geils Band). Peter wasn't afraid of frolicking in the tall grass, either. As a kid, he took painting lessons from Norman Rockwell and, in college, his roommate was filmmaker-to-be David Lynch. And the answer to part B is Georgie Fame. The song wasn't in the movie – Georgie was just taking advantage of the celluloid's celebrity status. If you're into Van Morrison, you already know that Fame was in Van's band for nearly 20 years and even helped on

the knob twistin' as a producer. And... If you're a Motown fan, you know that Georgie Fame and his band the Blue Flames were the only act from Britain summoned to perform with the first Motown Review when they toured the U.K.

233. Pat Boone, who also popularized Little Richard's "Tutti Frutti" and "Long Tall Sally" for the "white" market. To take that sterilization one step further, Pat even wanted to change the title of "Ain't that..." to "Isn't that a Shame".

234. Van Morrison. The "Lions" song I'm referring to is "Listen to the Lion" where, in the lyrics, he sings "And we sail, and we sail, way up to Caledonia." His fixation even spilled over into the Hollywood Bowl performance of *Astral Weeks* where he fell into this incantation about Caledonia during his performance of the song "Astral Weeks". What makes his big head so hard?

235. [c] Jim Brown (Cleveland Browns' running back). The FOD's roots were in Ray Charles' backing band the Hi-Fi's which also had Marilyn McCoo and Lamont McLemore before they took off to be in the 5th Dimension.

236. Frank Zappa for 60 seconds of snorks, gorks, and norks. Go find it on YouTube.

237. David Porter. Together they wrote "Soul Man", "Hold On, I'm Comin'", "When Something is Wrong with My Baby", "B-A-B-Y"... all told more than 200 tunes as a team. The partnership started to unwind with Isaac started wooin' the ladies with things like *Hot Buttered Soul*, so David

decided to do a solo thing, as well, not only under his own name but the pseudonyms of "Little David" and "Kenny Cain", as well.

238. [d] The Byrds' "Eight Miles High". The guy who played electric sitar on "Green Tambourine" – Vinnie Bell – also played it on Gene Pitney's "She's a Heartbreaker" and Freda Payne's "Band of Gold". You can also hear one in B.J. Thomas' "Hooked on a Feeling", Eric Burdon's "Monterey", and the Spinners' "It's a Shame".

239. [c] "Atom Heart Mother" (23:44 long). You a movie buff? Next time you watch *A Clockwork Orange*, keep an eye on the shelf in the music shop scene. The album is right there (the one with a big cow).

240. Essentially [a] Furay and Messina, who were cycling out of Buffalo Springfield to create Poco. When Poco was trying out players to be in the band, Gregg Allman spent a few days working out, but didn't make the cut.

241. [b] *Sweetheart of the Rodeo.* Before he did himself in with morphine and tequila at age 26, Gram (real name: Ingram Cecil Connor III) did a semester at Harvard studying Theology, joined the Byrds at 21, formed the Flying Burrito Brothers, befriended Jagger/Richards and turned them on to "country honk" and toured with 'em, and credited with the incubation of one Emmylou Harris.

242. [b] "Positively 4th Street", "Rainy Day Women #12 & #35". As the story goes, Dylan recorded "Rainy Day Women #12 & #35" high as a kite (listen to his

laugh) and if you multiply 12 by 35, you get 420, a number associated with marijuana (but, that's just as the story goes, mind you…).

243. The answer is Jimi ("gave us rainbows"), Janis (took a piece of our heart"), Otis ("took us to the dock of the bay"), Jim Croce, Bobby Darin, and Jim Morrison. Written by Alan O'Day who gave us "Undercover Angel" and the Righteous Brothers, who had been pursuing solo for seven years, got back together for the song.

244. They all feature a "whistling" break, as does "Games Without Frontiers" by Peter Gabriel, "Jealous Guy" by Lennon, "Lazy Sunday" by the Small Faces, "Wind Of Change" by the Scorpions, "I Was Kaiser Bill's Batman" by Whistling Jack Smith, "Walk Like An Egyptian" by the Bangles…

245. [a] "Purple Haze". Why the name "Wilburys"? Seems like George and Jeff coined the phrase when they were recording *Cloud Nine* as their expression for malfunctioning studio gear, as in "We'll bury 'em in the mix".

246. Phil Keaggy. There are variations on the rumor - Clapton, a magazine, etc. - but Keaggy (now a Contemporary Christian artist) is the answer most often given. The facts are that the tapes of the show were destroyed and most believe that Hendrix didn't say it and the Carson part is inaccurate as Flip Wilson was filling in. It's doubtful that Jimi knew of Phil, but Keaggy's band - Glass Harp - had recorded their first album at Jimi's Electric Ladyland Studios. If there's style

points for this question, it would be for those who gave (pre-ZZ Top) "Billy Gibbons" (then of the band revealed in Answer # 275) as a response because Jimi did sing his praises on the *Dick Cavett Show.*

247. [c] The 1983 arrival of one Natalie Rae Hynde was made possible by Ray Davies of the Kinks. While Chrissie and Ray never did the nuptial thang, she did exchange vows with Jim Kerr of Simple Minds and they, too, had a child - Yasmin - who came into this world alive and kicking in 1985.

248. [b] *Live from Max' Kansas City.* Bridget Polk (real name is Berlin), an "associate" of Warhol's and the daughter of the head of the Hearst media empire, was a taping freak and captured the performance on a little mono cassette recorder. Atlantic Records was unhappy with the sales of the Velvets first album and Danny Fields (who later discovered the Ramones) persuaded them to put this out as fulfillment of their two-LP commitment.

249. [a] Keith Richards has a daughter named "Dandelion". The kid wasn't crazy about it either and wound up changing it to Angela. She's one of three children Keith had with Anita Pallenberg, all without the benefit of clergy.

250. "Skydog" is Duane Allman; "No Show Jones" is George Jones (defined by his legacy of not showing up for gigs); "Motor City Madman" is Ted Nugent; "Bocephus" is Hank Williams, Jr.; "Thin White Duke" is David Bowie (in his *Station-*

to-Station persona of being a dapper fella); and the "Ice Man" is Jerry Butler.

251. [c] John Hammond (Sr.). John discovered some of the greatest talents in jazz, folk, blues and rock and roll during his 54-year association with Columbia Records. On the jazz and blues side, he played a major role in launching the careers of Billie Holiday, Count Basie, and Aretha Franklin. Among rock and roll fans, he will no doubt be best remembered for signing Bob Dylan, Stevie Ray Vaughn, and Bruce Springsteen. For those of you who cherish the almighty dollar, John was the great-grandson of William Henry Vanderbilt. For those of you who want me to drill down even further, his sister (Alice) married Benny Goodman and his son, John Hammond, Jr. is the only person alive who had the fortune of employing both Clapton and Hendrix in his band at the same time, albeit for five days in the '60s when Hammond was playing at NYC's Gaslight Café. The greater regret is that none of it was ever caught on tape.

252. [b] John Sebastian, the name changed to avoid contract hassles. John also played bass on Dylan's *Bringing It All Back Home*, harp on CSN&Y's *Déjà Vu*, guitar/harp on Lightfoot's "If You Could My Mind" sessions, Mama Cass records, BJ Thomas' "Rock and Roll Lullaby", yadda... John grew up in Greenwich Village where folkies like Burl Ives and Woody Guthrie would stop by to jam with his dad, a noted classical harmonica player. When little Johnny came into the world, his godmother

was none other than Vivian Vance, "Ethel" on *I Love Lucy.*

253. [b] Jeff Lynne. Trust me, you've never heard it and probably don't want to.

254. [a] The Who backed out so the Yardbirds stepped in. It's one of only two known recordings that featured the dual guitars of Page and Beck. The other being "Happenings Ten Years Ago Today".

255. Austin, Texas. They're all gone, 'cept Antone's, a Blues dig made famous by Clifford Antone and Stevie Ray Vaughan. Cliffie nurtured some of the Blues cats in and around Austin and when he found out that Stevie's dream was to play with Albert King, he asked Al if SRV could sit in one night. King said yes, was blown away, and the rest is a crosscut saw across the Blues landscape.

256. Martha Reeves & the Vandellas' "Heat Wave". It might sound a wee bit different to the, er, untrained ear, but John Sebastian himself says that's where he got the lick.

257. They're blind – *and* they can play their butts off!

258. Taj Mahal. If you want to sink your ears into something good, track down *The Rising Sons* album – it's Taj and Ry Cooder and Ed Cassidy (the bald drummer guy in Spirit). One of the first interracial badass jams (from 1965) before we knew there was such a thing.

259. "World's Largest Store" because it was owned by Sears & Roebuck which was, in effect, the world's largest store at the time of the station's origin,

1924. At the height of its heyday, WLS had more than four million listeners tuning in each week.

260. Little Stevie Wonder, Little Peggy March, Little Anthony (and the Imperials), Little Brenda Lee, Little Milton, Little Walter, Little Richard, and Little Eva (real name: Eva Narcissus Boyd, but named Little Eva after a character in *Uncle Tom's Cabin*) who was Carole King and Gerry Goffin's maid. Amused by her dancing style, Carole and Gerry wrote "Locomotion" about her but actually intended for Dee Dee Sharp to record it. Eva did the demo, Don Kirshner dug the sound, and she landed the gig.

261. Richard Milhaus Nixon. And the voices in the background? No, not Spiro Agnew's children – but the Jackson 5.

262. "Renegade" by Styx. Adam Sandler must be a big Styx fan. He used this song in *Billy Madison*, "Mr. Roboto" in *Eight Crazy Nights*, and "Blue Collar Man" in *Big Daddy*.

263. [b] *Hullabaloo*. It was sort of NBC's prime-time answer to *American Bandstand*. Some of the hosts included Sammy Davis Jr., Petula Clark, and Frankie Avalon and the artists who appeared on the show were folks like Sonny & Cher, Dionne Warwick, the Rolling Stones, Herman's Hermits, the Animals, the Supremes, and Marianne Faithfull. It was the prime-time show that *The Monkees* eventually replaced.

264. [d] Peter Gabriel, the same man who (in '67) started the group Genesis (named by Jonathan

King of "Everyone's Gone to the Moon" fame)... the same man who played flute on "Katmandu" on Cat Stevens' *Mona Bone Jakon* album in 1970... the same man who forbid any cymbals being used on his third album (aka "Scratch")... the same man who dated Rosanna Arquette that Toto's "Rosanna" was about... the same man who we *think* sings "She's so pop-u-lar" on "Games Without Frontiers" when the lyric is really "Jeux Sans Frontieres," which is French for "Games Without Frontiers"... the same man who wrote "Solsbury Hill" after seeing Bruce Springsteen in concert and wanted to write a song about his departure from Genesis.

265. [a] Hot on the heels of opening for Cream at the Royal Albert Hall for Cream's Farewell Concert, Yes released *Yes** – with the Beatles' "Every Little Thing" and the Byrds' "I See You". *Not to be confused with *The Yes Album,* the one with "I've Seen All Good People".

266. Bob Dylan, who performed two dates under the name of Elston Gunn with Bobby Vee in '59.

267. [b] Mr. "Games People Play", Joe South. Bobby Womack did the rest of the geetar parts, but the game at the front is the all Joe. You can also hear Joe's strums on Tommy Roe's "Sheila" and Dylan's *Blonde on Blonde*. Teenie? He's a member of the Hi Records rhythm section and co-wrote "Take Me to the River" and "Love and Happiness" with the Right Reverend Al Green.

268. [a] "Stairway to Heaven" – the biggest-selling single piece of sheet music ringing up about 15,000 copies every year – is the biggest record of all-time that was never released as a single. Some of you might wanna take me to task on this because you've seen a *promotional* 45 that were sent to radio stations but the song was never *commercially* released. Sidebar proffering: If you listen to Spirit's song "Taurus", you'll note an eerie resemblance to "Stairway". Maybe Jimmy picked up on the slant when Zeppelin opened for Spirit on one of their tours, 'ya think?

269. [a:3] Bobby Womack/"Across 100th Street"; [b:5] Steely Dan/"Brooklyn"; [c:4] Village Stompers/ "Washington Square"; [d:2] Neil Diamond/"Brooklyn Roads"; [e:10] Joni Mitchell/"Song for Sharon"; [f:7] 10cc/"Wall Street Shuffle"; [g:8] Tradewinds/"New York's a Lonely Town"; [h:1] Barry Manilow/"New York City Rhythm"; [i:9] Simon & Garfunkel/"Bleecker Street"; [j:6] Velvet Underground/"Chelsea Girls"

270. Bing Crosby. *TV Guide* listed the Crosby-Bowie duet as one of the 25 most memorable musical moments of 20th century television.

271. [a] "Dueling Banjos" (*Deliverance*) which is really a dust-off of a 1955 song called "Feudin' Banjos" by Arthur Smith but seems like Warners forgot to give Arthur credit on the soundtrack. Lawsuit? You betcha. It's on there, now! [b] Old & In the Way with Garcia, David Grisman, Vassar Clements, John Kahn, and Peter Rowan (he wrote

"Panama Red" for the New Riders among other ventures). [c] That bunch o' longhairs is the Nitty Gritty Dirt Band and the LP is *Will the Circle Be Unbroken* with Bluegrass originals Doc Watson, Maybelle Carter, Jimmy Martin, Merle Travis, Acuff, et al.

272. [b] Freddie Bell and the Bellboys. Elvis picked up on the song when he was in Vegas in '56 and Freddie Bell's band was playing The Sands and saw them do it live. Being a good, polite Southern boy, he asked them if they minded if he did the song in his set and the rest is history. BTW, the Presley version we're all used to hearing is a bit different from the original Big Mama Thornton version the way that Leiber & Stoller wrote it. In the original, the lyrics are more metaphoric and in the Presley version – the one that Freddie Bell rewrote – the lines were more literal. Example: "*Snoopin' round my door*" was replaced with "*cryin' all the time*", and "*You can wag your tail, but I ain't gonna feed you no more*" was replaced by "*You ain't never caught a rabbit, and you ain't no friend of mine.*"

273. Oui. Guitarist Iommi took on guitar duties for a short time after the departure of Mick Abrahams, appearing in Tull's line-up for *The Rolling Stones Rock and Roll Circus* (December '68) in which the group mimed "A Song For Jeffrey", but it was a one-time only arrangement and Tony returned to the group "Earth" (which later was renamed "Black Sabbath") after the gig.

274. [c] Norman "Hurricane" Smith: Producer of Pink Floyd's first, second, and fourth studio albums (*The Piper at the Gates of Dawn, A Saucerful of Secrets,* and *Ummagumma*). But, previous to Floyd, Smith was the engineer on all of the EMI studio recordings (about 100) by The Beatles up to '65 (the last being *Rubber Soul*) when EMI promoted him from engineer to producer.

275. The Moving Sidewalks. They recorded several singles and one album, *Flash*, which – for grins, if nothing else – is worth checking out for their Blue Cheer'ish version of "I Want to Hold Your Hand".

276. [c] The Byrds in their 1969 release, *Ballad of Easy Rider*. It was the second single but stalled at #97. The Doobies version was part of their '72 *Toulouse Street* album and, as a single, reached 35. The other bands you know, 'cept proably Clover. When Elvis Costello got signed, he didn't have a band, so Nick Lowe brought over Clover who he'd seen at L.A.'s Palamino club. Clover featured John McFee (future Doobie), one Huey Lewis (although Huey didn't play on the Costello sessions), and Alex Call, who wrote Tommy Tutone's "867-5309/Jenny". Dig – there is an annual project on the web called "JennyScan" where people who have no life call 867-5309 in every area code in the U.S. and document if there's life at the other end of the string. There's usually only one – Gem Plumbing and Heating in Rhode Island who laid hands on the number after Brown University gave it up in 2002. The lawyers among you will love this: Gem

actually owns (and has protected) the copyright on the number.

277. Steve Miller Band. Boz (William Royce) Scaggs was on the band's first two albums until Jann Wenner (*Rolling Stone*'s publisher) saw his cool persona in person, started singing his praises, and Boz split to be a solo act on Atlantic where his first album was done in Muscle Shoals with Duane Allman.

278. [a] *2112* (Maybe someday they'll do a whole side based on *The Secret Life of Bees*).

279. Sorry, it ain't like the 'ol "Who makes BIC pens" trick - Les Paul did not "officially" invent the Gibson "Les Paul". By "officially," I mean that you won't see his name on the patent (#2714326) but rather the name of Theodore (Ted) McCarty, the President of Gibson. Les did approach the company with a solid body design called "The Log" but it was rejected. Rejection led to opportunity and Les had a chance to give a bit of advice on the new model, specifically on the trapeze tailpiece and the colors of gold and black, although some Gibson sticklers will claim that Les was chiefly approached for the right to use his name on the headstock so the company could spur sales. And, before we leave the fold, I should inform you that Mr. McCarty couldn't play guitar (Leo Fender couldn't, either), but he loved to design 'em. Did the Flying V, the SG, and others. Now, on to part two... Keith Richards was supposedly the first rocker to use a Les Paul. He

(or someone) tried to auction it off at Christies in '04, but it went unsold. According to a report in *Newsday*, it's worth $400k.

280. Seger had a few Top 10'ers in the '70s under his own banner but his biggest chart success was as the co-writer (w/ Henley, Frey, J.D. Souther) of the Eagles' "Heartache Tonight", which hit #1. It came from *The Long Run*, the first LP to feature Timothy B. Schmidt and the last #1 album of the '70s.

281. They're all based on classical music themes. For example, "Groovy Kind of Love" was based on the Rondo from "Sonatina in G Major" by Muzio Clementi"; "Lover's Concerto" on Bach's "Minuet in G Major"; "All by Myself"* on Sergei Rachmaninoff's "Piano Concerto No. 2 in C minor, Opus 18"; "American Tune" (*and* Peter, Paul, and Mary's "Because All Men Are Brothers" which was penned by Tom Glazer, the guy who wrote "On Top of Spaghetti") is based on a melody line from Bach's chorale in "St. Matthew Passion". Other classical rips include "Because" by the Beatles, based on Beethoven's "Moonlight Sonata" – *backwards* – and "A Whiter Shade of Pale" which got its lift from Bach's cantata, "Sleepers Awake".

*Eric Carmen thought the tune was in the public domain but found out all too late that there was still someone in the Rachmaninoff family keeping an eye on their stuff and he had to fork over the royalties from the melody portion of the song.

282. The Capitol Records building in Hollywood. Slyly nicknamed "The House That Nat Built" in honor of the enormous financial contributions Nat "King" Cole lent to the company, the President of

Capitol – Alan Livingston* – had a beacon built on top that spells out "Hollywood" in Morse code.

*Livingston is also the guy who signed the Beatles <u>and</u> created the character of Bozo the Clown.

283. Believe it or not, a folk song originally done by Kingston Trio and specifically written for them by Ervin Drake, who wrote the song within an hour! The diff between what he penned and what we know by 'Ol Blue Eyes is that his original has a flamenco chord structure.

284. True. I don't know which is worse, shooting yourself in the foot or marrying Cher, but it's not fair to pile on to any man who's been married at least six times, now, is it?

285. While the Alpha Phi's among you were hoping it was *"Chi O, Chi O, it's off to bed we go!"*, it was both [a] <u>and</u> [c]. The actual inspiration was Boz Scaggs' girlfriend (who Dickey Betts may have been shagging in Macon's Rose Hill cemetery) but Betts felt he couldn't use her real name so he used "Elizabeth Reed" off a tombstone in the cemetery where he used to write (or saw while shaggin').

286. She be the lovely Linda McCartney. Later, Paul taught her how to play keyboards and she became an official "Wing". Often taunted and never really appreciated but, still, a Wing. There's actually a Linda McCartney album out – one Paul finished after her death – called *Wide Prairie* and includes tracks she did with Wings in Nawlins during *Venus & Mars,* a McGuire Sisters cover, and a

single she did in '77 as Suzy & the Red Stripes called "Seaside Woman".

287. [d] Gordon Lightfoot but while Billy didn't wax as to why, my research says that the influence might be more "structural"* than anything else (let's hope it wasn't for his looks!). "She's Always..." is from *The Stranger* which overtook Simon & Garfunkel's *Bridge Over Troubled Water* as Columbia Records' best-selling album (at that point, anyway). * Things like utilizing the second inversion of a pure triad, ascending to its suspended 4th, then back, finally down to its 2nd in Gordy's "Carefree Highway". Go listen...

288. [d] All are true (What! You haven't heard Babs' "You Don't Bring Me the Fez Anymore"?). Fagen and Becker wrote "I Mean to Shine" on Streisand's *Barbra Joan Streisand* album and Fagen played organ on the track, along with Joe Cocker's horn guys, three-fourths of the chicks from Fanny, and the guy who played half of "Dueling Banjos" (Eric Weissberg).

289. [c] Tom Waits. "Chuck E" is Chuck Weiss, who's also a musician and the guy who created the famous Viper Room in L.A. with Johnny Depp.

290. [b] and [d] Keith Moon and Mama Cass Elliott and they died in a flat owned by Harry Nilsson! She died in her sleep of a heart attack; Keith of a drug overdose. We don't know what Cass' last words were, but Keith's were, "If you don't like it, you can fuck off". It stems from him asking asked his girlfriend Annette Walter-Lax to cook him a steak

and she complained about cooking him another meal. So much for last suppers.

291. "Eight Miles High". The tune came about while the Byrds were touring England in 1965 and the title was a result of rhyming more than anything else since planes normally don't fly higher than seven miles. The irony in it is that the band's chief songwriter, Gene Clark, had a phobia about flying and left the band after it became and hit and the band never had another Top 20 song again.

292. [b] "Get Ready" which peaked at #29 ("My Girl" hit #1). And (because I do such things), an interesting tidbit about "I Wish It Would Rain": The guy who wrote that - Roger Penzabene - wrote the follow-up, "I Could Never Love Another (After Loving You)", two songs that illustrate depression if I ever heard it. The songs came from Roger finding out that his wife was cheating on him, and a week after "I Wish It Would Rain" was released, he committed suicide.

293. The leader of the band that John Lennon once punned as "Book a Table and the Maitre D's" - Booker T. Jones. *Just as I Am* was done in just three sessions and features none other than Stephen Stills on guitar (yes, that's him on "Ain't No Sunshine"). Incidentally, did you know that Booker T's first ever session at STAX was not playing organ, but rather playing baritone sax on "Cause I Love You", by Rufus Thomas and Carla Thomas? Did you know that Booker was married to Priscilla Coolidge, Rita's sister? And get this:

Ever heard "Stoned" by the Rolling Stones? The instrumental track is based on Booker T. & the MGs' "Green Onions", a record the M.G.s recorded during a break in the action while in the studio as the session band for a set with Rockabilly dude, Billy Lee Riley. Did you know that I'm going to stop spewing forth Booker T. Jones trivia right about... now?

294. Little Richard, Joey Dee and the Starlighters, Curtis Knight and the Squires, Chuck Jackson, Slim Harpo, Sam Cooke, Jackie Wilson, and the Isley Brothers where he did his first successful studio session on the Isley's "Testify".

295. [a] "The Look of Love". A lot of folks have recorded the song (Claudine Longet, Sergio Mendes, Zombies, Tony Joe White, et al), but Isaac Hayes version gets the most props, these days. It's been sampled by Jay-Z, Ashanti, Snoop, Speshul Ed, Smif N' Wessun and other hip-hop'ers and candy rappers.

296. [b] Teddy Bears, who were pretty much a one-and-done deal because Spector wanted to play producer and not artist. The female lead in the group – Annette Kleinbard, p/k/a Carol Connors – went on to write/co-write the theme to *Rocky* ("Gonna Fly Now"), "Hey Little Cobra" by the Rip Chords, and "With You I'm Born Again", the Billy Preston/Syreeta Wright duet.

297. [c] Set up record labels Invictus and Hot Wax (Freda Payne, Flaming Ember, et al).

298. [b] Grand Trunk Western Railroad, who also broke the attendance record, previously set by the Beatles' at Shea Stadium, selling out in 72 hours.

299. [a] and [c] are True; [b] ain't. I'll flesh it out for you... They used to be called "The Iveys" and even released their first single – "Maybe Tomorrow" – as The Iveys on Apple Records. After being confused with "The Ivy League", they were renamed Badfinger after "Badfinger Boogie", the original title of "With a Little Help From My Friends". Ray Davies did, in fact, produce several demos for them at the request of Pye Records and Todd Rundgren produced *Straight Up* (after Geoff Emerick's version was turned down by Apple and Harrison pulled out due to his commitments to his Bangla Desh project). Other morsels include the fact that some of the members sang backup on Ringo's "It Don't Come Easy" ... their "Come and Get It" was a McCartney tune he had written for the movie *Magic Christian* ... the band served as a backing group for the Concert for Bangla Desh ... a couple of 'em performed on Lennon's *Imagine* ... the two guys who wrote "Without You*" (the Nilsson hit) – Pete Ham and Tom Evans – hanged themselves, a tidbit most of you buffs already know. * Did you know that Gary Wright (Spooky Tooth, "Dream Weaver") played the piano part on Nilsson's version?

300. [b] Graham Gouldman, later of 10cc. He also wrote and sang lead vocals on "Sausalito (Is the Place to Go)" under the name of the Ohio Express.

301. [c] Bassist. She started out as a guitar player but one day when she was doing a Sam Cooke session,

the bass player failed to show and she volunteered to give it a try. You can hear her on "Good Vibrations", "Homeward Bound", "I'm a Believer", "Wichita Lineman", "The Way We Were", "Suspicious Minds", "You've Lost That Lovin' Feeling", the Mothers' *Freak Out!*, etc.

302. [c] 1975, a turning point in what we heard on the radio. It was that year that six songs hit #1 on both the Pop *and* Country charts: "Before the Next Teardrop Falls"; "(Hey Won't You Play) Another Somebody Done Somebody Wrong Song" by B.J. Thomas; "Rhinestone Cowboy" by Glen Campbell; "Thank God I'm a Country Boy" and the double-sided hit "I'm Sorry"/"Calypso," by John Denver; and "Convoy" by C.W. McCall.

303. [d] Lou Reed's double LP of recorded feedback loops (four songs, each about 20 min. long). No one knows if he was serious or it was some contractual obligation, but we do know he was very stoned while making it. *Rolling Stone* said it sounded like "the tubular groaning of a galactic refrigerator" and "as displeasing to experience as 'a night in a bus terminal'". I listened to half of it once. I now opt for having my wisdom teeth removed when I want to feel that bad.

304. [f] All of them, as well as Aretha Franklin's 1986 LP *Aretha*, and Lennon's *Menlove Avenue*. If you wanna find the first album cover Andy did, look for of John Wallowitch's debut album from '64. Oh, yeah – do you remember Warhol playing the bartender in the Cars' video for "Hello Again"?

305. [c] Tom Johnston of the Doobie Brothers. Tom's the one we hear singing "Listen to the Music", "Take Me in Your Arms", "China Grove", and "Long Train Running". He got sick the night before the Doobies' 1975 tour, so they recruited McDonald whose influence completely changed the band's direction. Michael came from Steely Dan who had already lost Jeff "Skunk" Baxter to the Doobs.

306. [c] Bad Company. Kirke came with Paul Rodgers from Free and Burrell came from King Crimson and was the one selected to replace Roger Daltrey in the Who when Entwistle/Townshend/Moon were on the verge of firing Daltrey, which ultimately (and gleefully) didn't happen.

307. [d] Love. Originally, *Forever Changes* was to be produced by Bruce Botnick (the Doors) and Neil Young, but Neil Baby gracefully bowed out because of his commitments to Buffalo Springfield. However, he did hang around to do the arrangements on the track "The Daily Planet".

308. [a] Unlike most other rock groups, the drummer — Dave Clark — was the leader of the group. And, unlike most other groups, Dave was large and in charge. He played with his drums at stage front, lining up the guitarists and keyboard to the rear and sides. While the band was originally a partnership, during its heyday he employed the group's members, paying their wages, paying for the recordings, and owning all the copyrights.

309. [b] "Give a Damn". When they performed it live on *The Smothers Brothers Comedy Hour*, CBS got a bunch of complaints about the song being played during "family time". Supposedly, even President Nixon beefed about it.

310. *Thick as a Brick* by Jethro Tull. It was Ian Anderson's little trou drop to all the critics who had (mistakenly) called *Aqualung* a "concept" album. TAAB was essentially him saying, "You want a concept album? I'll show you a %@^#*&! concept album. Ian even stated in an interview with Redbeard on *In the Studio* that the album was "a spoof to the albums of Yes and Emerson, Lake & Palmer much like what the movie *Airplane!* had been to *Airport*".

311. Bert Berns together with his partners from Atlantic Records: Ahmet Ertegün, Nesuhi Ertegün and Jerry Wexler (Gerald). BANG had Van Morrison, Neil Diamond, the McCoys among others. Bert wrote "Piece of My Heart", co-wrote "Twist & Shout", produced "Under the Boardwalk", etc. The other three were Atlantic Records president (Ahmet), his brother (Nesuhi who was head of Atlantic's Jazz division) [their dad was Turkey's ambassador to the US], and their ace producer, Jerry Wexler (Aretha, Cream, etc.). Bert married a go-go dancer named Ilene, had three kids, then kicked the bucket with Ilene left to handle everything at the tender age of 24. She moved the company to Atlanta, signed up Brick, Paul Davis, Nigel Olsson (who she also dated), and Peabo

Bryson, sold the label to Columbia, but kept Bert's publishing. Wouldn't you?

312. [c] *Naked in the Shade*, although the Stones had a set called *Made in the Shade*. The others belonged to Black Sabbath, Lennon, and Peter Gabriel.

313. [d] None of them have a song that matches the LP's title, although there is a song called "Question" and one called "The Balance" on *A Question of Balance*. That album is probably the most stripped-down of all the Moodies' stuff because they were having a hard time replicating their highly-involved studio recordings in concert and wanted to keep the distance between recorded and live as short as possible.

314. [b, d, e, f, g, h] (American) Indian, cowboy, policeman, biker, soldier, construction worker. The classified ad they ran for the auditions read, "Macho Types Wanted: Must Dance and Have a Moustache". The Navy – not realizing that the act had a decided gay lean to it – asked to use "In the Navy" as a recruitment campaign and the band's producers agreed if the Navy would help them shoot a video for the song. Sure enough, the Navy brought 'em to San Diego to film a rendition on an aircraft carrier. Someone finally tipped the Navy off, they got their dress whites in a knot, and the ad campaign was cancelled.

315. "Long Cool Woman in a Black Dress" by the Hollies, a song co-written, sung, and guitar'ed (is that a word?) by Allan Clarke even though he had left the band for a solo career.

316. Sir Douglas Quintet, led by one Doug Sahm who, in '73, Jerry Wexler bought the contract of and took him into the studio with Dylan, Dr. John, David Bromberg, jazzer David "Fathead" Newman, and put together one of the rare five-star ratings that AllMusic.com gives an album.

317. Hit me with your rhythm stick... Hit me, hit me!

Player	Drums or Bass	Group
Geddy Lee	Bass	Rush
Al Jackson	Drums	Booker T. & the MGs
Peter Cetera	Bass	Chicago
Tom Hamilton	Bass	Aerosmith
Artimus Pyle	Drums	Lynyrd Skynyrd
Stu Cook	Bass	CCR

318. [d] "In-a-Gadda-Da-Vida", baby, around 9:20 in.

319. Friday. A lot of us – maybe you, too – mistakenly call the song "Stormy Monday Blues" or "Stormy Monday" because that's what the Allmans called it on their *Fillmore* disc. However "Stormy Monday Blues" is actually another song that Earl Hines and Billy Eckstine had a hit with in '42. "Call It Stormy Monday (But Tuesday Is Just As Bad)" is the correct title and T-Bone Walker wrote it, not Bobby Bland as the Allmans would have us believe. We Allmans fans also got screwed on the *real* version. When Tom Dowd edited it, he cut out a harmonica solo by Thom "Ace" Doucette, who played with the band for almost 30 years and even offered a

slot in the group but refused because he thought it would be like a real job.

320. Glen Campbell. Glenner also played guitar on *Pet Sounds,* not to mention on Sinatra's "Strangers in the Night", the Righteous Brothers' "You've Lost That Lovin' Feeling", and "I'm a Believer" by the Monkees.

321. [b] Longbranch Pennywhistle which was really a duo with John David Souther (co-writer of "Best of My Love" and "New Kid in Town") . If you can find a copy of the movie *Vanishing Point,* you'll find a song called "I Can't Believe It" that they co-wrote with a young Bob Seger and an even younger Jackson Browne. It's not on the soundtrack – just in the movie. Delaney, Bonnie & Friends had a tiny role as a Gospel music band that included singer Rita Coolidge and Bread's David Gates at the piano.

322. [c] Peter Green. Although he did have the honor of replacing Clapton in John Mayall's Bluesbreakers and, then, after one album, split with Mick Fleetwood and John McVie to form Fleetwood Mac. His biggest paycheck came from writing "Black Magic Woman".

323. Rainbow (or Blackmore's Rainbow). The band featured Ronnie James Dio on vocals for four albums, then Ronnie moved over to Black Sabbath to take Ozzy's place.

324. [a:1] "Mary, Queen of Arkansas"/Bruce Springsteen; [b:2] "Mary Lou"/Steve Miller Band; [c:3] "Marianne"/Stephen Stills; [d:4] "Mary,

Mary"/Butterfield Blues Band (a song that Michael Nesmith wrote).

325. [e] All of these are true, I promise. The GTOs (Girls Together Outrageously) were an all-groupie group featuring Pamela Des Barres and six other expert plaster casters. Their only album, *Permanent Damage*, was released in '69 (not a pun, folks) and had studio help from Jeff Beck, Zappa, Davy Jones, Lowell George, and Rod Stewart (on "The Ghost Chained To the Past, Present, and Future").

326. 1) Entwistle played French horn on *Tommy*; 2) Sonny Boy Williamson II wrote "Eyesight to the Blind"; 3) Nicholson played "The Specialist" (who confirms who confirms that Tommy's problems are psychosomatic) in the movie version. There are around 25 differences between the album and the movie versions. For instance, 1) On the album, Captain Walker returns from the WW1 to find his wife with a new lover and murders him, but in the film the lover comes home from WW2 and kills Walker in front of Tommy; 2) "Pinball Wizard" has extra lyrics; 3) Leslie West (Mountain) plays lead guitar on "Acid Queen", Mott the Hoople is the backing band on "1951/What about the Boy", and Paul Nicholas (yep, the same guy who did that sappy "Heaven on the 7th Floor") sang "Cousin Kevin". That's enough for now... if you're truly curious, look the rest of 'em up.

327. [a] Because the group refused to add his friend Peter Frampton (from the Herd). I step aside to bring you this important piece of useless

knowledge: Marriott was alleged to have been Page's point of reference when looking for a vocalist for Led Zep, and "Whole Lotta Love" is thought by some to be a direct rip of Marriott's version of Muddy Waters' "You Need Lovin'" (written by Willie Dixon). Go listen and you'll see.

328. Elvis Presley, Johnny Cash, Jerry Lee Lewis, and Carl Perkins. As happenstance goes, Perkins had come in to work on "Matchbox" and Sam Phillips, in an effort to fatten up the arrangement, brought in relative unknown Jerry Lee Lewis to play piano. Sometime that afternoon, Elvis (now on RCA) dropped by to see his old Sun chums. He listened to Carl's tracks and, then, went into the studio where the jam began. Later on, Cash dropped by and history was written. At some point when Jerry Lewis was settin' the place on fire, Elvis, er, left the building, because as Johnny says in *Cash,* "no one wanted to follow Jerry Lee, not even Elvis." 40-odd songs were captured that day, including several gospel numbers, a coupla Christmas tunes, four Bill Monroe bluegrass numbers, and Chuck Berry's "Brown-Eyed Handsome Man" and "Too Much Monkey Business".

329. "Jingle Bells" by the Singing Dogs. The song was created by a Danish recording engineer, Carl Weismann. Carl's fascination wasn't with recording dogs but with birds and being a neat freak, wanted all the stupid barking out of his recordings. So, after snipping all the little barks out, he decided to have some fun rather than put his little pile of tape clippings into file 13. He

pasted the barks in their different tones, goosed 'em with a variable speed control, and set about crafting a medley of tunes sung by the Dogs, beginning with "Pat-A-Cake", "Three Blind Mice", and winding up with "Jingle Bells". Most of us don't remember the original 1955 version that sold a half-million copies, but we do remember the 1970 adaptation where RCA Records took the original minute-long segment of "Jingle Bells" and cut and pasted part of its middle to the ending (just like what happened in Answer #331).
And those of you who said "The Chipmunks" as being the only "animal" act with a hit record? I've got some swamp land in Florida I think you'd like.

330. [c] Mike Oldfield, with *Tubular Bells.* Virgin Records actually started out as a little record store in Notting Hill Gate and grew from there. The guy who introduces all the instruments on *Tubular Bells* was Vivian Stanshell, who also co-wrote "Arc of a Diver" with Stevie Winwood for the LP of the same name and founding father of Bonzo Dog's Doo-Dah Circus.

331. You might say because the Gentrys had Jimmy Hart, who went on to become a (very?) famous wrestling manager, as a vocalist; or you could say that although the group had Hart and Bruce Bowles as "vocalists"-only (no instruments), but that the song was actually sung by *guitarist* Larry Raspberry; but neither is what I call the real twist. That would be that they had to get the length of a typical single, they had to take the song and copy/paste it onto itself because the original

recording was only about a minute long. In the final analysis, it's just one song played twice.

332. "Land of 1,000 Dances". Chris Kenner (the writer and original artist) had all 16 dances in his, but Wilson Pickett cut those in half so he could get in more squeelin'.

333. [c] Procol Harum. 'Twas the one that had "Conquistador" on it which led it to become their best-selling album as well as the first orchestral recording to achieve international platinum sales.

334. "Talking John Birch Society Blues". Whoever was in charge of all that's "good and proper" at CBS considered the song potentially libelous to the John Birch Society, and rather than sing another rousing version of "Blowin' in the Wind" or something else, Dylan said "nay" to his appearance. It's not known whether Topo Gigio, the Italian mouse, stepped in to fill the void or not.

335. "Maybellene", but you won't find Freed listed anymore. Berry, not immune to a good shell game, is thought to have ripped an old Bob Wills song for the basic idea. According to Johnnie Johnson, Chuck's piano player, it happened at the suggestion from Leonard Chess. "It was an old fiddle tune called 'Ida Red'. I changed the music and re-arranged it, Chuck re-wrote the words, and the rest, as they say, was history. At that time, someone else already had a song out by the same name, so we had to change our version. We noticed a mascara box in the corner, so we changed the name to 'Maybellene'."

336. Gene Pitney, who was all that and a bag of chips! After writing hits for the Crystals, Ricky Nelson ("Hello Mary Lou"), and Bobby Vee, he was certain he could sing as well as write, so he set out to do groundbreaking things like multi-tracking his own vocals and playing most of the instruments on "(I Wanna) Love My Life Away"; using Indian instruments in '63 on "Mecca"; crossed over to Country where he did two albums with George Jones and they were named Country music's "Most Promising Duo of the Year"; recorded songs in Italian, German, and Spanish; and reignited his career in '89 when he redid "Something's Gotten Hold of My Heart" with Soft Cell's Marc Almond and took it to #1 in the U.K. Oh, one more - Gene's hit "It Hurts to Be in Love": It was recorded by Neil Sedaka but RCA wouldn't release it because it was recorded outside RCA and violated his contract. So the writers just replaced Neil's voice with Gene's and he had the hit with it, instead!

337. [c] Los Angeles. If I went in to the whole sordid story about Sam's death, it would take up several pages, so best find it on your own watch. Suffice it to say it's got "grassy knoll" conspiracy theory written all over it - something about naked with only a sports coat and a single shoe, a gun, a woman named Bertha, and a broomstick.

338. [b] "She Just Satisfies" by one James Patrick Page. Some will proffer that it's a copy of a song written by Ray Davies and (Kinks' manager) Larry Page called "Revenge" off their first album, one that

Jimmy played on and was inspired to write the own song. I dunno and I ain't passin' judgment.

339. [a] There were two Sonny Boy Williamsons. The first one – John Lee Curtis Williamson –wrote "Good Morning Little Schoolgirl" and was the "Northern" version, born in '14 and died in '48; and Aleck 'Rice' Miller who appropriated his name (often referred to as "Sonny Boy II"), born around 1912, hung around the Delta, wrote "One Way Out", "Bring It On Home", and "Eyesight to the Blind", and did live albums with the Animals and the Yardbirds, and died in '65,.

340. [d] "Sad-Eyed Lady of the Lowlands". Sara was born Shirley Marlin Noznisky, but changed her name at the request of her first husband, a photographer (Sara used to be a Playboy playmate and fashion model, so that's where she and the photog probably met). Besides "Sad-Eyed Lady...", Sara was the focus of "Sara" on Dylan's *Desire* album, a tune he wrote to try and reconcile their differences. And, yes, all you family tree types – she is the mother of Jakob Dylan of the Wallflowers.

341. [c] "The black Elvis". February 25, 1968, Sunday edition of the *New York Times*.

342. [d] Gibraltar. The lovebirds spent their honeymoon in Amsterdam, drinking coffee (ha!) and campaigning for an international "Bed-In" for peace. After Amsterdam, they wanted to do another "Bed-in" in the lower 50, but were denied entry, so they went to Montréal, did their "Bed-In"

at the Queen Elizabeth Hotel recorded "Give Peace a Chance". All we are saying...

343. [b] Hotlegs/"Neanderthal Man". And, before they were Hotlegs, Eric Stewart (the vocalist) was heard as the singer on "Groovy Kind of Love" by the Mindbenders and Kevin Godley even masqueraded as the lead singer on "There Ain't No Umbopo", one of (studio creation) Crazy Elephant's failed follow-ups to "Gimme Gimme Good Lovin'".

344. Jack Nitzsche. And you probably saw him on the TV show *COPS*, too. He was seen waving a gun at some youths who had stolen his hat. While he was being arrested, you can hear Jack trying to explain to the officers that he was an Academy Award winner (for his co-write on "Best Song" for "Up Where We Belong" from *An Officer and a Gentleman*).

345. [a] Hoyt Axton was the son of Mae Axton who wrote "Heartbreak Hotel". Together they were the only mother and son *songwriters* to have written #1 songs.

346. Elephant's Memory. They also did time on a couple of John & Yoko's albums and some live gigs. Earlier in their career, they placed two songs on the soundtrack of *Midnight Cowboy* and waaaaaaay earlier in their career ('68), they had Carly Simon as their vocalist for about a six-month stretch.

347. When Grand Funk fired their manager, Terry Knight, they hired Paul McCartney's father-in-law, John Eastman.

348. [c] "Nutbush City Limits". Nutbush, Tennessee was the birthplace of Tina Turner. Marc Bolan (T. Rex) played guitar on the tune.

349. [b] Heart failure during open heart surgery. Darin was travelling with Bobby Kennedy on the campaign trail and was with him the night RFK was murdered in L.A. Darin was so freaked by the incident, sold his house and most of his possessions and moved into a trailer near Big Sur and lived there in seclusion for about a year.

350. Dead (at least of this writing, she is). Her parents were able to prove that Pam and Jim were a "common law" couple and they inherited Morrison's fortune. Since there were more than 20 paternity suits against the Lizard King when he died – and since he had bedded the best of the breasts like Janis, Grace Slick, and Nico – you'd think that someone would either raise their hand and stake a claim or one of the rock star grrrls would show up, bun in oven with some golden child offspring. One kid actually did say came from Jim's loins, but he was found to be a fraud. Not sure if he had to make his mojo rise to prove Morrison was his daddy or not...

351. [c] Tower Theatre in Philly. Bowie commented that the record was the "death of Ziggy" as he started to segue into his more dapper suit and kerchief

persona. It's also the first time we saw his version of "All the Young Dudes" on record.

352. [e] Ardent Studios*. Chips started his rise in Memphis at STAX where he did Carla's "Gee Whiz" and produced a group called The Triumphs that featured a young Al Green. He and STAX got crossways on money, however, so he built his own place - American Sound Studios - where he brought in cats like Bobby Womack to be his session guitarist, and turned out classics like *From Elvis in Memphis* ("In the Ghetto" and "Suspicious Minds") and *Dusty in Memphis* as well as hits by the Box Tops, Merliee Rush, et al. At one point, Moman's success was such that during one particular week, over a quarter of Billboard's Hot 100 hits were generated at American. Around the same time, he travelled to Muscle Shoals and FAME Studios where he wrote "Do Right Woman" for Aretha and "Dark End of the Street"for James Carr. He later closed American in Memphis and moved everything to Nashville where he also wrote "Luckenbach, Texas". He married Toni Wine who wrote "Groovy Kind of Love" and "Candida" and sang the female voice on "Sugar, Sugar" ("I'm gonna make your life so sweet"). * Ardent is, however, where Zeppelin *III* was done, as well as 12-inch'ers from Dylan, Stevie Ray Vaughn, ZZ Top, Big Star, White Stripes, and a zillion others. The studio was founded by three guys - one of whom was Fred Smith who went on to found Fed Ex.

353. [c] It was Bill Wyman's 1974 LP, *Monkey Grip*. He got help from Dr. John, Gwen McCrae, Leon Russell, Danny Kortchmar, Lowell George, et al.

354. *Physical Graffiti*. For we recording studio phreaks, this just in: The album was (partially*) recorded at Ronnie Lane's (he being a Small Face) Mobile Studio, a pioneer in mobile recording studios, equipped with a 16-track studio housed in a 26' Airstream trailer. After he left the Faces in '73, Ronnie based the studio on his farm, Fishpool, and used the studio to record his first solo album *Anymore for Anymore* as well as *One for the Road*. Besides using the studio himself, Lane leased it to numerous other artists for their own recordings, including: *Quadrophenia* and *the Who by Numbers*, *Bad Company* and *Straight Shooter*, Clapton's *Rainbow Concert*, and the aforementioned *Physical Graffiti*. * John Paul Jones got sick and they had to resume at Headley Grange months later because Bad Co. had come in to *Straight Shooter*.

355. [a] We purists raise our hands for Mr. Nesmith. While Pittman had a hand in the *launch* of MTV, his boss had shepherded the *Pop Clips* thang with Nesmith years before. But this chicken and egg story goes back even further to 1976 in New Zealand where there was a show called *Radio With Pictures*; even even further to the syndicated *Now Explosion* around '71-'72; and even even even further back to Mason Williams who pitched an idea to CBS for a TV program that featured "video-radio" when he was with *The Smothers Brothers*.

356. *Wish You Were Here*. The original record was intended to be packaged in an unidentified, all-black plastic wrapper, but the president of

Columbia Records threw a hissy and Hipgnosis (the design firm) and the band relented and an image with "Pink Floyd" over the top of two robotic hands was included as a sticker on top. This was also the album where they paid tribute to Syd Barrett (via "Shine On, You Crazy Diamond") and part of the melody from Syd's "hit", "See Emily Play", was played on a Moog at the tail end of "Shine On...".

357. [c] Power plant. And "*Gostaria de comer fora de hummus Julie Andrews da barriga se ela iria deixar-me*" is Portuguese for "I would eat hummus off of Julie Andrews' belly if she'd let me".

358. "The Night the Lights Went Out in Georgia", a hit by Vicki Lawrence. Vicki's husband - Bobby Russell (the guy who wrote "Honey") - didn't even record a demo for the song because he didn't like it, but Vicki believed in the song and did the demo herself. The publisher first pitched the tune to Liza Minnelli, then Cher (but Sonny thought it would offend her Southern fans) so, without a marquee name to record it, Lawrence went back to the studio and recorded the song herself.

359. [d] Witnessing the birth of his son, Sean.

360. *Fly Like an Eagle*. Most people miss the connection because they're not familiar with Miller's earlier stuff, but the guitar hook on "Fly..." is the same one Steve used on "My Dark Hour" from *Brave New World* (listen starting at :00:16).

361. [d] Peter & Gordon. Nonetheless, the lads had a direct connection to the Fab Four because Peter's

sister, Jane Asher, was Paul's galfriend. Paul gave Peter & Gordon several songs he wrote (without Lennon, although he's still credited): "A World Without Love", "Nobody I Know", "I Don't Want To See You Again", and "Woman" (it says "Bernard Webb" wrote "Woman" but that was just an alias for McCartney).

362. Cactus. They were initially conceived in 1969 by the Vanilla Fudge rhythm section of bassist Tim Bogert and drummer Carmine Appice with guitarist Jeff Beck and singer Rod Stewart who were available since the Jeff Beck Group had dissolved. But Appice and Bogert didn't want to wait out the time for Beck to rehab and Rod got the call from Ron Wood to do the Faces, so Jim McCarty and Rusty Day signed up.

363. [c] A penis transplant. Some cat named Bennett had his wee-wee damaged in a car wreck and they had to amputate it and he got some womanizer's (larger) digit in its place. Elke Sommer and Britt Ekland were in the movie, I guess in the role of having to identify the, uh, third party.

364. Mickey Hart. It was his first album and done while he had temporarily left the Dead, but Garcia, Weir, and Lesh helped out as well as some other buds like Stephen Stills, Grace Slick, and David Frieberg (Quicksilver Messenger Service), most of who helped him mix the album.

365. [b] Marx Brothers' movies, *A Day at the Races* and *A Night at the Opera*. If you say the secret word,

you can find Groucho on the cover of Alice Cooper's *Greatest Hits*, too.

366. [b] Guitarist. Davey Johnstone didn't join in until '72, so it was just Elton, Nigel Olsson (drums), and Dee Murray (bass), both of who came to Elton from the Spencer Davis Group, and were released from the lineup after *Captain Fantastic* for several years because Elton was looking for a different sound. They did come back, however, in '81.

367. [c] Devo. The legend goes that the group Devo came up with the "rust never sleeps" slogan as part of an ad campaign for Rustoleum. Neil corroborates the story about getting the phrase from Devo, but no confirmation, yet, on if Devo had really created it for an ad campaign.

368. *V* (five). And, btw, there really wasn't a "[Roman numeral] *I* or *IV* – the first one was *Chicago Transit Authority*; the fourth one was *Live at Carnegie Hall*. All of the rest of the official U.S. releases were numbered until *Hot Streets* (the debut of Donnie Dacus as the replacement for Terry Kath) came along in '78.

369. Herb Alpert wrote "What a Wonderful World" for Sam Cooke, not to mention "Alley-Oop" for the Hollywood Argyles. Herb being the "A" in "A&M" Records and Jerry Moss – owner of Kentucky Derby winner Giacomo (named after Sting's son) – being the "M".

370. Sonny Bono – and Debbie Harry played his wife, Velma Von Tussle. And why do we creative dogs love Sonny? Because of the "Sonny Bono

Copyright Term Extension Act", a copyright lasts the life of the author plus 70 years (and a little longer for corporate copyrights).

371. Billy Preston (along with Bruce Fisher, who also co-wrote "Nothing From Nothing"). Billy did his version first (and a little more up-tempo) on *The Kids and Me.*

372. Paul Williams. Another guy - like Stephen Stills - who auditioned for, but didn't land a part in the Monkees. Undaunted, he (w/ Roger Nichols) wrote the band's "Someday Man". Paul's brother - Mentor - is the guy who wrote "Drift Away" (Dobie Gray, Uncle Kracker).

373. [d] "American Pie", clocking in at 8:33. "Taxi" about 6:33, "Layla" 7:05, "Roundabout" 8:29 <u>but</u> none of those hit #1, either.

374. [a] Leon Russell's Shelter Records. Tom formed Mudcrutch in 1970 with Tom Leadon, kid brother of Bernie Leadon of the Eagles.

375. "Louie, Louie". The year was 1955 and Richard Berry heard a song "El Loco Cha Cha" by Ricky Rillera and the Rhythm Rockers. The tune was written originally as the cha-cha'ish "Amarren Al Loco" (which means "Tie up the crazy guy") by Cuban bandleader Rosendo Ruiz Jr. In Berry's fertile mind, he kept hearing the words "Louie Louie" layered over the bass riff. Lyrically, he wrote from the first person person perspective, kinda like a customer talking to a bartender. Then, he picked up some of Chuck Berry's (no relation) speech cadence and Jamaican references from

"Havana Moon". Richard Berry eventually records the tune with the band The Pharohs and got a little regional action on the West Coast. One bad break led to another and, eventually, Berry gave up and sold his publishing to the head of Flip Records for $750. Years later, the Kingsmen put down $36 to rent a studio in Portland, Oregon for an hour, lay down their version and the rest is history. The garbled lyrics on the Kingsmen's version led to a witch hunt by the FBI who was looking to hang an obscenity rap on someone but came up empty. And since Berry sold his rights cheaply, the 1,000+ versions that were released over time put most of the money in someone else's pocket. Nonetheless, he got a small but consistent dribble off his BMI rights but, finally, in '86 (and, again, in '93), he was able to get the belated compensation he deserved before dying in '96.

376. Someone (I take it a Gino Vannelli fan) said they all wore chest wigs, but that's not right. The real answer is that they're all from Canada.

377. [c] Robbie Robertson on *Blonde on Blonde*. Dylan was familiar with the Hawks by hearing their work on John Hammond Jr.'s *So Many Roads* and soon after Newport started to assemble some replacements for Bloomfield (guitar) and Bobby Gregg (drums) who weren't available. The first audition went to Robertson who passed the smell test but when the drummer wasn't really working out, he suggested Levon Helm who came in and things grew organically on from there.

378. [c] Even though Jackson was in the Dirt Band when he was 17, his first real *songwriting* success came after he moved to Greenwich Village and Nico recorded "These Days", a song Browne had written at 16. He even got to play on it, courtesy of a nudge from Andy Warhol.

379. [b] William "Bootsy" Collins. He and his bro', Catfish, toiled for the Godfather of Soul for only 11 months and played on things like "Get Up (I Feel Like Being a) Sex Machine".

380. Bill Wyman, living sex legend* and bassist for the Rolling Stones. *He's reputed to have bedded more than 1,000 women (or 19,000 shy of Wilt Chamberlain).

381. [c] Dixie Hummingbirds

382. If you <u>do</u> buy that, you're good. The owner of a pub the band was rehearsing in, remarked on Peter Noone's resemblance to the character Sherman in *Peabody's Improbable History*, one of the supporting cartoons in *The Rocky and Bullwinkle Show*. Noone thought he said "Herman" and, well, the rest is a fractured fairytale, so to speak.

383. [a] Mick Ronson. The Revue's backing band also included T-Bone Burnett, violinist Scarlet Rivera (who'd been on Bob's *Desire* LP), David Mansfield (who you'll find in the first version of Bruce Hornsby and the Range), bassist Rob Stoner (bass and bg vocs on "American Pie"), and drummer Howie Wyeth (yes, of the famous artsy Wyeth family).

384. [b] Dino Valente is the pen name for Chet Powers (his other pseudonyms are Jackie Powers and Jessie Orris Farrow). When Chet first got busted for possession, he sold the rights to "Get Together" to the Kingston Trio*'s manager to help pay for his defense. * The Kingston Trio was the first to record "Get Together".

385. [b] Quicksilver Messenger Service and [e] The Youngbloods. Yes, it's true that David Freiberg who was originally in QMS *eventually* became a member of Jefferson Starship, but that wasn't the question, now, was it? Skip Spence moved on to Moby Grape; Spencer Dryden to the New Riders; Jorma and Jack, of course, to Hot Tuna. How'd the Tuna get that wacky name? Well, according to the FAQs @ HotTuna.com, Jack & Jorma and the rest of Jefferson Airplane were driving down St. Marks Place in Greenwich Village when they passed one of New York's finest street employees walking down the sidewalk. The question from the back of the car was "What's that smell like fish, oh baby?" "Hot tuna!" was the response and it's stuck ever since. Hush yo' mouth.

386. Give yourself points for either [e] Billy Preston *or* [c] Janis Ian as they were both on. Billy performed "Nothing from Nothing" and "Fancy Lady"; and Janis did "At Seventeen" and "In the Winter". If you want to be real specific about who was the first one to play, well, the script says Billy. Paul Simon? Yes, he *was* on that episode, but it was a cameo and he didn't sing or play.

387. [b] Barry/Greenwich. They also took a neophyte named Neil Leslie Diamond under their wing and formed a publishing company with Neil and produced Cherry, Cherry" and "Kentucky Woman".

388. [d] Bette Midler, as well as Dionne Warwick and Rosemary Clooney. I think one of the most interesting tidbits about Barry is a letter he wrote to *Playboy* (Dec. '65) when he was 22, asking for advice on whether he should purse music fulltime. He wrote, "My musical wild oats are screaming to be sown, but it means giving up my secure job. ... Any suggestions?" and the response was go and "sow your notes".

389. [a] Cherilyn. Cherilyn Sarkisian to be exact.

390. "Black and White" was originally done by a U.K.-based reggae group called Greyhound and Blondie covered the Paragons' original "The Tide is High". The Blondie tune became anthemic across the good state of Alabama in the Fall of '80 where every radio station blasted it in anticipation of the Crimson Tide's game versus Notre Dame. Debbie Harry even did an interview in Birmingham and wished the team good luck, but it was all for naught as the Fighting Irish won, 7-zip.

391. [d] Ronnie Montrose. Same cat that first worked with Herbie Hancock on *Mwandishi* and Van Morrison on *Tupelo Honey* and *St. Dominic's Preview* and, then, formed his own band with Sammy Hagar on the mic.

392. Queen, and the logo was designed by the Virgo faerie in the group (hey, it's what it is), Freddie Mercury, who snagged a diploma in Illustration and Graphic Design from London's Ealing Art College (Pete Townshend and Ronnie Wood are alums).

393. [a] Phil Rizzuto did all the metaphors. Thank goodness we were saved from a "switch hitter", "designated hitter", "drag bunt" or "fan interference" reference.

394. Johnny Jenkins/"Walk on Gilded Splinters". Mister Jenkins not on your radar? Well, then, a little history: He used to be the leader of the Pinetoppers who had a singer named Otis Redding. One day, during a recording session, Johnny left about 40 minutes of studio time unused and Redding took advantage of the opportunity to record a little ditty called "These Arms of Mine" (which Jenkins played guitar on), and the rest, as they say, is history.

395. Cat Stevens wrote it and PP Arnold had the original Brit hit. PP is a lady named "Pat" Arnold who Mick Jagger discovered while she was a singer with Ike & Tina Turner who was opening for a Stones tour in '66.

396. False. It was Mickey Thomas, who went on to become a lead vocalist with Jefferson Starship and do the do on "Jane", "We Built This City", "Nothing's Gonna Stop Us Now", y mas.

397. [c] Van Morrison's ex-wife, as well as the chick on bareback on the cover of "Tupelo Honey", and the designer of *His Band and Street Choir*.

398. [d] Stevie Wonder, although he actually *co-wrote* "Until You Come Back to Me" with Morris Broadnax and Clarence Paul.

399. [a] "Everything's Alright" sung by Yvonne Elliman on the album, on Broadway, and in the movie version. Yvonne went on to be Eric Clapton's background vocalist ("I Shot the Sheriff" and "Lay Down Sally") as well as his girlfriend for a spell. And, of course, her monster hit from *Saturday Night Fever*, "If I Can't Have You". "Jesus is a Soul Man" was a regional Top 40 hit by Lawrence Reynolds and "Jesus Was a Crossmaker" was a Judee Sill nugget. "Love Him, Love Him, Love"? Nuttin' that I know – I just pulled the title outta my butt.

400. Al Green. Bunches of people have recorded it – among them, the Dead, Levon Helm, Annie Lennox, Dave Matthews Band, Bryan Ferry, Delbert McClinton, Gov't Mule, and Phish.

401. "Brown Sugar". Rolling Stones Records was initially headed up by Marshall Chess, the son of Leonard Chess, Chess Records founder. Kracker was the first act signed (Cuban rock group whose record came in a very ornate cigar box package), Peter Tosh did some stuff, and John Phillips (Mamas & Papas) got a deal and did some recording but Mick and the boys lost interest and finally cut off the pipeline.

402. [d] Springsteen. 1976 while he was playing Memphis. The Boss actually jumped the fence and got all the way to the door. When they answered the knock, he asked if Elvis was home and they told him, no, he was in Tahoe. Bruce tried to explain who he was – that he'd recently been on the cover of *TIME* and *Newsweek* – but it fell on deaf ears and they sent him packin'.

403. Bill "Wolfgang" Graham, founder of the Fillmore (East and West). After his death (helicopter crash as he was leaving a concert), his assets were picked up by SFX Entertainment who, in a swap o' stuff, sold it to Clear Channel who wanted the concert biz but had no idea what to do with all of Graham's boxes of memorabilia so they decided to sell it. A guy named Bill Sagan was able to buy everything for something like $5 million. Since Graham kept virtually everything – like posters, tapes of the shows – Sagan turned "Wolfgang's Vault" into an online treasure chest that's now worth an estimated $100 million.

404. [c] *Saturday Night Fever*. The reason why the world was given Samantha Sang's "Emotion" was that it – along with three Bee Gees' tunes (including "If I Can't Have You" and the one that wound up in Andy's mouth "(Our Love) Don't Throw It All Away") – were recorded for the soundtrack but never used.

405. [d] Ry Cooder. Yessir – the man who played mandolin on the Stones' "Love in Vain" and the

slide guitar on "Sister Morphine" – recorded *Bop 'Til You Drop* with all 1s and 0s.

406. [c] The movie *Bad* Company, a 1972 acid Western, a reworking of *Oliver Twist* set in Civil War-era America, with Jeff Bridges as the Artful Dodger.

407. Robin and Maurice. Robin's the one who had a child with his housekeeper, 26 years his junior; Maurice is the one who married Lulu and opened up a paintball shop in Miami Beach. Like you cared...

408. [d] Ray Charles. In his first incarnation, Joe used the persona Vance Arnold, a name he combined from Vance Everett, the Elvis character in *Jailhouse Rock* and Eddy Arnold. His band was "Vance Arnold and the Avengers".

409. Dennis, the surfing Beach Boy whose death came by drowning. Hmm...

410. [a:2] Deutschendorf is Denver; [b:3] Osterberg is Pop; [c:1] Westover is Shannon; [d:5] Cohen is Mama Cass; [e:4] Paul Crosby is Jerry Jeff; [f:7] Pauline Matthews is Kiki Dee (did you know she was the first Caucasian British female singer to be signed to Motown?); [g:8] Arnold Dorsey is Engelbert; and [h:6] Stevens is Chaka, Chaka, Chaka [Khan], a name she adopted while working as a volunteer on the Black Panthers' Free Breakfast for Children program in Chicago. And, puhleeze, don't ask me why someone would take on the name of Engelbert Humperdinck unless they were trying to channel the opera composer of the same name or has the same gingerbread jones

that the characters did in his namesake's opera, *Hansel & Gretel*.

411. [b] Baritones. Michael McDonald and Tom Jones are baritones, too.

412. [b] Jim Kweskin's Jug Band. Her husband, Geoff, was in the band, too.

413. "El Condor Pasa". Talk about what would be a sampling no-no in today's world, Paul took the *original* recording (the whole enchilada) of the tune from an album the Los Incas did, used it as the instrumentation, and just layered his lyrics over top of it. Go and look up "Los Incas + El Condor Pasa" on YouTube and you'll see for yourself.

414. [c] Seatrain which was the first act to feature an electric violin (played by Bill Monroe alum, Richard Greene). While Sir George had done some other Pop acts (i.e., Matt Monro, Cilla Black), the second Seatrain album was the first time he had acted as the producer of a Rock act since his work with the Beatles. He also produced their follow-up *Marblehead Messenger*, before moving on to do production work for America, Ultravox, Jeff Beck, Kenny Rogers, Cheap Trick, et al.

415. Not written by Kris? "She Left Me While I Slept" (written by me in my sleep) and "What Made Milwaukee Famous" (a country hit by Jerry Lee Lewis [riffing on the Schlitz Beer ad] and written by Glenn Sutton who produced Lynn Anderson's "Rose Garden").

416. "While My Guitar Gently Weeps", where we find yet another clue to the "Paul is dead" theory towards the end of the song. During the Clapton solo, George Harrison cries out a groan that sounds like "Paul, oh Paul, oh Paul," as if George was mourning for him. And, although he was quit the band for a brief time, leaving bassist McCartney to perform drums on some of the album's songs, Ringo still owns the serial # "1"copy of the album's consecutively-numbered pressings.

417. [b]Daltrey played the lead in *Lisztomania*. Rick Wakeman composed the soundtrack and appears in the movie as Thor, god of thunder, and Ringo Starr appears as the Pope.

418. [a] He should be back in school. You know, I've always wondered who played mandolin on that song (as well as "Mandolin Wind") so I looked it up. The answer is Ray Jackson of Lindisfarne. He was paid £15 for his part in the studio. Bonus nonsense: Some poetry devotees would like to take Rod into an alley somewhere and shove a volume of Carl Sandburg's verse down his throat. Ever look at Sandburg's poem "Mag"? Its story is suspiciously close to the one of "Maggie May".

419. Ike & Tina Turner's "River Deep, Mountain High", produced by Phil Spector on the Philles label. The story goes that Spector knew what a control freak Ike Turner was, so he drew up a rather unusual contract where Ike would be credited as half of the listed artist (meaning "Ike and Tina Turner") if Ike

would stay *out* of the studio. The single featured Leon Russell on keyboards, Jim Horn on sax, Barney Kessel (known for the intro on "Wouldn't It Be Nice" by the Beach Boys and for being the namesake of a track on Pete Townshend's *Scoop*) and Glen Campbell on guitar, Hal Blaine and Earl Palmer on drums, and Carol Kaye on bass. Sting claims to have lost his virginity to the tune. And *yours* was lost to what song, pray tell?

420. [a] "Tomorrow Never Knows". John Lennon wrote the song in January of 1966, adapting it from The Psychedelic Experience by Timothy Leary, Richard Alpert, and Ralph Metzner, which they based on the *Tibetan Book of the Dead*. While it was the last track on the *Revolver* album, it was actually the first track recorded.

421. [b] Vincent Ford was a friend of Marley's who ran a soup kitchen in Trenchtown, Jamaica where Marley grew up. The royalty checks that went to Ford ensured the survival and continual running of his soup kitchen.

422. True – and Dead fans know the song all too well since they've played it 300+ times in concert.

423. *Blind Faith*. We Americans originally got the khaki tacky pic of the group on the cover while the rest of our planet's hipsters got Little Miss Nekkid. The rumor mill had it that she was Ginger Baker's daughter or some sex slave of the band, but neither was true. Bob Seidemann, a San Fran photog whose fame came from his shots of Janis (the nude one with the beads), Garcia's first solo

cover, and Jackson Browne's *Late for the Sky* cover, came up with the idea. His version of the layout is "To symbolize the achievement of human creativity and its expression through technology a space ship was the material object. To carry this new spore into the universe innocence would be the ideal bearer, a young girl, a girl as young as Shakespeare's Juliet. The space ship would be the fruit of the tree of knowledge and the girl, the fruit of the tree of life." Mum and dad gave their permish, and Seidemann and Stanley Mouse (Journey, Dead, Steve Miller art) set about capturing the image. When the girl was asked what fee she wanted for modeling, she said a horse, so Robert Stigwood bought her one. The photogs entitled the photo "Blind Faith" and, then, Clapton named the band after the photo! It was also EC's idea to keep the name of the band off the cover which had never been done before.

424. [c] My girl can't get no satisfaction. While "My Girl" seems out of place alongside "Have You Seen Your Mother, Baby, Standing in the Shadows", "Mother's Little Helper", and "Let's Spend the Night Together" on *Flowers*, there it was! But it's not the *only* Motown song the Stones covered. I know six – how 'bout you? For the bean counters among you, the original or cover of "My Girl" has been found its way to vinyl or CD 1,600+ times according to AllMusic.com while "(I Can't Get No) Satisfaction" shows up 470 times (the Phyllis Diller version being the most painful, I reckon).

425. [a] Barry McGuire. The Mamas and Papas had already done the background tracks to McGuire's version on the elpee *This Precious Time* and were given a chance to record their lead on the track. It was so good, Dunhill decided to release it.

426. "Domino" (for Fats Domino) and it's Van's biggest single, getting to #9 on the American charts.

427. [b] *Here We Go 'Round the Mulberry Bush* by the Spencer Davis Group – Winwood's previous band – who made an appearance and provided some music as well. It's nice when divorces go this sweetly, isn't it?

428. He was left-handed, but usually played right-handed guitars flipped upside-down which meant the strings were in reverse, too, leaving the low E string on the bottom.

429. [b] Boston. Original name: "Mothers Milk".

430. [c] Ray (the ultra-sexual) and Dave (the bi-sexual) Davies and Dave's actually the one with more solo success given his "Death of a Clown"* that hit #2 in Britain. He thought chart life was so grand that he might just do the solo thing fulltime. A few flops later, he changed his mind. *Yes, the same one that's on *Something Else*.

431. [d] "Mercy Mercy Me". The chick singers in the background – the Andantes – are the same ones you hear on "Baby, I Need Your Loving", "Reach Out", and "I Can't Help Myself (Sugar Pie Honey Bunch)" by the Four Tops.

432. [b] Laura Nyro (born Laura Nigro), writer of "And When I Die", "Stoned Soul Picnic", "Eli's Coming", "Wedding Bell Blues", "Stoney End", etc. The first song she sold was "And When I Die", for five thou to Peter, Paul and Mary. And, when Al Kooper split from BS&T, Laura was offered the lead singer role, but turned it down. Who the heck is Dory Previn? Used to be Andre's wife... co-wrote the theme to *Valley of the Dolls* and *The Sterile Cuckoo* ("Come Saturday Morning"). Dory got a little peeved when she found out that Mia Farrow was having Andre's baby and kicked his hiney to the curb.

433. *Let's Dance.* When Bowie first witnessed the power of SRV, he and Jackson Browne were both in the audience. Browne offered the band 72 hours of free studio time at his studio and Bowie also offered Stevie to play on his upcoming album. Guess which one he took...

434. [c] Eric Clapton and Blackie (for its black finish) is his favorite Fender Stratocaster. His first Strat was nicknamed "Brownie" (it had a sunburst brown finish), and he used it on his first solo LP as well as *Layla*. In 1970, Clapton bought six vintage Strats for a $100 each and gave one each to Harrison, Townshend, and Winwood. With the other three, he took their best parts and built Blackie. Eric put the instrument up on the block in '04 at a Christie's auction to raise money for his Crossroads Centre. It pulled in $959k, the largest amount ever for a guitar at the time.

435. [b] Chad Mitchell Trio. Mitchell left the Trio in 1965 to play the life of a solo performer and he was replaced by a young John Denver, but the group retained the well-known "Mitchell Trio" name. Other permutations of the group included Michael Johnson who had a 70s hit with "Bluer Than Blue" and Roger (er, Jim) McGuinn of the Byrds.

436. [d] Jimmy Nicol, who was an little known British drummer and lucky enough to be called on to sub for Ringo who was down and out with tonsillitis and couldn't make two short tours of Scandinavia and the South Pacific in the summer of 1964.

437. While the lyrics certainly make a good case given that Petty's from Gainesville, the home of the University of Florida and "441" is the highway that runs by Beatty Towers, but the answer would be a resounding "no". There are no balconies on the dorm and Hwy 441 stretches from Florida to Tennessee so the geography is transportable. Tom will as much as tell you that he wrote the song while living in Encino and that he was inspired more by the cars going by on the freeway outside his apartment.

438. Tom and Jerry. If you look hard enough, you might find their MGM single, "Hey, Schoolgirl" in some thrift shop somewhere.

439. [b] Buddy Holly and the Crickets. They played a whole week at the Apollo – August 16-22, 1956

440. [a] Frank Beard (the drummer). He wore a manicured little beard during one ZZ period, but mostly he's the mustachioed one in the bunch.

441. [b] Donovan who came up with the "sky of blue, sea of green" line. For his help, Paul helped him with some of the bass parts on his *Mellow Yellow* elpee. The chatter and party noises on "Yellow Sub" were from a motley crew that included (among others) Pattie Boyd, Marianne Faithfull, Donovan, and Brian Jones.

442. Delaney and Bonnie. Fleshing things out: Harrison did sign them to Apple, but D&B already had a pre-existing deal with Elektra which they failed to tell Georgie about and had to void the Apple deal (Delaney also taught Harrison how to play slide guitar)... he produced and his band played on Clapton's self-titled album... and Bonnie co-wrote (with Leon Russell) "Superstar" that the Carpenters had a Top Ten hit with. BTW, the original title of that song is "(Groupie) Superstar".

443. ELO (Electric Light Orchestra). The American version of the first ELO album was titled *No Answer* because someone at United Artists Records called Harvest Records (ELO's U.K. label) to find out what the title was supposed to be (which was *The Electric Light Orchestra*), but no one answered the call, so the UA person wrote down "No Answer". Pretty much the same thing happened for the Byrds' *Untitled* album when their producer/manager wrote "Untitled" on the info sheet the label was pushing him for, meaning that the group had yet to decide on one.

444. John Entwistle. 'Twas the album with "Squeeze Box" which was originally intended for a Who

television special where the Who would perform the song accompanied by 100 topless lady accordionists! Dang, I hate when that happens...

445. Their handiwork was on all but [d] "If I Can Dream" (although they did write "Hound Dog"). The other songs they either produced or wrote as well as: "Ruby Baby", "Kansas City", "Yakety Yak", "Jailhouse Rock", "Youngblood", "Spanish Harlem", "Searchin'", on and on and on and on.

446. Black Oak Arkansas in the *Raunch 'N' Roll Live* album. Black Oak, who by my count, has had 38 different members in their lineup, got their start as the Knowbody Else. Under that banner both good and bad happened. The good is that they were signed as one of the rare white acts by STAX; the bad being that they stole the PA from a local high school. They were charged in absentia, sentenced to 26 years at the Tucker Prison Farm, and got off with a suspended sentence. What the world would've been without Jim Dandy to our rescue!

447. [a] The New York Dolls. Their first LP was produced by Todd Rundgren; their second by Shadow Morton, the guy who did the Shangri-Las' "Leader of the Pack", the first two Vanilla Fudge albums, and Janis Ian's "Society's Child".

448. [a] T. Rex. The song was "Get It On" (Bang a Gong). Did you know that Marc Bolan played guitar on ELO's "Showdown", and Alice Cooper's "Elected", "Hello Hooray", and "Billion Dollar Babies"? And, and, and did you know that he had a child (named Rolan Bolan) with Gloria Jones, the

lady who had out the first version of "Tainted Love" as well as co-writing "If I Were Your Woman" for Gladys Knight & the Pips?

449. "Dirty Deeds Done Dirt Cheap" which is homage to one of Angus Young's favorite childhood cartoons, *Beany and Cecil* where the character Dishonest John carried a business card reading, "Dirty Deeds Done Dirt Cheap. Holidays, Sundays, and Special Rates."

450. [b] Frank Marino (Mahogany Rush). These days, Marino claims his Hendrix relationship was created by the press, but he also tries to explain that "Mahogany Rush" was a condition his LSD trips produced, so believe what you want.

451. "If you look closer, it's easy to trace the tracks of my tears ", one of several Miracles songs that were on Lennon's jukebox that he bought to take on tour with him in '65. Smokey's perfect reading of the word "substitute" is said to have inspired Pete Townshend so much that he wrote "Substitute" in its honor. The guitar lick of another one the tunes on the jukebox – Bobby Parker's "Watch Your Step" – might be a dead-ringin' revelation for the lick in "I Feel Fine". Go find it on YouTube and see fer yasef...

452. [b] Bad Company/*Bad Company*, recorded at Headley Grange where Zep recorded many a track including "Black Dog" named after a black lab that was hanging around the building; and [c] Black Sabbath/*Black Sabbath*, an album recorded in a

single day and, then, released on Friday the 13th, February 1970.

453. [b] Rick James. Other members/incarnations included Goldie McJohn and Nick St Nicholas, who both went on to Steppenwolf; Bruce Cockburn; and Bruce Palmer who would go on to Buffalo Springfield with Neil Young. They signed a seven-year deal with Motown but Rick got arrested for deserting the Navy and Motown gave up and never released the album. However, you can find a single, "It's My Time" on iTunes.

454. Charlie Watts. The title came from "Get Yer Ya-Ya's Out" by Blind Boy Fuller, but the line used in Fuller's song was "get your ya-ya's out the door". The same line I think Jerry Hall used once. 'Ya think that's why she became the worldwide spokesperson for Levitra?

455. Usually, keyboardist Ray Manzarek played the parts on a Fender Rhodes piano Bass*. Ray was a fan of jazz, too, and based the solo in "Light My Fire" on John Coltrane's version of "My Favorite Things". * There were a couple of instances where Bread's keyboard-player-to-be Larry Knechtel played bass to fill in the gap. Lar' also played bass on the Byrds' "Mr. Tambourine Man" and the piano part on "Bridge Over Troubled Water" for Paul & Artie.

456. [d] "D'yer Mak'er", one of the few Zeppelin songs where all members share the composer credit. The sleeve on the album also gives tribute to Rosie and the Originals, a reference to the doo-wop influence which was evident in the song's style. If you listen

to Rosie's "Angel Baby" and speed up the tempo in your mind, you'll see the relationship.

457. Meatloaf, who – for 12 years – was actually a vegetarian, but with *Bat Out of Hell* selling about 200,000 copies a year, he can eat any damn thing he wants. And, yes, this is the same Meatloaf who was on Motown Records believe it or not as the beefy half of "Stoney & Meatloaf". "Stoney" was Shaun Murphy who recorded with Seger, Clapton, the Moodies, others, and took Craig Fuller's place in Little Feat when he stepped down.

458. *Play Misty For Me* where Eastwood played deejay David "Dave" Garver. And who wrote "Misty"? The silky cool Errol Garner.

459. [b] The Raspberries first album (the one with "Go All the Way" – another song banned by the BBC [too sexual]).

460. [c] Roy Orbison. For those of you who thought he wore those sunglasses because he was blind, well, he wasn't. His identification with those trademark Wayfarer shades began when he was on a tour of Britain in the early Sixties (maybe the same one with the Beatles), and forgot his regular specs.

461. Waylon Jennings. Big Bopper (J.P. Richardson, Jr.) was fighting the flu and didn't feel at ease on the group's bus so Jennings agreed to give up his seat to him. If you missed this one, you have to drink four shots of Jägermeister and listen to Enya for an hour.

462. [a] "I Got a Name" which was written by the same guys who wrote "Killing Me Softly", and the themes to *Laverne & Shirley* and *Happy Days* – Norman Gimbel and Charles Fox.

463. [b] Elton John. Neil Diamond made the earliest recording of "He Ain't Heavy..." (on *Taproot Manuscript*), but it wasn't released until *after* the Hollies' version and typically mistaken as a cover. The song was written by Bobby Scott, the guy who wrote "A Taste of Honey" and Bob Russell who wrote the lyrics (Duke Ellington did the melody) for "Don't Get Around Much Anymore".

464. [c] Let's spend some <u>time</u> together. Ed Sullivan thinking the lyrics were suggestive in '67 was mildly understandable but, in 2006 for the Stones first gig in China, the government prevented the band from singing the song for the very same reasons. Keep that birthrate down, boys.

465. [d] Billie Jean King. Her professional tennis team was called the "Philadelphia Freedom".

466. "Pink Houses". Edwards used it without any problem; McCain used it (and "This is Our Country") without permission and got his little weenie slapped; Reagan asked to use it and was denied. The song's roots are very happenstance if we're to believe Mellencamp's interview in *Rolling Stone*: Seems the inspiration came when Mellencamp was driving across an overpass on his way home to Bloomington from the airport in Indy. And what did he see but an old Black man sitting on the porch outside his little pink shotgun

house with a cat in his arms, at complete peace despite all the cars speeding by. "He waved, and I waved back." Ain't that America?

467. [d] Aretha Franklin. She went in the *second* round of inductees – 1987.

468. [a] Bobby Gregg who had played on *Bringing It All Back Home* and *Highway 61 Revisited*. He lasted a month, then Sandy Konikoff came in, then Mickey Jones – the same Mickey Jones that you hear pounding the beat on all of the Kenny Rogers and First Edition records, some old John Lee Hooker and Johnny Rivers records, that Dylan *Live at the Royal Albert Hall** bootleg you're hiding from the feds, and the one you saw in a recurring role on *Home Improvement*. *Some diggin' will reveal claims that the bootleg recording isn't all from the RAH, either, but at the Free Trade Hall in Manchester.

469. Joni Mitchell from the song "California" (from her fourth album, *Blue*; James Taylor plays guitar). Best as I can tell, the "Sunset pig" is a cop on Sunset Boulevard.

470. [b] *One of These Nights*, the one where he wrote "Journey of the Sorcerer" (theme music for the radio, TV, and movie versions of *The Hitchhiker's Guide to the Galaxy*), and co-wrote "Hollywood Waltz" (with his brother, Tom, plus Frey and Henley), and "I Wish You Peace" (with Patti Davis, Ronald Reagan's daughter, and Bernie's girlfriend at the time).

471. KISS. Thank God it was a comic book and not in those Pez dispensers I bought!

472. [c] David Crosby, born in L.A. to Aliph Van Cortlandt Whitehead and Floyd Crosby, who was a cinematographer on *High Noon* and *The Pit and the Pendulum*. Clyde Jackson Browne was born in Germany, Glenn Frey in Detroit, Zevon in Chicago (to William "Stumpy" Zevon [original name was "Zivotovsky"] and Beverly Cope Simmons, a nice Mormon girl from Utah).

473. [a] Sugar Hill, whose first claim to fame was "Rapper's Delight" by Sugarhill Gang (also the first Top 40 hip-hop single), followed by Grandmaster Flash, Melle Mel, et al. The label was founded in 1974 by Joe and Sylvia Robinson (she had a hit with "Pillow Talk") with a guy named Milton Malden and a little green from Morris Levy, owner of Roulette Records.

474. [b] The Ramones. "Ramones" was just a stage name they made up from the pseudonym that McCartney used to use when checking into hotels ("Paul Ramon"). Fanny was led by June Millington and sis, Jean, and were the first all-female band to release an album on a major label (Reprise). Bowie said, "They were one of the finest... rock bands of their time... as important as anybody else who's ever been" and, without them, folks like Joan Jett and Courtney Love might have never had a prayer. You probably already had the Sly and Carpenter thing figured out or, at least, should have.

475. [c] "Teddy Bear", Red Sovine's saga of a disabled boy who lost his truck drivin' dad in a highway

mishap and keeps his CB radio as his only companion, rose to #1 in seven weeks – the fastest rise to the #1 on the Country charts for any single ever released. Another Sovine tune – "Phantom 309" – the story of a hitchhiker who thumbs a ride with a trucker who turns out to be the ghost of a guy who died when he gave his life to save a school bus full of kids from a horrifying crash with his rig, was tailored by Tom Waits into "Big Joe and Phantom 309" for *Nighthawks At The Diner*.

476. Edgar Winter. "Shabby" being a synonym for "trash" as in Edgar Winter's White Trash. Quick pieces of trivia: 1) Edgar Winter Group was the opener on the Skynyrd tour ended by their plane crash; 2) One of Edgar's more recent productions is *Mission Earth*, an album where the words/music were written by Scientology founder L. Ron Hubbard who ostensibly left comprehensive instructions and audio tapes for the musicians and producers to follow in putting the album together.

477. Ok, geo gnomes, here are your answers...

"San Francisco"	Scott McKenzie
"Indiana Wants Me"	R. Dean Taylor (also wrote the Supremes' "Love Child" and the Temps' "All I Need")
"Massachusetts"	Bee Gees
"Kentucky Woman"	Neil Diamond or Deep Purple
"Honolulu Lulu"	Jan & Dean

"L.A. Goodbye"	Ides of March
"Detroit City"	Bobby Bare
"Tulsa Time"	Eric Clapton (or Don Williams)
"Dallas"	Steely Dan (it was their very first single and Poco covered it on *Head Over Heels*)
"Houston"	Dean Martin
"Jackson"	Nancy Sinatra & Lee Hazlewood or Johnny Cash and June Carter
"Memphis"	Chuck Berry (among others)
"Nashville Cats"	Lovin' Spoonful
"Galveston"	Glen Campbell
"Vienna"	Billy Joel
"Kansas City"	Wilbert Harrison (or the Beatles)
"London Calling	The Clash
"Oh, Atlanta"	Little Feat (although Bad Co. had a song by the same name)
"Alta Mira"	Edgar Winter Group
"Brooklyn Roads"	Neil Diamond
"Bowling Green"	Everly Bros. or Jesse Winchester
"Doraville"	Atlanta Rhythm Section

"El Paso"	Marty Robbins or the Grateful Dead
"Funky Nassau"	The Beginning of the End
"He Went to Paris"	Jimmy Buffett (or Waylon Jennings)
"Bristol Stomp"	The Dovells

478. McGear – "gear" being the Liverpudlian meaning of "fab". Get it? Mike was also in The Scaffold who did one of my fave pub songs of all-time – the U.K. #1 "Lily the Pink". In the lyrics of that song, they say "Jennifer Eccles had terrible freckles" as a nod to The Hollies because Graham Nash sang background vocals, as well as Sir Elton. Jack Bruce played bass.

479. Well, there IS a Sheriff *Andy* Taylor as well as the one in Duran Duran, but James didn't have a sibling named [c] Andrew. All of JT's sibs except brother Hugh (meaning Livingston, Kate, and Alex) were signed to various Atlantic Records labels (Capricorn, Cotillion, etc.) who released all of their debut albums at exactly the same time.

480. [c] Seven: Alan, Wayne, Merrill, Jay, Donny, Marie, and that Long-haired Lover from Liverpool, Jimmy.

481. [d] Stevie Wonder (with producer Hank Cosby). Playing Santa, Stevie gave Smokey Robinson the instrumental track as a present at the 1966 Motown Christmas party. BTW, Andy Kim and Jeff Barry wrote "Sugar, Sugar", the #1 song for the whole dang year of 1969.

482. [c] The Canadian group Klaatu (named after the extraterrestrial of the same name in the film *The Day the Earth Stood Still*). Their sound was fairly Beatlesque (especially on the song "Sub-Rosa Subway"), but their first album had no biographical details, and that alone spurred rumors that the album was an anonymous project by the Beatles. Their best-known song, "Calling Occupants of Interplanetary Craft", was covered by the Carpenters using a crew of 160 musicians. Yikes! More maple leaf twaddle: Klaatu was produced by the same guy who produced Rush's second through eighth albums – Terry Brown.

483. [c] The Dirty Mac. It was the first time Lennon had ever publicly stepped outside of the Beatles to play and he came up with the name as a rip on Fleetwood Mac. Recordings? Well, they (plus violinist Ivry Gitlis) did do a version of "Yer Blues" and some kitchen sink'y Blues jam called "Whole Lotta Yoko".

484. Zombies. The lead singer of Argent – Russ Ballard – is the cat who wrote their songs "Liar" that Three Dog Night covered and "God Gave Rock and Roll to You" that KISS covered. He also wrote Santana's "Winning", "You Can Do Magic" for America, "I Know There's Something Going On" for Frida (of ABBA), Ace Frehley's "New York Groove", et al.

485. [b] Honda Motorcycles. The person referred to as "Sugar Plum Fairy" in the song was Joe Campbell, who was Harvey Milk's lover for seven years and,

then, the partner of Oliver "Billy" Sipple, the man who knocked the gun out of Sara Jane Moore's hand when she pointed it at Gerald Ford during a NYC speech.

486. They're all songs that have "stuttering" in them. Randy Bachman swears up and down that "You Ain't Seen Nothin' Yet" was done as a gag for his stuttering brother, Gary, and only intended to record it once with the stutter and send the only recording to Gary. But, ah, yes, those guys at the label smelled hit! When Randy tried to do it sans stutter it came out sounding like a lounge act, so he finally relented. Gary's stutter? Gone now. The miracle of music science.

487. [a] When he was a child, his family moved to New Orleans. Sorry, but "Short People" ain't on *Trouble in Paradise'*— it's on *Little Criminals.* People in Maryland can't take a joke, evidently, because someone with grubby little fingers and tiny little teeth introduced legislation to make playing the song on the radio illegal in the state, though the bill failed to pass.

488. [b] "I'd Like to Teach the World to Sing". Anyone among the living Seventies grads remembers it becoming a smash Coke jingle, produced by Billy Davis who co-wrote "Lonely Teardrops" with Berry Gordy, and went on to do Coke's "It's the Real Thing" and "Things Go Better" as well as "If You've Got the Time" for Miller Beer. The idea for the Coke angle came to the songwriters, Cook and Greenaway, while they were at Shannon Airport

and witnessed some folks laughing and joking standing at a Coke machine waiting for their drinks to roll out.

489. [a] 3 days (October 17, '77). The original cover of the album shows the band standing in flames, with an even spookier shot of Steve Gaines where his eyes were closed and his head surrounded by flames. After the crash, the cover was modified to an alternate photo with an solid black background in respect of the three lost in the crash. By the way, this was Steve Gaines' only gig with the band and the only time anyone other than Ronnie Van Zant did lead vocals on a song ("Ain't No Good Life") in pre-crash Skynyrd.

490. [d] *Quadrophenia* and [a] *Who Are You*. *Who Are You* was kept out of first place by the soundtrack to *Grease* and *Quadrophenia* by *Goodbye, Yellow Brick Road*.

491. [c] The Strangeloves were in real life Bob Feldman, Jerry Goldstein, and Richard Gottehrer posing as Giles, Miles, and Niles Strangelove. Their game even included a story about some rare sheep breed they developed called "the Gottehrer". Their big hit was "I Want Candy" but, earlier, in their real lives as songwriters, they had written "My Boyfriend's Back" for the Angels. While the Strangeloves were on tour with the Dave Clark Five, the DC5 told them they were going to cover their version of "Hang on Sloopy" (written about Dorothy Sloop, a Nawlins jazz pianist), so Bob/Jerry/Richard recruited a group from Dayton

called Rick and the Raiders, changed their name to the McCoys (to avoid confusion with the Paul Revere Raiders) and their lead singer's name from Zehringer to Derringer, stripped off the existing vocals from their version of "Sloopy" and had Rick re-record the vocal, and beat the DC5 to the record bins. Gottehrer went on to produce the first Blondie album and co-found Sire Records. Goldstein is responsible for putting Eric Burdon and WAR together. Feldman headed up the classic folk label Red House Records until his death.

492. Everly Brothers who recorded it on *A Date with...* but never released it as a single. Orbison put it on the flip of "Running Scared", too. In Nazareth's version, they changed the line *"love is like a stove, it burns you when it's hot"* to *"love is like a flame..."*. Nazareth took their name from "The Weight".

493. Jackie Wilson. The stroke happened as he was singing the line "My heart is crying..." during "Lonely Teardrops".

494. [c] "Walk On". The referring lines are... *"I hear some people been talkin' me down, Bring up my name, pass it 'round. They don't mention happy times... They do their thing, I'll do mine."*

495. [d] Duke Ellington with "Sir Duke". The cat on guitar was Michael Sembello, who brought us that *Flashdance* gem, "Maniac".

496. [b] Right after the Second World War, John Lee Hooker and his producer, Bernard Besman, wrote a song called "Boogie Chillen" which Hooker recorded twice by himself and once with Canned

Heat. In the early '90s, Besman (who was 89 at the time) heard "LaGrange" and his BS detector went off. He sued but while the accusation was true in premise, the proof didn't hold up in court because the judge found the 1958 and 1950 recordings to be in the public domain because copyrights (at the time) were only good for 28 years and they didn't renew the copyright for the *Hooker 'n Heat* album, so they lost the case. The funny thing is that Chrysler used a "LaGrange" rip-off for a commercial in the late '90s and ZZ Top sued *them*. Chrysler argued that, even if some parts of "LaGrange" are original and copyrightable, the song's guitar riff is not and there were seven other songs (including "Spirit in the Sky" [huh?]) where the riffs are similar in pitch and rhythm… *and* another court had already proved the song was in the public domain! Sorry, but I need more billable hours to go any further...

497. Smash Records, where JB released three vocal recordings (including "Out of Sight") before going back to King, but all of his band's instrumental recordings between 1964 and 1967 stayed on Smash as part of the kiss-and-make-up deal.

498. [b] *The Button-Down Mind of Bob Newhart* (1960) was the first comedy album to ever top the *Billboard* chart. It also won George Robert Newhart a Grammy for Album of the Year and Best New Artist and, with that, it became the first comedy album to win Album of the Year, and the only time a comedian has won Best New Artist. It also

saved Warner Brothers Records who was bleeding red ink like a gun-shot pig.

499. [a] Bryan Ferry/*Let's Stick Together*. It happened during a time when Roxy Music had temporarily disbanded, so Ferry pulled out some songs he'd already done with the band and added some cabaret versions of Everly Brothers, Beatles, Jimmy Reed, Marvin Gaye, and Wilbert Harrison songs.

500. Jimmy Buffett — as a play on the (original Atlantic City version of) Monopoly spot "Marven Gardens" (which is a real place in Margate, New Jersey). He posed next to John Prine in the cover photo of Steve Goodman's *Somebody Else's Troubles* in that persona and "Why Don't We Get Drunk" was credited to Mr. Gardens. Jimmy has even masqueraded as "Freddie Fishsticks", and God knows who else.

501. [b] Electric Light Orchestra who did the Move's "Do 'Ya" (Jeff Lynne having been in the Move with Roy Wood, the co-creator of ELO). All-knowing Lynne/Petty campers are nodding yes to the supposition that Tom Petty took his inspiration for "Change of Heart" from this song.

502. [a] and [b] "Black Mountain Side" and "Over the Hills and Far Away". Jimmy, Jimmy, Jimmy – what a great "copy & paste" job you did. Folks, go seek out Davey Graham's "She Moved Through the Fair" from '63 and dial up "White Summer" from the Yardbirds' *Little Games* album and, then, those two Zep cuts and see if you don't see a straight line connecting all of those little dots. And

those Davey Graham dots keep going – right up to Simon & Garfunkel's cover of his "Anji" and the Chumbawamba's sample of that song for "Jacob's Ladder". At least, Paul and Artie gave him credit. Jimmy? Nah.

503. [c] "Ready for Love". Mick's original version was on Mott the Hoople's *All the Young Dudes* album as the medley "Ready for Love/After Lights". Mick's first hit for Bad Co. – "Can't Get Enough" – was written for Mott, but Ian Hunter's vocal range couldn't handle it.

504. [a] *Give 'Em Enough Rope*. The title probably comes from the expression "give them enough rope and they'll hang themselves" which echoed the Clash' conviction that the bands who came before them were desperately outdated and irrelevant. It was voted "Album of the Year" ('78) by both *TIME* and *Rolling Stone*.

505. "Last Train to Clarksville". Most of us geography and Army "useless info" people would say that it refers to Clarksville, Tennessee because it's close to Fort Campbell, Kentucky, home to 101st Airborne Division, but Bobby Hart — who wrote the song with Tommy Boyce — says that was just coincidence as "Clarksville" was settled on because of the say it sounded.

506. Chic. In what may have been the birth of hip-hop, you can hear the line from Chic's "Good Times" all over "Rapper's Delight" and its catchy bass hook as the influence for "Another One Bites the Dust". When Chic was hittin' homers on almost

everything they tried, Atlantic Records gave Chic's Bernard Edwards and Nile Rodgers to op to produce *anyone* on the label. Their first choice? Sister Sledge's "We Are Family". From there, it was a field day – Diana Ross, Power Station, Jagger, Bowie, Madonna's first album, etc.

507. [e] All of 'em. Tony must love Apple "seeds", too! He was married to both Mary Hopkin (Apple artist of "Those Were the Days" fame) *and* May Pang (who achieved fame as the apple of John Lennon's eye during his split from Yoko).

508. [b] George Benson. In 1976, he won two Grammys – one for "Best Pop *Instrumental*" ("Breezin'" [on Warner Bros.]*) and one for "Best R&B *Instrumental*" ("The Theme from Good King Bad" [on CTI]) as well as the award for "Record of the Year", the Leon Russell-written "This Masquerade". Two years later ('78), the live take of "On Broadway", from *Weekend in L.A.*, also won a Grammy for "Best R&B *Vocal*". * "Breezin'" is a track Bobby Womack wrote for jazz guitarist Gabor Szabo in '71

509. Vee-Jay. The Beatles, you say? Yessir. They had a deal with EMI which gave them access to product that Capitol turned down and when Capitol gave the thumbs-down to the early Beatles stuff, Vee-Jay didn't and released "Please, Please Me" and "From Me to You" without luck, but when the band did finally hit, they returned with "Love Me Do" and gave the Beatles their fourth #1.

510. Irving Azoff, manager of the Eagles and countless others, former prez of MCA, onto Big Wig @ Ticketmaster, and so on. "Son of a band director" and "turned to stone" refers to songs from Dan Fogelberg and Joe Walsh who he took with him to L.A.. "Giant" refers to the label he created.

511. The Byrds' hit "Turn! Turn! Turn! (to Everything There is a Season)" – a song taken almost entirely (the exception being the last line) from the the Bible's book of Ecclesiastes (a book traditionally ascribed to King Solomon) and set to music by Pete Seeger in 1959. 'Ol Pete waited until 1962 to record it, however, when he put it on his elpee *The Bitter and The Sweet*. God love Pete – 45% of the royalties for this song (because, as he says, "I did write six words" [in addition to the music]) are donated to the Israeli Committee Against House Demolitions.

512. Area Code 615 or Barefoot Jerry. Several members of Area Code 615 appeared on the aforementioned *Nashville Skyline* as well as *Blonde on Blonde*. Member Wayne Moss did the unforgettable guitar riff on "Oh, Pretty Woman" and Mac Gayden did the wah-wah on J.J. Cale's "Crazy Mama" and co-wrote "Everlasting Love." Moss, Gayden, and Buttrey went on to form Barefoot Jerry who gets a shout-out in Charlie Daniel's "The South is Gonna Do It Again." As in "all the good people in Tennessee are diggin' Barefoot Jerry and CDB".

513. They all appeared 'cept for [d] Tull, although their music was played over the PA system. If you were

lucky enough to see *Hair* on Broadway, Sommer was in the play as "Woof". He also was in the Left Banke for awhile, had a mid-charter with "We're All Playing in the Same Band", co-wrote the Cherry People's hit "And Suddenly", and wrote five songs for the Vagrants, Leslie West's precursor to Mountain.

514. It could be [a] Don Gibson and Buck Owens <u>or</u> [b] Kitty Wells and Buck Owens. Reason being is that "I Can't Stop Loving You" was a hit first by Don Gibson, then by Kitty Wells. Ray's Buck Owens cover was "Crying Time".

515. "Good Girls Don't". I guess "*An in-between age madness that you know you can't erase 'til she's sitting on your face*" was a bit over the top, eh? The Knack's lead singer – Doug Fieger – is the younger brother of Jeffrey Fieger, the lawyer who represented Dr. Kevorkian. Only someone at Capitol could tell us if the Knack suffered an assisted suicide or not.

516. Nils Lofgren. Whose place did he take in the E-Street Band? Steve VanZandt's and, then, when Bruce reformed the band after his solo respite, both Nils <u>and</u> Steve came back into the fold.

517. [e] DC-8. And the Six Teens? They were a doo-wop group that had a Top 25 Pop single and a Top 10 R&B hit called "A Casual Look".

518. [a] Who else, but Memphis-born and music's most identifiable draft-dodger*, Jesse Winchester. Many of you probably haven't heard Jesse, but you should seek him out. His first album was

produced by Robbie Robertson and engineered by Todd Rundgren… Jimmy Buffett, Emmylou Harris, Elvis Costello are counted among the people who've covered songs out of his catalog like "Biloxi" and "Brand New Tennessee Waltz"… I personally heard Lyle Lovett call him his favorite songwriter and you can find quotes of Dylan echoing equally muscular praise. The album he did with Willie Mitchell isn't necessarily his best, but for a kid who grew up in Memphis and to be able to record with the same guy who did all the Al Green stuff was a pretty special moment for Jesse. *Yep, he got drafted right out of Williams College and bought a one-way ticket to Montreal where he stayed for 21 years until Jimmy Carter's amnesty legislation was passed.

519. [a] The Runaways. And what happened to all that "jailbait on the run"? Joan Jett, you know about... Sandy West became a drum teacher, worked with John Entwistle, died from cancer... Micki Steele joined the Bangles... Lita Ford signed on with Sharon Osbourne and had some hits with Ozzy... Cherie Currie was in *Foxes* with Jodi Foster and *Parasite* with Demi Moore... Vickie Blue became a producer for *Entertainment Tonight*... Jackie Fox went to Harvard and became a lawyer. As I write this, there's talk of a Runaways movie with Dakota Fanning, of all people, slated to play Currie.

520. "I'm Gonna Make You Love Me" and "Expressway to Your Heart". Dee Dee Warwick did "I'm Gonna…" first, then Jerry Butler, Jay & the Techniques, then it was offered to Dusty Springfield who passed it along to her background

vocalist Madeline Bell who had a decent-sized hit with it, but the one most people remember is by the Supremes and Temps. Gamble and Huff didn't have their hands on any of those versions but they did have their hands all over the Soul Survivors "Expressway…" and it became big enough of a hit that ATCO signed them and brought in Duane Allman to help out on a few tracks.

521. Emerson, Lake, & Palmer. A chewy tidbit is that prior to agreeing on Carl Palmer, they approached Mitch Mitchell (Hendrix). Mitch wasn't interested but passed the idea to Jimi who was getting tired of the Experience and desirous of doing something different. Supposedly, he actually expressed some interest in playing with Emerson and Lake. Now, if they could've recruited Patty Labelle, they could've been called HELL. Bad...

522. Tis' true – the good Captain's first two singles on A&M. Pre-Beefheart, Gates wrote "Popsicles and Icicles" for the Murmaids, "Saturday's Child" done by the Monkees, and produced the Glenn Yarbrough hit, "Baby, the Rain Must Fall."

523. [b] Public Image Ltd. and the point where Johnny Rotten became John Lydon. Following the Sex Pistols' breakup, Johnny hung out for three weeks in Jamaica with Virgin Records head Richard Branson, scouting for emerging reggae musicians. Branson also brought Devo down to Jamaica, trying to get them to sign Lydon on as their lead singer. Devo declined the offer. "Whip It" would've never been the same.

524. [e]] Chad Allen & the Expressions became the Guess Who; and Pud evolved into the Doobie Brothers. The backstory on the Chad Allen evolution is that Quality Records released "Shakin' All Over" and as a promotional stunt credited the single to "Guess Who?" and that eventually became their name.

525. [a] "Fools Overture" off of *Even in the Quietest Moments*. The song is about WWII England and the lessons the country learned from that conflict. The song has all sorts of little twists on top of Churchill's "never surrender" speech – snippets of Holst's "The Planets", a reading of a Wm. Blake poem, and a short detour where they play their own "Dreamer". …*Quietest Moments* was an album that was recorded at Caribou Ranch Studios where Chicago did *VI, VII, VIII, X*; Joe Walsh did *Barnstorm*; Elton did three albums (*Caribou*, et al); and EW&F did *That's the Way of the World*. Caribou Ranch was owned by James William Guercio, the guy who's listed as a "contributor" to Zappa's *Freak Out*, produced the Buckinghams' hits, the 2nd BS&T album, most of the Chicago ones, and even owned CMT for about 10 years.

526. [a] True (well, kinda). The original inspiration for the song was poster angel Farah Fawcett, long before she adorned every teenage boy's bedroom wall. Jim Weatherly, the song's writer, knew Lee Majors and had a short exchange with Fawcett who was Majors' girlfriend. In their chat, Fawcett mentioned that she was going to take a midnight plane to Houston to visit her folks. The words

"midnight plane to Houston" stuck with Weatherly and he used it as the basis for the train/Georgia version. [b] is False. It's actually Sir Georg Solti (Chicago Symphony) with 31, but Quincy is second with 27 little golden gramophones. U2 is the leader among "bands" with 22 (as of 2009). [c] is very True.

527. John Henry Ramistella p/k/a/Johnny Rivers. Billy Lee Riley played harp on "Mountain of Love"; the U.S. version of the U.K.'s *Danger Man* theme was "Secret Agent Man"; discovered the 5th Dimension or what he called the "Black Mamas & Papas"; publishes Jim Webb's early hits (like "By the Time I Get to Phoenix" which he did on his *Changes* LP before Glen Campbell); and the Willie Dixon tune? "Seventh Son", a tune Johnny freely admits owing a debt of gratitude for the vocal phrasing and styling to Mose Allison who Johnny used to catch at the Down Beat Club in Gulfport, Mississippi.

528. Peter (Yarrow), Paul (Stookey), and Mary (Travers), who were so blistering hot in the doth-I-protest-too-loudly movement that their first three albums were all in the Top Ten the week JFK was assassinated. The John Denver song was "Leaving on a Jet Plane", the Seeger "If I Had a Hammer", and the Dylan "Blowin' in the Wind". The group's "Puff (the Magic Dragon)" was written by one of Yarrow's Cornell buds (Lenny Lipton, who went on to invent 3D movie technology like we see in *The Nightmare Before Christmas*) who got the inspiration from an Ogden Nash poem, "Custard the Dragon".

529. Jefferson Airplane's *Bark* and Led Zeppelin's *In Through the Out Door*. Remember, *Bark* had a big "JA" on the cover, a rip-off of the A&P logo? That album marked a big shift for the band, being the first *without* Marty Balin and the first *with* violinist Papa John Creach. For Zeppelin, they named the album as a way of describing their recent struggles concerning the death of Robert Plant's son and the taxation exile the band took from England which kept them off the Queen's terra firma for more than two years. In their way of thinking, getting back into the public's conscious was like "trying to get in through the 'out' door." The Braille-enhanced covers were Stevie Wonder's *Talking Book* and Wings' *Red Rose Speedway* which had a special "We love ya baby" message for Stevie in Braille on the back cover. And you don't need to go searching for Alice Cooper's *School's Out* for the undies because the album was recalled due to the panties not being flame-retardant, which I'm sure one of you can vouch for, right?

530. Anyone who's ever been to Mary Majors Tiny Castle in Eddyville, Kentucky will tell you that polk salad looks like [b] a turnip green.

531. Motown grad, Junior Walker. The version we hear, tho', wasn't blown in one shot. The solo was cobbled together from a variety of takes.

532. Well, I'll tell 'ya, now – if you went with the obvious ones, you probably blew it. [a] Go Now, Bessie Banks; [b] Hanky Panky, the Raindrops ; [c] Somethin' Stupid, Carson & Gaile (Carson Parks is

the older brother of Van Dyke Parks) ; [d] Rock Around the Clock, Sonny (or Sunny) Dae & the Knights; e. Little Bit O' Soul, the Little Darlings; [f] Wild Thing, the Wild Ones; [g] Richard Chamberlain (yessir, Dr. Kildare – flip side of "Blue Guitar").

533. "Ol' 55". Waits' version of the tune was on his debut and produced by Jerry Yester, who cut his production chops producing the Turtles, the Association, and Tim Buckley (Tim covered "Martha", the first ever cover of a Tom Waits song by a known artist), playing piano on the Spoonful's "Do You Believe in Magic"(he later replaced Zal Yanovsky), and featured on some Monkees tracks on *Headquarters*. Back to Waits... If you have the album, listen to the song "Midnight Lullaby". It scrounges its opening line from the nursery rhyme "Sing a Song of Sixpence".

534. The name came from a (envelope please) steamroller. One was parked outside Barry Friedman's* house where Stephen Stills and Richie Furay were staying. The backstory on "For What it's Worth"? I've heard Richie Furay tell it like this: Ahmet Ertegun (head of Atlantic Records) wasn't all that wow'ed with how the first album was doing out of the box, so he gathered the group together in LA to hear what new songs they had. After they finished and were packing up, Stephen turned to Ahmet and said, "Oh, I have another song for what it's worth". A song with a title not even referenced in the lyrics. * Don't know Barry, you say? He was the publicist for the Beatles gig at the Hollywood

Bowl, produced Nico's *The Marble Index,* a couple of tracks on Butterfield's *East-West*, among others. Now known as Frazier Mohawk.

535. [b] The first single to be certified "Platinum" by the RIAA, not to mention the first #1 hit to include the word "disco" in its title. Among the players on the song were three members of Parliament-Funkadelic (bassist Bootsy Collins, keyboardist Bernie Worrell, guitarist Glen Goins), as well as Telma Hopkins from Tony Orlando & Dawn.

536. Seals & Crofts, who were in the Champs who did "Tequila" and, as Seals & Crofts, they did "Hummingbird". While I'm not a religious studies scholar, it's my understanding that the hummingbird is considered sacred in Seals & Crofts' Baha'i faith and quotes from its scriptures. After they hung up their rock and roll shoes, Seals branched out and operated a coffee farm in Costa Rica and Crofts raised Arabian horses. BTW, the guy who produced their hit records – Louie Shelton – is the guy who played the flamenco-style intro and solo on The Monkees' "Valleri".

537. [b] Steppenwolf ("The Pusher" and "Born to be Wild") and Roger McGuinn ("Ballad of Easy Rider" and "It's Alright, Ma, I'm Only Bleeding"). They approached Dylan, but he was reluctant, so instead of writing a completely new song, he simply jotted down the first verse of "Ballad of Easy Rider", handed it to the filmmakers and said, *"Give this to McGuinn, he'll know what to do with it."*

538. George Harrison, who formed the production company Handmade Films to help out when EMI

got cold feet on the subject matter and backed out of their offer to finance the film. If you look closely, you'll see Harrison in a cameo role as the owner of the Mount.

539. Alan Parsons was an engineer on both *Abbey Road* and *Dark Side of the Moon* (and Pink Floyd's *Atom Heart Mother*), engineered and produced *Year of the Cat*. The Chicago Bulls connection? Well, make that a connection with about half of the sports teams in the world. Alan Parsons Project's "Sirius" (off of *Eye in the Sky*) is the intro song for the Bulls (at least when Jordan was there), the Nebraska Cornhuskers, even wrestler Ricky "The Steamboat" Dragon.

540. [b] Leo Sayer (writer) and Three Dog Night's "The Show Must Go On". Yes, Mr. Quizmaster, there is a reference to the circus in the Peggy Lee song but hers is more of an existentialist thing. I actually wish "Is That All There Is" was the answer so I could drop in a tidbit about Randy Newman arranging the song years before he hit our awareness (1969).

541. [b] Heatwave ("Boogie Nights", "Grooveline", "Always and Forever", etc.). Rod wrote "Rock With You", "Off the Wall" for Michael, "Yah Mo Be There" for Michael McDonald/James Ingram, "Stomp" for the Brothers Johnson and others.

542. [a:2] Shirelles/"Boys"; [b:5] Cookies/"Chains"; [c:3] Dr. Feelgood*/"Mr. Moonlight"; [d:4] Donays/"Devil in Her Heart"; [e:1] Buck Owens/"Act Naturally"; [f:8] The Top Notes

/"Twist & Shout"; [g:7] Carl Perkins/"Honey Don't"; [h:6] Barrett Strong/"Money"; [i:9] "Till There Was You" which was sung my Shirley Jones (mama Partridge) in *The Music Man*. I know you think I'm a stinker about the Top Notes and "Twist & Shout" but, historically, I'm correct (and, yes, a stinker). I quote the "The Atlantic Story": "Phil Spector produced a group called the Top Notes with the original version of "Twist and Shout", although "Twist and Shout" was one of Spector's glaring failures. The record stiffed, and Bert Berns, the song's writer, was incensed when he heard it. Berns felt Spector had ruined his song, and went out to show Spector how the song should be done. Berns recorded the Isley Brothers doing it the way he thought it should sound, and it was a huge hit."

* William "Willie" Lee Perryman performed sometimes as "Dr. Feelgood" and sometimes as "Piano Red". The Lovin' Spoonful covered his version of "Bald Head Lena" authored under his Piano Red pen name. There was also a '70s British pub rock band called "Dr. Feelgood".

543. [b] Hurley Girlies (sorry, Weasel Spagnola was in the Electric Prunes [guitar on "I Had Too Much to Dream Last Night"] so he qualifies as an "artist").

544. The Buckinghams did a <u>lyrical</u> version of Cannonball Adderley "Mercy, Mercy, Mercy", which was actually written by Adderley's pianist, Joe Zawinul, who a) played his part on an used electric piano he got from Ray Charles; b) later formed Weather Report. The Buckinghams hit #5 and Cannonball's version topped out at #11.

545. [b] Playboy Records. They were listed as "Björn & Benny (with Svenska Flicka)".

546. [d] Both! You're saying whatttttt? Yes, my friend, pre-Love, the group was called the Grass Roots until they found out that there was *another* band in L.A. by the same name, so he really was in both. You hate me when I do trick questions, I know.

547. a: "*Blue* Velvet" (Bobby Vinton); b: "*Green* Manalishi" by Fleetwood Mac; c: CCR's "*Green* River" or "Yellow River" by Christie; d: Elvis Costello's "(Angels Wanna Wear My) *Red* Shoes"; e: "*Black* is *Black*" by Los Bravos; f: "Old *Brown* Shoe" by the Beatles; g: Ram Jam's "*Black* Betty" which while it - and the band - sounds like a precursor to the White Stripes, the song was actually a folk tune made popular by Leadbelly in the '40s and the band was produced by the bubblegum music kings, Kasenetz and Katz.

548. Pat Benatar - on her debut *In the Heat of the Night* which was part of the natural path of seeing Liza Minnelli live and being inspired enough to quit her job as a bank teller, then landing a roll in Harry Chapin's futuristic musical *Zinger*, and gaining attention on Halloween night '77 when she came straight from a party dressed as a vampire and in her black tights, short top, and eyeliner and rather than change clothes, she went on stage and got more applause than she ever had so she hung onto those trimmings and rode 'em into the land of milk and honey.

549. Jackie (Sigmund Esco "Jackie" Jackson) was born in '51 and the *second* official Jackson child (Rebbie was first).

550. [a:2] Bell is the big sis to Amy (Lee Dorsey's "Working in the Coal Mine" was on Amy); [b:3] Decca to Brunswick (Jackie Wilson); [c:1] Chess to Checker; [d:5] Liberty to Imperial (Cher, Classics IV, Johnny Rivers); [e:4] Mercury to Smash; [f:6] STAX is the big bro to Volt (Otis Redding's label) Other STAX subordinates included Enterprise, the gospel label Chalice, Hip, and Safice; [g:7] Parrot was home to Tom Jones, Them, Engelbert, etc. It died in '73 and, now, Polydor manages the catalog.

551. [c] Kitten. There really was a Cugini - had a record called "Let Me Sleep Alone" in '79.

552. [a:5] Alvin & Ric Lee were in Ten Years After; [b:3] Jimmy, Jack & Donna Hall were in Wet Willie; [c:1] Ron & Scott Asheton were together in the Stooges; [d:2] Soupy's kids, Hunt & Tony Sales were in Tin Machine with Bowie (they were also the rhythm section pounding out Iggy Pop's "Lust for Life"; [e:4] Bobby & Cecil Womack were part of the Valentinos.

553. [b] Isaac Hayes & David Porter. Ike wound up being the one with the moxie, which lead to (among other things) becoming the first African American composer to win an Oscar for Best Original Song for "Theme from Shaft". The flip side of that moxie is probably what lead to him filing bankruptcy, too.

554. They're all true 'cept [c] the Noel Harrison one. The Belafonte session is the very first appearance of Mr. Zimmerman on record. The Booker T. & Priscilla track was a single in '73, not on any LP.

555. [c] Vinegar Joe. Most of we Yanks know about Robert Palmer and his string of successes, but Elkie is huge across the pond, having released 20 LPs and named by the *Guinness Book of World Records* as the most charted British Female artist of the last 30 years. Pre-Vinegar Joe, she helped the Small Faces get gigs in their infancy and was an opener for the Beatles at one of their Xmas shows.

556. Capricorn, which was also the home of the Allmans, Wet Willie, Jonathan Edwards, Marshall Tucker Band, etc. It was founded by Phil Walden (with brother Alan, and Frank Fenter). Phil was Otis Redding's lifelong manager and wound up with the publishing rights to "Respect", "I Can't Turn You Loose", "Sweet Soul Music", and "Dock of the Bay". Phil also managed the careers of Jim Varney ("Hey, Vern!") and Billy Bob Thornton (we'll forgive him), and Alan also roped in the publishing to "When a Man Loves a Woman, "Free Bird", and "Sweet Home Alabama".

557. [e] Hound Dog Taylor. Mr. Taylor wasn't exactly a ne'er-do-well. Freddie King admitted his classic, "Hideaway" (a tune you've heard Clapton do), was inspired by an unnamed instrumental he had heard Taylor perform at a Chicago clubs in the Fifties. Howlin' Wolf is the answer many of you guessed (wrongly!) because most of us consider

the Wolf to be a Chess Records act, but Sam Phillips cut the masters on Wolf's "How Many More Years" and "Moanin' at Midnight" at Sun and turned around and sold 'em to Chess. A-ha!

558. [c] Kaleidoscope. I'm not sure I can imagine Buffalo Bob (and Howdy Doody) entertaining the hashified crowd at the Fillmore, but the facts speak for themselves. Kaleidoscope was a band that featured David Lindley who went on to be Jackson Browne's guitar sidekick and the guy who sings the high part of JB's "(Load Out)/Stay".

559. [b] Frijid Pink whose debut LP did, in fact, hit the Top Ten and sold a million. Led Zep even opened for 'em ... *once*. Who are (Terry) Cashman & (Tommy) West, you say? Well, Cashman wrote "Sunday Will Never Be the Same" for Spanky and Our Gang; both guys masqueraded as two-thirds of the Buchanan Brothers (w/ Gene Pistilli [who went on to form the Manhattan Transfer] and they hit with "Medicine Man"); and they both signed Jim & Ingrid Croce to a recording deal and, then, produced most of Jim Croce's hits. They also had one tune – "American City Suite" – that hit # 27 on the Top 40.

560. Naomi Neville. The pseudonym-driven songs included "Fortune Teller" (Rolling Stones and, more recently, Plant/Krauss), "A Certain Girl" (Yardbirds), and "Pain in My Heart" (Otis Redding). Toussaint gave the name up after a while and went on to pen "Yes We Can Can", "Southern Nights", et al under his real name.

561. A bottle of Southern Comfort (or "Honey Poo" to you North Texans) was kept on stage for Janis, just in case she need some, uh, encouragement? And, Pigpen? He was so devoted to Thunderbird and SoCo that, at age 27, he died of "gastrointestinal hemorrhage". Southern Comfort is the same bar juice referenced as one of Morrison's addiction problems in Oliver Stone's *The Doors*, as well.

562. The Turtles' "Elenore". "You're my pride and joy, et cetera...". It was the band's next to last hit* and came off of their concept album *The Turtles Present the Battle of the Bands.* * "You Showed Me" was their last *real* hit and authored by Roger McGuinn and Gene Clark of the Byrds.

563. [c] "It Doesn't Matter Anymore" and who wrote it? You'll find out when you get to the answer to question 725...

564. Del Shannon. Tom Petty loved Del – quoted him in "Runnin' Down a Dream" and produced Del's coulda-been-a-comeback album and Jeff Lynne had worked with Del when Shannon did some recording with ELO. When Roy passed, the rumor was that Del would take his place but Prozac won out. Nonetheless, the Wilburys honored him with their version of "Runaway".

565. [b] Dr. John was never on *Chico and the Man*, but he was on *Touched by an Angel.*

566. [b] Bassist, Big John Wallace. John had a decent vocal range, too – he also sang the baritone parts in "Mr. Tanner" and "30,000 Pounds of Bananas".

567. "I got worries" from We Five's "You Were on My Mind"; "thinking about our fortune" from the Moody Blues' "Story in Your Eyes" and "All across the nation" from "San Francisco (Be Sure to Wear Some Flowers in Your Hair)" by Scott McKenzie.

568. [b] Terry Jacks' "Seasons in the Sun". Terry (and soon-to-be ex-wife, Susan) had worked with the Beach Boys to record the song but the Beachies decided to abandon the project mid-stream so Jacks decided to record the song himself. The version we hear is a bit different than the way it was originally written – in Jacks' version, the part about the wife's infidelity is left out.

569. *Urban Cowboy* which grossed more than 80 mil, making it more popular than *Saturday Night Fever*. Travolta outdoes Travolta...

570. [a] Paul Revere and the Raiders. Their guitarist, Freddy Weller, had a C&W hit with "Games People Play" and a co-write on Tommy Roe's "Dizzy" and "Jam Up and Jelly Tight" after he left the band.

571. 4o seconds according to my watch. Give yourself credit if you're within five secs, ok? John, Paul, Ringo, and Mal Evans* shared three different pianos and played an E-major chord simultaneously. *Mal also did the ticking clock and the counting in the song.

572. (US) Springsteen's *Born in the USA*; (UK) ABBA's *The Visitors* and a recording of Herbert von

Karajan conducting the *Alpine Symphony* by Richard Strauss.

573. [c] Dire Straits/*Brothers in Arms*. It was the first album to sell a million in the CD format as well as outsell its vinyl counterpart. If you do have an album version of it, though, did you know it was different from the CD? Four of the songs were trimmed down so everything would fit ("So Far Away" [a little more than a minute shorter], "Money for Nothing" [about a minute and a half shorter], "Your Latest Trick" [about 2:00 shorter], and "Why Worry" [about 3:00 shorter].

574. "Mony, Mony" by Tommy James and the Shondells. As Tommy tells it, "True story: I had the track done before I had a title. I wanted something catchy like "Sloopy" or "Bony Maroney," but everything sounded so stupid. So Ritchie Cordell and I were writing in New York City, and we were about to throw in the towel when I went out onto the terrace, looked up and saw the Mutual of New York building (which has its initials illuminated in red at its top). I said, "That's gotta be it! Ritchie, come here, you've gotta see this!" It's almost as if God Himself had said, "Here's the title." I've always thought that if I had looked the other way, it might have been called "Hotel Taft"." Bobby Bloom – who had a hit with "Montego Bay – is credited with being one of the non-Shondell writers on the song.

575. 230 pounds.

576. Atlantic offered $25,000 but RCA laid down $40,000 and won out. Elvis got $5k, Sam got the rest. Why did he sell? He says he simply needed the money to promote his other acts (Orbison, Cash, Perkins, et al).

577. Supertramp/*Breakfast in America*. The World Trade Center's twin towers appear as two stacks of boxes and the plate of breakfast represents Battery Park, the departure point for the Staten Island Ferry.

578. Joe Walsh. It was a 1959 Gibson Les Paul Sunburst.

579. [a] Percy Sledge. But the Bee Gees recorded - and had the hit with it - instead of Percy. However, Percyman did finally record the tune and it's on some of his compilations.

580. Quincy Jones... and, because not a single one of you asked for it, here's my personal collection of Leslie Gore trivia: a) Marvin Hamlisch wrote her "Sunshine, Lollipops, and Rainbows". b) Leslie didn't chase the rainbow like most of her peers did and instead of movies and TV, she opted to go to college at Sarah Lawrence. c) We might've heard more hits from her, but the man who became her producer - Shelby Singleton - refused to let her record "A Groovy Kind of Love" because it had the word "groovy" so the Mindbenders grabbed the opportunity and had the hit. d) But, she did record "Wedding Bell Blues" before the 5th Dimension. It's just that hers flopped and theirs didn't. e) Oh, yeah - and her kid brother, Michael Gore, is the guy who wrote the soundtrack to the movie *Fame*.

581. [d] We Five. The lead male voice was Michael Stewart who wound up producing Billy Joel's *Piano Man* album. And, for those of you who think that the We Five's "You Were on My Mind" was original to them, it wasn't – folkies Richard and Mimi (Joan Baez' sister) Farina did it first.

582. [c] A Leslie speaker. You've probably seen 'em next to a Hammond or Wurlitzer organ. It has a speaker that spins around and gives sort of a Doppler effect.

583. Emerson, Lake, and Palmer/*Brain Salad Surgery.* We've got more than enough ELP trivia so let me dispense with some Dr. John juju: The guitar solo on "Right Place..." was by David Spinoza, who a) produced James Taylor's *Walking Man* album, b) played on McCartney's *Ram* and Lennon's *Mind Games,* and c) dated Yoko when she and John were splitsville for a year. The horn section was the "Bonnaroo Horns" and provided the creative juice (along with Dr. John's follow-up, *Desitively Bonnaroo*) for the festival of the same name.

584. Chip Taylor. "Wild Thing", "Angel of the Morning", "Take Me for a Little While" all came out of his pen. And, if you've ever heard Shaggy's "Angel", it's built around of "Angel of the Morning" and Steve Miller's "The Joker" which meant that both got the songwriter credit *and* Chip got his second #1 35 years after "Wild Thing".

585. Stevie Wonder with "Fingertips (part 2)" (part 1 was the flip). Stevie was 13 years 1 month at the

time. It was Motown's second #1 pop hit (Marvelettes' "Please Mr. Postman" was the first).

586. [c] "I Think We're Alone Now". He got the idea when it was accidentally played backwards during a writing session.

587. "Mother and Child Reunion". Paul did the tune in Jamaica using Jimmy Cliff's band and Whitney Houston's mom, Cissy, on background vocals.

588. *The Last Waltz*. Most of what you see on the video really happened that night, but post-concert, Scorsese filmed more on an MGM studio soundstage with The Band, Staple Singers, and Emmylou Harris.

589. Billy Preston – the label of the "Get Back" single credits the artists on the record as "The Beatles *with* Billy Preston".

590. The only mother and son to both have a number one hit on the *Billboard* Hot 100 are Shirley Jones, who sang on the Partridge Family's "I Think I Love You" in November, 1970 and her son Shaun Cassidy for "Da Do Ron Ron" in July 1977

591. [d] America. Yep. Sergio Mendes covered "After Midnight", Skynyrd did "Call Me the Breeze", "I Got the Same Old Blues", "I Know a Little"; Kansas did "Bringing It Back"; Feliciano and Poco did "Magnolia".

592. [a] Ray Brown, who played bass on *Countdown to Ecstasy*. Ray was married to Ella Fitzgerald, managed a young Quincy Jones, and found Diana Krall playing in a restaurant in British Columbia.

He wasn't the only jazz cat to lay down some grooves for Rock acts. Michael Brecker played the sax solo on Paul Simon's "Have a Good Time" and James Taylor's "Don't Let Me Be Lonely Tonight", and Phil Woods played the sax solo on Billy Joel's "Just the Way You Are" and on Steely Dan's "Dr. Wu". Phil's such a jazz stud, he even married Charlie Parker's ("Bird") widow (more useless information that only music extremists would give a hoot about...). And, why did I include Elliott Randall in that list? Because I'm Steely greedy, that's why, and wanted to get this bit in somehow: Mr. Randall is the guy who did what Jimmy Page called his favorite guitar solo of all-time – the one in "Reelin' in the Years" (he also did the blistering solo on Irene Cara's "Fame", but that's another subject). Hmm… and you thought it was Larry Carlton who did "Reelin'…"? Nope. He did the axe flight on "Kid Charlemagne".

593. [d] My best research says "Ron Dunbar & Edith Wayne" were Invictus Records staffer Ronald Dunbar and Holland-Dozier-Holland disguising themselves as "Edith". Not only did they play the name game for Payne's hit, but for the Chairmen of the Board's "Give Me Just a Little More Time". Incidentally, Ray Parker, Jr. ("Ghostbusters") plays lead guitar on "Band of Gold".

594. [a:3] "Save Your Kisses for Me" by Brotherhood of Man; [b:1] "You To Me Are Everything" by the Real Thing; [c:2] "I Love to Love" by Tina Charles; [d:5] "Mississippi" by the all-girl band Pussycat, the first Dutch act to top the British charts; [e:4]

"When a Child is Born" by Johnny Mathis, his only #1 in the British Isles and despite there being absolutely no reference to the season, a song that gets played primarily at Christmas. It's gotta be the allusions it makes...

595. False – the correct answer would be Bobby McFerrin's "Don't Worry, Be Happy" (apologies for stretching this far into the '80s). Nonetheless, while most everyone's fond of "Mercedes Benz", it never hit #1 as a single, just as part of *Pearl*. It was a song Janis recorded in one take and that – plus a couple of rowdy verses of "Happy Birthday" sung for John Lennon – were the last things she ever recorded. She died three days later.

596. [b] "I think I've got it, got the strength to carry on, yeah...". The first time H&O released "She's Gone", in '73, it stiffed at #50 on the charts. Then, Tavares released an R&B version that topped the Soul charts. Later, on the coattails of "Sara Smile", in 1976, it was released again and got up to #4.

597. The answer is [f (both b & c)]. Linda Lawrence was both the lady who gave Brian Jones an illegitimate son, Julian Brian Lawrence, <u>and</u>, eventually, became Donovan's wife. The Jan & Dean song "Linda" was written in the '40s, but was about Linda (Eastman) McCartney, the daughter of the songwriter's (Jack Lawrence) attorney... and Linda Thompson was the girl Elvis dated, (she wound up marrying Bruce Jenner, then David Foster with whom she wrote "No Explanation" for the movie, *Pretty Woman*).

598. Judy Collins' "Amazing Grace". 'Ol Judy started a trend with it, too. After her, there were versions from Aretha, Crystal Gayle, Kylie Minogue, Joan Baez, et al. Judy, being a playful one, even did a song on the same album as "Amazing Grace" called "Farewell to Tarwathie", where she sang to the accompaniment of humpback whales. Sorry, but that's just a bit over the top for me...

599. Death by plane crash. Denver in California, Croce in Louisiana. Nelson in Texas. Otis is Wisconsin. Lake Monona in Madison, Wisconsin, on December 10, 1967 to be exact. The only survivor was Ben Cauley, a member of the Bar-Kays, Otis' backing band. There was another Bar-Kay, James Alexander, who lived but it was his turn to take a commercial flight (because there were eight people and only seven seats) that landed safely.

600. Motor City (those of you who said Methadone Clinic lose 10 points). Their guitarist, Fred "Sonic" Smith went on to marry Patti Smith and whose nickname Sonic Youth borrowed for their name.

601. Atlanta Rhythm Section (1979), who was built out of Roy Orbison's backup group, the Candymen, <u>and</u> members of the Classics IV who did the original *vocal* version of "Spooky" in '68 but the very first version was an instrumental by saxman Mike Sharpe in 1967.

602. The answer to part (a) is [e] Television's *Marquee Moon** LP didn't chart at all in America, but the Brits must love it – NME named it the 4th best album of all-time (ahead of *Revolver*).** The answer

to part (b) is [f] *Exodus* was the best of the bunch in America, hitting #20 on the *Billboard* LP charts. *I have to give props to Television's Tom Verlaine for one thing that, as a Jazz fan, I find very cool. He wanted to record the album with noted Jazz engineer Rudy Van Gelder because Rudy had done Coltrane's *A Love Supreme,* the LP that was a turning point for Verlaine. The pairing didn't happen, but it's the thought that counts. **#1: *The Stone Roses* by the Stone Roses; #2: *Doolittle* by the Pixies; #3: Beach Boys' *Pet Sounds.*

603. Elektra (the butterfly holding the "E") and Chrysalis. There may be others, but it beats me who they are.

604. They're (just about all of the) guitar players in the history of Fleetwood Mac. Yes, Mick Fleetwood has been in every incarnation of the band, but no for John McVie. He actually got cold feet at the inception of the band and a guy named Bob Brunning initially was their bassist with the understanding if McVie changed his mind, Brunning was out. It only lasted three weeks and a gig or two and McVie finally joined. Brunning got in enough studio time, though, to ink his licks on "Long Grey Mare" on the first Mac LP.

605. Providence, Rhode Island, as told in the song "The Last Resort" (on *Hotel California*). The track was about the demise of society, about how we're all screwing up paradise. And, unlike the Eagles, there were none of their typical lead or rhythm guitars on the track, just a pedal steel that Don Felder played. Frey played piano, Henley sang and played synths with Walsh.

606. Otis Redding's "Try a Little Tenderness". The other Rock-era tie in the movie was provided by the Danny Hutton Hitters – Hutton of Three Dog Night fame. After Three Dog Night broke up, Hutton managed Punk bands and personally seized the chance to cover Nik Kershaw's "Wouldn't It Be Good" for *Pretty in Pink*.

607. Lake Geneva and the Rolling Stones had the mobile recording thang. Here's the lowdown on what happened: Deep Purple was recording in Montreux using the Stones remote facility which was parked at the Montreux Casino. The night before the recording session, a Zappa and Mothers gig was going on inside at the casino's theatre. During the show, a fire broke out due to some butthead in the audience firing a flare gun into the ceiling. The fire destroyed the whole complex, with the Mothers' equipment to boot. Roger Glover, DP's bassist, had a dream a coupla days later where the title of the song "appeared" to him as he flashed back to watching the smoke from the fire spreading over Lake Geneva.

608. Francis Albert Sinatra.

609. [c] English. Britain's first family of harmony (or disco) was born on the Isle of Man to some nice English parents, then lived in Chorlton-cum-Hardy, Manchester, England.

610. [b] Santana – "Evil Ways" and "Black Magic Woman"(Santana's keyboard player Gregg Rolie sang lead on "Black Magic Woman" – the same Gregg Rolie who joined Journey in '73).

611. [d] Brian Peter George St. John le Baptiste de la Salle Eno. Mssr. Eno is the fella who also wrote the six-second start-up music-sound of the Windows 95 operating system– working on a Mac, no less.

612. True. Very true. Ron Dante's his name and he also pretended to be Veronica (or Betty) on the Archies' "Jingle Jangle" by singing falsetto. And, bonus useless knowledge while we're at it: he's also the voice of the Cuff Links ("Tracy") and in the Detergents for "Leader of the Laundromat".

613. [b] Smoking in the boys' room. The line "Who calls the English teacher 'Daddy-o'?" may well be a reference to the '50s flick *Blackboard Jungle* where the students poke fun at the surname of their new teacher, Richard Dadier, by changing "Dadier" to "Daddy-o".

614. [a] Mr. Acker* Bilk or, to the more formal of you, Bernard Stanley Bilk, with that clarinet ditty "Stranger on the Shore", which he wrote for a British TV series. And being one who believes in equal rights, Vera Lynn was the first *female* British artist to top the U.S. charts with "Auf Wiederseh'n Sweetheart" in 1952. *"Acker" comes from Brit slang for friend or mate. Note: it's "Acker", not "Wanker".

615. [d] Sex Pistols. Despite Glen co-writing 10 of the 12 tracks on *Never Mind the Bollocks* (he did the music while Johnny Rotten did the lyrics), Glen either got disgusted with the whole lot of bullocks and left on his own or replaced (by Sid Vicious) for admitting the liked John, Paul, Ringo, and George*. The Beatles reference makes for a better

legend, don't you think? Of course, Rotten named Sid after his pet hamster, so it was probably an insect vs. mammal controversy.

616. Dave Mason. One version has it that Mason had invited Jimi to a party where Hendrix first heard the song; another version being that Hendrix had been given a tape of the Dylan song by one of Albert Grossman's (Dylan's managers) lackeys. What we do know is that Dave did to the acoustic part and when Noel Redding got pissed off halfway through the sessions, Mason took over on the bass part. Nevertheless, Hendrix went back in and redid all the bass lines himself.

617. Ok, follow... Truman Capote wrote *In Cold Blood* which Quincy Jones did the score for... Quincy produced the Brothers Johnson who recorded Shuggie Otis' "Strawberry Letter 23"... Shuggie's father, Johnny Otis (whose goatee was the inspiration for Zappa's), wrote "Willie and the Hand Jive" which Clapton recorded on *461 Ocean Boulevard*. Perry Mason would be proud if you got this one right.

618. [a] The Nelsons: Ozzie (Nelson and His Orchestra) who had a #1 hit with "And Then Some" in 1935; Ricky ("Poor Little Fool"), and Matthew & Gunnar p/k/a Nelson (["Can't Live Without Your] Love and Affection").

619. Yes, Dog was. You know if you got this right exactly *why* you got it right and those of you who guessed right, leave now. "Was Dog a Doughnut" was an instrumental – and a single (peaked @ 53) –

off of Cat Stevens' comeback/rebound *Izitso* album. Cat laid everything on the line for *Izitso* after the substantial failure of *Numbers*. It was recorded in all the hot spots at the time – Memphis, Muscle Shoals, and at Sound 80 in Minneapolis where Dylan had done parts of *Blood on the Tracks* – using all the hot hired hands like the Swampers, even Chick Corea who did the keyboard work on "Was Dog a Doughnut".

620. [b] The Godfather of Soul, Mr. James Brown, holds that illustrious record – 99 chart entries without a #1 song. CCR holds the record for the most #2 hits (five) without ever reaching the top spot.

621. Shelter Records (Leon Russell, J.J. Cale, Tom Petty [Mudcrutch], Freddie King, Phoebe Snow, et al). DC Comics got a bit peeved, sued, and so Shelter started blacking out the man of steel's "S" and eventually replaced it with a hand-scrawled, puny-arse "S".

622. They're all the 60s/70s folks who did theme songs to the James Bond movies, Shirley Bassey getting to do the dirty deed three times!

623. [b] "Crystal". Believe it or not, despite the marquee value of the two, the *Buckingham Nicks* album has yet to been released on CD in the U.S. (at least, by this '09 writing).

624. Yeah, but it took 'er awhile. She co-wrote two on 1976' *Hasten Down the Wind* and the follow-up, *Simple Dreams*. Linda probably isn't worried about getting mailbox money from songwriting – her grandfather is the cat who invented an early form

of the toaster, the grease gun, the first electric stove, one of the original varieties of the microwave oven, and the love of every lush's life, the flexible rubber ice cube tray.

625. [c] It was the messenger guy, Guy. Our homework says this is the biggest instrumental hit EJ had, although he does mutter "Life isn't everything" repeatedly at the end.

626. Well, you get some choices: "The World's Most Flexible Record Label"... "We came. We saw. We left."... "If It Ain't Stiff, It Ain't Worth a Fuck" ... and "When You Kill Time, You Murder Success". If you ask me, any label that gave Elvis Costello and Ian Dury their start can call themselves whatever they like and be as stiff as they want.

627. [d] Status Quo. They first moved to "Traffic Jam" but wound up as the Quo.

628. Plant wrote the lyrics, copping references to [a] "The Stroll", [b] "Book of Love", and [d] "Walking in the Moonlight", adding a verbal layer to a jam session that came out of the band trying to finish "Four Sticks". There are several Fifties licks in the tune – some hear a rip of Little Richard's "Keep a-knockin'" or a little "Good Golly Miss Molly". The song also featured Rolling Stones co-founder, Ian Stewart, on keys (he also did "Boogie With Stu" from *Physical Graffiti*).

629. I am Bobbie Gentry (real name Roberta Streeter), the voice and ink behind "Ode to Billie Joe". What's with the wordplay in the question? "Having enough germs to catch pneumonia" was

a line from "I'll Never Fall in Love Again", the hit Bobbie had in the U.K. and "swamper" refers to Jim Stafford who had a hit with "Swamp Witch" and "My Girl Bill".

630. Lorne Greene's "Ringo". Hit #1 in '64, it did. Was it about Ringo STARR? No (probably about outlaw *Johnny* Ringo), but timing is everything, isn't it?

631. C'mon, do the verbal math… repeat after me "Ten… Years… After". Duh.

632. [b] When all the Stones collab'ed on a song, they would list the songwriter credits as "Nanker/Phelge" or "Nanker Phelge" and, being the loving bunch they were, would share all the royalties from the track. Examples include: "Play with Fire" and "2120 South Michigan Avenue". According to Wikipedia, Phelge came from Edith Grove flatmate Jimmy Phelge, while a Nanker was a revolting face that band members would pull.

633. The Platters ("Only You"*, "The Great Pretender"). All the eight-plus permutations – so 'n so & The Platters, etc. – was a novel-length legal wrangling and made lawyers across America a lot of money with everyone claiming to be the "official" version. There's now a law called "Truth in Music" in 33 states that requires performing groups to have at least one member of the recording group that they claim a connection to and a legal right to use the name. Or else they must label the production a "tribute" or "salute" or else own the recording group's trademark or have its authorization. The answer to the

question's hint? Besides writing the hits, the creator of the group was Buck Ram who also co-wrote "I'll Be Home for Christmas". He also had his paws in the writing, production, or arranging for the Coasters, The Drifters, Ike & Tina, Ike Cole, Duke Ellington, Glenn Miller, Ella Fitzgerald, and others. * Song written by Ram for the Ink Spots but considered unreleasable by the Ink Spots label (Federal).

634. Martha Reeves and the Vandellas (get it – VANdyke and DELLAreese?). Most don't realize that it's also the same bunch of girls who can be heard in the background on Marvin Gaye's "Stubborn Kind of Fellow", "Hitch Hike", and "Pride and Joy" – all tunes they did session work before they started their own career.

635. [c] Albert King (aka "the Velvet Bulldozer"). The tuneage was written by Booker T. Jones (of the MGs) and William Bell (whose "I Forgot to Be Your Lover" was remade into a pop hit by Billy Idol in as "To Be a Lover").

636. [d] Scot Halpin was the lad's name. It happened November 20, 1973, at the Cow Palace in San Fran during the Quadrophenia tour. Seems like the horse tranquilizers Keith had taken got the better of him and he collapsed an hour or so into the gig. The band went on as a three-piece for awhile until Pete asked if there was anyone in the audience who could play drums (and well). 19-year old Halpin, sitting down front, was outed by a pal as the go-to guy, was summed up on stage and played a coupla tunes in Moon's absence.

637. "Teen Angel" by Mark Dinning, a song so morbid the deejays at the BBC refused to play it.

638. [h] They all featured twin leads... and Duane Allman appeared in *two* of those configurations – Derek & the Dominos and ABB.

639. "Also Sprach Zarathustra" (the *2001* theme) by Deodato. CTI was founded by Creed Taylor, who had also served as founder of Impulse! Records (Ray Charles, John Coltrane, etc.) and, as a producer at Verve Records, is widely acknowledged for starting the Bossa Nova movement through the likes of Antonio Carlos Jobim, Astrud Gilberto, and others.

640. [a] Roxy Music coz there was already a band in the States called "Roxy". Herman's Hermits used to be called "Pete Novak and the Heartbeats" but I don't think there's any band who wanted *that* name.

641. [b] Soft Machine, same as the Burroughs novel's title. Andy Summers, pre-Police, was in the Softs, and during that stint, the band opened for Hendrix on a string of dates back in '68.

642. [b] Jeff Beck (yes, AC/DC turned the line into a whole *song* but that wasn't the question). The phrase originates from the Willie Dixon/J.B. Lenoir classic "You Shook Me". While Muddy Waters had first recorded the song in '61, Jeff Beck was first on the scene for the Rock audience via the song's appearance on *Truth,* but by the hair of his chinny chin chin. *Truth* was recorded in August of '68 and the first Zep LP with the same song was recorded mere months later. And although Page

and Plant had kinship through their time in the Yardbirds and John Paul Jones had played on both versions, neither Beck nor Page knew that the other had recorded the song. Needless to say, both were pissed and it started a long feud between them. Believe it or not, Kenny Chesney did the tune as an encore on his '05 tour. Don't even...

643. [a] It was originally written as a reggae tune *and* [b] it was banned by several archdioceses (St. Louis et al). The ban, of course, fueled interest in the song, and Billy wrote to several archbishops and asked them to please ban his *next* record, too!

644. Well, it's true – in a way. Let me explain: When Townshend was in the midst of transitioning the Lifehouse project into *Who's Next*, he went to NYC to do some sessions. From what I've been able to track down, early versions of "Behind Blue Eyes" and "Won't Get Fooled Again" were recorded at the Record Plant in March of '71. Both included guest shots from Al Kooper on organ and Leslie West on guitar (Leslie played on the Who's cover of the Motown classic "Baby, Don't You Do It") and produced by Felix Pappalardi (future producer/bassist for Mountain). There are bootlegs from this and Townshend acknowledged much of this in the deluxe edition's liner notes.

645. Felix and his wife, Gail (the one who shot him to death), not only wrote "Strange Brew", but "World of Pain"... <u>and</u> Felix produced *Wheels of Fire, Disraeli Gears,* and *Goodbye.*

646. Trigger. The instrument is a Martin N-20 and the reason it's got a big 'ol hole in it – well, other than being played so much – is that it has no pick-guard since classical guitars are meant to be played fingerstyle instead of with flat-picks.

647. A Hank Williams cover. It was Hank's first major Country hit, reaching #4.

648. [a] Steely Dan's "Time Out of Mind". Becker & Fagen hired the guitar slinger after they heard him wailin' away on "Sultans of Swing". The tune – from the Dan's *Gaucho* album, had a bit of controversy, according to Wikipedia (and I quote), "The title track was intended as a tribute to Keith Jarrett, and was originally credited only to Fagen and Becker. However, after hearing the album, Jarrett insisted that the track uses a part of his composition "Long As You Know You're Living Yours," and threatened the Dan with legal action. Becker & Fagen were then forced to add his name to the credits and include him in future royalties."

649. [c] (Nick) Ashford and (Valerie) Simpson, who also wrote "Let's Go Get Stoned" (Ray Charles), "I Don't Need No Doctor" (Humble Pie, et al), "I'm Every Woman" (Chaka Khan), and they even get (more) mailbox money (geez, I love this term, don't I?) out of the Amy Winehouse LP *Back to Black* for the single "Tears Dry On Their Own" which is based on "Ain't No Mountain High Enough". And, if you're an Oprah fan, you probably saw 'em accompanying Ms. Winfrey to Africa when she opened up her girls school.

650. [b] *Trick of the Tail*, however it's not the first *song* on which Phil Collins sang lead, which was "More Fool Me" on *Selling England by the Pound.*

651. [a] Kate Bush/"Wuthering Heights". She did it in 1978 at age 19, after being discovered by David Gilmour of Pink Floyd. Another first? She was the first singer to use a wireless headphone/ microphone on stage.

652. I have to believe it's "I'm Not in Love" since everything I read says it has 240 or 256 and "BoRhap" had 180. It took 10cc three friggin' weeks to record all the vocal parts for a pure chromatic scale so they could turn them into loops and create whatever harmonies they wanted so they could pop 'em in anywhere in the song.

653. "Timothy" by the Buoys, a song written by Rupert Holmes who, in '79, had a hit with the "Piña Colada Song", did the lead vocals on "Jennifer Tompkins" by the Street People, wrote a couple of tracks on the soundtrack to *A Star is Born*, and was the playwright behind the Broadway hits *Drood* and *Say Goodnight, Gracie.*

654. Yessir, the man who wrote the lyrics to most of Elton's songs also did co-writes with [b] Alice Cooper (the *From the Inside* LP), [c] Heart ("These Dreams"), and [d] Brian Wilson ("What I Really Want for Christmas"). And, uh, well, he also co-wrote a track with Courtney Love which might cost him a week in purgatory. What's the boy do with all his royalties? He bought a bucking bull named Little Yellow Jacket (an unprecedented

three-time world champion), opened a restaurant in LA called Cicada, and swoons his wife who happens to be Rene Russo's sister.

655. [c] Alvin Tostig is Levon's father and "Jesus" (not the real one) is Alvin's grandson/Levon's son. Was Levon (born Lavon, christened Levon) Helm the inspiration for the song? According to Bernie Taupin, the answer is yes, but Alvin is pure fiction.

656. Maurice White, the genius behind Earth, Wind & Fire. After graduating from Tennessee State, Mo' moved to ChiTown and became a session drummer for Chess and Okeh, and THE guy behind Fontella Bass' "Rescue Me" and Billy Stewart's "Summertime". About '66, he became the full-time drummer for the Ramsey Lewis Trio before moving on to the Salty Peppers whose name and direction eventually grew into EW&F.

657. Nick Mason, the Floyd's drummer, has played on every single record the band has done. He and the missus vacation in the home (manor… estate?) that the Prince Phil's wild thing, Camilla Parker Bowles, used to live in.

658. Blue Oyster Cult's "Don't Fear the Reaper" off of *Agents of Fortune*, an album featuring a young Patti Smith on lyrics and vocals (she was the keyboardist's, Allen Lanier, girlfriend at the time). The character Walken's part was based on was BOC's producer Sandy Pearlman (although they mistakenly referred to him as another producer, Bruce Dickinson).

659. [a] is Tiny Tim/"Tiptoe Through the Tulips"; [b] is "They're Coming to Take Me Away, Ha-Haaa!" by Napoleon XIV (real name: Jerry Samuels who actually spent eight months in a mental institution. The flip side of the record was the A side backwards); [c] is Steve Martin's "King Tut" ("untamed and fanatical chap" = "wild and crazy guy") that he debuted on *Saturday Night Live*, a show which (at this writing), he holds the title for hosting the most number of times – 15 (Alec Baldwin is #2 with 14); [d] is Ray Stevens' "Ahab the Arab". Ray has said, as much, that "Clyde" the camel was named after R&B singer Clyde McPhatter, original lead singer of the Drifters.

660. "Snoopy vs. the Red Baron". Charles Schulz, *Peanuts* creator, was a wittle bit touchy about his beloved Snoopy being turned into a hit record without his permish, sued the band, and won all the publishing proceeds from the record. Natch, Schulz did allow the group to write more Snoopy songs but when they released the tune in Canada, they re-lyric'ed it as "Squeaky vs. the Black Knight" to avoid legal hassles. Unfortunately, the maple leaf citizenry didn't bite and the record died. The hit song was produced and written by Phil Gernhard, who produced "Stay" for Maurice Williams and the Zodiacs as well as Lobo's hits and Dick Holler who penned Dion's tribute to Lincoln, King, and Kennedy.

661. "Martha My Dear" is about Paul's sheepdog (a purely platonic relationship, we take it); "Dear Prudence" was written about Mia Farrow's sister

who accompanied the boys to India to see El Maharishi. The lore goes that Pru would stay in her room all day and Lennon, fearing she was depressed, penned this little tune to try and pry her out of her isolation; "Hey Jude" was written by Paul to bolster the spirits of Julian Lennon during his parents' divorce. Originally titled "Hey Jules", it was the first single released on Apple.

662. "Creeque Alley", named after a club in the Virgin Islands where the Mamas & the Papas hung out. In the song, they reference fellow musicians Zal Yanovsky and John Sebastian of the Lovin' Spoonful, Roger McGuinn (Byrds), Barry McGuire ("Eve of Destruction"), The Mugwumps (Zal Yanovsky, Cass Elliott, Denny Doherty, Jim Hendricks [he wrote Johnny Rivers' hit, "Summer Rain", as well as the theme to the TV show *Then Came Bronson* ("Long Lonesome Highway" by Michael Parks [aka Earl McGraw in Tarantino's *Kill Bill* flicks]). Some explanations on the various lines: *Zal and Denny workin' for a penny tryin' to get a fish on the line* refers to when they were working in Nova Scotia as part of the Halifax Three; the line *Let's go South* was about getting out of Nova Scotia and going South to New York; *Duffy's good vibrations* refers to Hugh Duffy who owned Creeque Alley; and while Cass was a smart lass (IQ of 165), she wasn't planning to go to Swarthmore. She actually dropped out of high school mere weeks before graduation (the show biz bug got her), then later enrolled at American University (in D.C.). In reality, she had planned to

transfer to Goucher College (in Maryland and named the home of the "most happy" students by Newsweek ['04]) but John Phillips couldn't rhyme Goucher with much of anything so we wound up with Swathmore.

663. [a] is from "I Am the Walrush" and [b] from "Mrs. Robinson" (the *Bookends* version, not the earlier version in *The Graduate*). "Walrus" came about from a slew of different things – for one, a student wrote to him telling him that the teacher was having them analyze Beatles lyrics so John decided he'd have a little fun by writing the most confusing lyrics he could. Then, he copped that "yellow matter custard" stuff from a playground rhyme he used to sing. There was also an allusion to the Lewis Carroll verse, "The Walrus and the Carpenter," from *Through the Looking-Glass* (the "eggman" paying homage to Humpty Dumpy from the same book). Later, in a 1980 edition of *Playboy*, Lennon further 'splained that "The first line was written on one acid trip one weekend. The second line was written on the next acid trip the next weekend, and it was filled in after I met Yoko... I'd seen Allen Ginsberg and some other people who liked Dylan and Jesus going on about Hare Krishna. It was Ginsburg, in particular, I was referring to. The words "Element'ry penguin" meant that it's naïve to just go around chanting Hare Krishna or putting all your faith in one idol. In those days I was writing obscurely, a la Dylan."

664. [b] *Captain Fantastic and the Brown Dirt Cowboy*, the album that contained "Someone Saved My Life

Tonight" which, we understand, is somewhat of an autobiographical narrative about Elton's catastrophic engagement to Linda Woodrow, and his related suicide attempt. Who's the "Someone" he refers to? That would be Long John Baldry (whom EJ refers to as "Sugar Bear"). Baldry persuaded him to break off the engagement because saving his music career was a better bet and trying to save a miserable marriage.

665. Ransom Eli Olds' company made the "REO Speed Wagon". Mr. Olds also went on to greater heights with his OLDSmobile and REO took it on the run after their beginnings as a covers band in '67 at the University of Illinois in Chambana.

666. [a] It was Woody Guthrie's "This Land is Your Land", a tune whose melody was based, in part, on the Carter Family's "Little Darlin' Pal of Mine" and has grown from the folk circuit to glee clubs, Springsteen, Ford and United Airlines ads, and the theme song to McGovern's presidential campaign. Woody a liberal? Methinks so, but Arlo switched parties and became a registered Republican around the turn of the 21st century.

667. Ann & Nancy Wilson, p/k/a Heart. In '77, their label, Mushroom Records, ran an ad in *Rolling Stone* stirring up rumors that the sisters were lesbian lovers. The ad showed the sisters bare-shouldered – as they appear on the *Dreamboat Annie* cover – with a suggestive caption of "It was only our first time".

668. [b] A Farfisa (organ). John Paul Jones also used a Farfisa on "Dancing Days" and there was one on "Wooly Bully". Some may contend that there was one on "96 Tears" and "In-a-Gadda-Da-Vida" but the purists will tell you that those were "Vox" organs, not Farfisas.

669. No and no... the Walker Brothers weren't brothers *or* named Walker but rather Engle, Leeds, and Maus. It's a far cry from Milli Vanilli, but three guys from L.A. who had been in groups like the Routers and the Standells pulled the act off pretty well and had two #1s in the U.K. plus another two Top Ten'ers, one of which was an peculiar cover of Tom Rush's "No Regrets". Scott Engle was the most interesting of the lot and David Bowie was the executive producer on a 2006 film called *Scott Walker: 30 Century Man* that featured performers that Engle (er, Walker) had an impact on, including Radiohead, Sting, Brian Eno, Johnny Marr of the Smiths, among others.

670. [b] Main Ingredient ("Just Don't Want to Be Lonely" and "Everybody Plays the Fool"). The rare name "Cuba" goes back to when grandpa Dudley Gooding, a Barbados native who had moved to Havana in the '30s, and married a woman there who was later killed because of her association with Marcus Garvey. On her deathbed, Dudley promised his wife that he would name his first son "Cuba". And, as Paul Harvey would say, now you know the rest of the story.

671. Neil's given serious credit for the rise of Bubblegum music beginning with his days at Cameo-Parkway (home of the first Ohio Express single) and, then, cresting the opportunity at Buddah* with the deployment of the Lemon Pipers, 1910 Fruitgum Company, Ohio Express, Kasenetz-Katz Singing Orchestral Circus, Crazy Elephant, et al. * Spelling freaks will notice that the spelling of "Buddah" is wrong, but that's the way the company had it until Sony/BMG bought the catalogue and started spelling it the correct (enlightened) way.

672. ABBA/"S.O.S". Lennon claimed it as one of his faves and Pete Townshend says it probably is his favorite pop record of all-time.

673. [b] The key word is "hit" because both the Marvin Rainwater song *and* the Don Fardon song are the same song (written by John Loudermilk ["Tobacco Road"], but titled differently, styled just a bit differently, and with Fardon having a Top 20 hit in the States and hitting #3 in the U.K. The Raiders version was actually cut at a Mark Lindsay solo session but no matter who got the credit, it went on to sell six million copies and was Columbia Records biggest selling single for almost a decade.

674. Edwin Starr's "War" and the Jackson 5's "ABC". "War" was first recorded by the Temps but the label thought releasing it as a single would alienate their fans, so Norman Whitfield cut a deal with Berry Gordy where it would be released but with someone else doing the vocals, hence Starr's version (w/ Undisputed Truth on the bg vocs).

675. [b] Pat Boone* had six #1s during that period, pale to Elvis' 17 chart toppers. Vinton had four during the same period. * You a basketball fan? Can you tell me what ABA team Pat was majority owner of? (Oakland Oaks, winners of the ABA title in '69)

676. Woodstock. It arose from the audience lighting candles during her set. On the track, Melanie was backed by the Edwin Hawkins Singers. After "Brand New Key", Melanie got glossed over by most of us in the 70s but Ahmet Ertegun personally signed her to Atlantic and oversaw the production of *Photograph*, an LP heralded by the *New York Times* as one of the best of '76.

677. [b] The "Spanish Castle" was a club in Des Moines, just south of Seattle. Hendrix used to go there as a teen to watch bands and, then, began jammin' there with others. The phrase "Takes 'bout a half a day to get there" came from him riding to the club in one of his friend's beat-up car that seemed to break down every few miles.

678. [a] "Blue Suede Shoes". The origin of the tune comes from two different angles: When Carl Perkins was on tour with Johnny Cash, Johnny told him about a black airman who he'd met while stationed in Germany who referred to his regulation flying shoes as "blue suede shoes" and suggested to Perkins that he write a tune about 'em. Well, heck, Carl didn't know anything about shoes and passed on the idea until he was playing a dance one day and noticed a young couple in front of him whose male half was wearing, duh, blue suede shoes and who was warning his date

not to step on his "blue suedes". And, that's how songs are born, children. Oh, before I wander away – why did Sam Phillips let Elvis cover "Blue Suede Shoes"? 'Cause Carl had been in a car wreck and couldn't tour and Elvis' popularity could spur royalties that Perkins (and the label) would've never seen otherwise. Most people would assume that Elvis' version was bigger than Carl's but the fact is that Carl's hit #1 on the C&W charts, #2 on the Pop charts, and Elvis' barely made the Top 20.

679. [b] Their hair was too long, and geez, they wouldn't even let them off the dang airplane! It was Valentine's Day, for cryin' out loud. Why wasn't anyone feelin' the luv? Maybe Page was subconsciously moved by the event because he shaved his beard a couple of days later and never grew it back while a Zeppelinite.

680. "Ballet for a Girl in Buchannon" off of Chicago *II*. Although Terry Kath sang lead on both songs, the 13 min. suite was written by trombonist, James Pankow, who, according to the grapevine, wrote it for his girlfriend when she left for school at West Virginia Wesleyan College in Buckhannon (correct spelling), West By God Virginia. One interesting postscript about Kath: After his death, his wife married Kiefer Sutherland, 14 years her junior.

681. The Monkees' "Daydream Believer". Penned by John Stewart (Kingston Trio and future hitmaker with "Gold"), arranged by Peter Tork (his only appearance on *The Birds, The Bees, and The Monkees*), and the band's last *Billboard* #1.

682. The real answer is [f] the Benny Goodman album, but, since we're trying to stick with rock 'n roll purity, we should go with [a] *Blonde on Blonde* if you like. *Freak Out!* was released just a coupla months after *Blonde...*

683. The original cover showed drummer Don Stephenson flipping the bird so, those things being taboo for the day, Columbia went back in and airbrushed it out on all subsequent albums. The LP was heralded for many things, not the least of which being a marketing feat by the label releasing five singles at once when the album came out.

684. Lloyd's first version had Stagger Lee and Billy gambling with Stagger Lee shooting Billy at the end. Then, after ABC-Paramount caught hell from the public, they recut another version where Stagger and Billy are arguing over a girlfriend, who goes back to Stagger at the end. The tune was built on the Blues standard "Ballad of Stack-o-Lee" of which there are some 200 different versions from Taj Mahal, Doc Watson, even Samuel L. Jackson in the movie *Black Cat Moan*.

685. [a] RCA in 1951 where he recorded four singles, then on to Peacock for two more, then Specialty where he had all of his hits ("Tutti Frutti", etc.). In '64-65, he found a little-known guitarist who called himself "Maurice James" and took him in to be his touring guitarist and used him on at least 12 recordings. Maurice went on to become Jimi Hendrix. For those of you who haven't given away your copy of BTO's *Head On* to Goodwill, dig it

out and check out "Take It Like a Man" – that's Little Richard on piano.

686. [d] Tim Hardin. Not much in the way of clever I can write about a guy who quit high school to join the military, discovered heroin in 'Nam, and let his addiction eventually run his life. Sorry.

687. [c] Teacher. As a matter of fact, the first African-American student teacher at an all-white school near Chevy Chase, Maryland. After graduating from Howard University she took a job teaching music and English for $2800 a year in North Carolina, then moved back to DC to teach Junior High. All the while, she played music at nightclubs and got a chance to do her own thing in between sets. One night when she was doing a benefit gig, jazz saxman Les McCann caught her act and arranged for an audition with Atlantic Records, where she did 40+ songs in 3 hours for Joel Dorn, one of the label's producers. And when she got signed the speed-of-sound continued, recording *First Take* in a mind-blowing 10 hours.

688. Johnny Cash. Now, we have to admit that the good Mister Cash certainly seems like the type and he did land his butt in *jail* seven times for misdemeanors, but he was never in for more than a night. He did come dang close once when the Feds collared him for what they thought was heroin he was bringing into El Paso from across the border but it turned out to be prescription narcotics and amphetamines and he got off with a suspended sentence. Ike Turner? Weapons. Sid?

Assault (on Patti Smith's brother). Berry? Armed robbery, the Mann Act, tax evasion. James B? Theft, assault, drugs. Gary Glitter? Don't ask.

689. [a] and [d] Straight and Bizarre. The original idea was to put the more mainstream acts on Straight and the more bizarre ones on (you guessed it!) Bizarre, but things didn't work out that way, completely. Zappa, Capt. Beefheart, Lenny Bruce, and Wild Man Fischer were on Bizarre, with Alice Cooper, Tim Buckley, and the Persuasions on Straight. If you said, "...but where is DiscReet Records", they came into the picture after Zappa and Cohen dissolved Straight and Bizarre. It was Frank's intention for DiscReet to be a quadraphonic-based label ("discrete" - get it?).

690. [b] The Olympics. To hear Felix Cavaliere tell it, he heard the original on one of NYC's R&B stations, dug it, and the band started to do an up-tempo version as part of their live act. Tom Dowd, their producer, liked what he heard and had them try and replicate it in the studio. The band thought it sucked, but the band wasn't in charge of what got released, was it? The bonus brownie points? If you guessed that the similarity was that "Good Lovin'", "Paperback Writer", and "Monday, Monday" all had a false ending, you'd be right.

691. [a] "Red Rubber Ball" which became the Cyrkle's first of two hits ("Turn-Down Day" the other). The band's bassist (Tom Dawes) was the tour bassist for Simon & Garfunkel and Paul offered it to the band who was managed by Brian Epstein and

whose name had been crafted by John Lennon. Luckily, they didn't look a gift horse in the mouth and recorded it. Epstein, then, secured them the opening slot on the Beatles '66 Summer tour. Dawes went on to write jingles like "Plop, Plop, Fizz, Fizz" for Alka-Seltzer and produce Foghat.

692. "Papa Was a Rolling Stone" ("...Talkin' about saving souls and all the time leeching") [dadgumit]. The opening line – about the "3rd of September, the day my daddy died" – was a little thorny for Temp Dennis Edwards since his pa did die on September 3rd and producer Norman Whitfield wasn't going to let him back off of it until he got the full brunt of Dennis' anguish over having to sing the line down on tape.

693. [c] *Tumbleweed Connection*. It's also one of the rare occasions that there was a song written by someone other than Elton (and Bernie). In this case, "Love Song" by Lesley Duncan who had previously appeared as a singer on the Floyd's *Dark Side of the Moon*.

694. The City and Jo Mama. The City was Carole, hubby Charles Larkey, and Danny Kortchmar (w/ Jim Gordon on drums) and had one LP on Ode in '69 which debuted "Hi De Ho" and "Wasn't Born to Follow". Jo Mama had two albums on Atlantic – *Jo Mama* and *J is for Jump* – and also had Larkey and Kortchmar, plus Abigail Haness on vocals with Carole guesting on bg vocs on *J is for Jump* which also has the first known version of "Smackwater Jack" that showed up later on

Tapestry and "Machine Gun Kelly" that JT picked up for *Mud Slide Slim*. Flick freaks will note that both Jo Mama and Kortchmar had a moment in *This is Spinal Tap* – there was a character named Joe "Mama" Besser and Kortchmar had a cameo as Ronnie Pudding, the Tap's former bass player.

695. [a] Sugarloaf in "Don't Call Us, We'll Call You". Pissed at CBS for turning them down ("Green-eyed Lady" wasn't big enough, I presume), the band added in the touch tones of a phone number at Columbia as well as a public number at the White House. To further run their angst up the label's hind end, they added riffs from the Beatles' "I Feel Fine" and Stevie Wonder's "Superstition".

696. [c] Jackie Wilson's "Higher and Higher". There is a string that runs through all of the multiple choices, though – a guy named Carl Davis who produced all of the tunes. But, I digress... the Funk Bros. were studio cats who played on what has to be every single Motown hit but never credited until Marvin Gaye's *What's Going On* (Marvin was even one of the group's drummers in the early '60s). Go back further and you'll find them billed as "Earl Van Dyke & the Soul Brothers", because Berry Gordy didn't like the word "funk". They were a creative bunch, too, using snow chains as percussion on Martha & the Vandellas' "Nowhere to Run" and a tire iron on "Dancing in the Streets".

697. Andrew Gold's "Thank You for Being a Friend". Andrew comes from good stock – his dad was Ernest Gold who scored more than 100 movies

(*Exodus, On the Beach*, etc.) and his mom, Marni Nixon, dubbed many of the singing parts for screen stars like Marilyn Monroe (*Diamonds Are a Girl's Best Friend*), Natalie Wood's part in *West Side Story*, and Audrey Hepburn's part in *My Fair Lady*. Andrew has the distinction of being the first human voice to be heard on the Mars when his version of the sitcom *Mad About You* theme song ("Final Frontier") was played as a wake-up call for the '96 Mars Pathfinder mission.

698. Second. Dave Evans was the first, but the band thought he was a little too "glam" and kicked him to the ground after about a year. Interestingly enough, the man who replaced Scott after his death by misadventure, Brian Johnson, came from Geordie, a British glam band.

699. [d – a, b, *and* c] Stanley "Bear" Owsley was the sound guy and acid supplier for the Dead, as well as the guy who came with the skull and lightning logo (w/ bud Bob Thomas)... plus, he was the guy who inspired "Kid Charlemagne" by Steely Dan, "Who Needs the Peace Corps" by the Mothers of Invention, Jefferson Airplane's "Bear Melt" and "Mexico", and the Dead's "Alice D. Millionaire" (when Mr. Owsley was busted with 350,000 doses of LSD and sent off to prison, a headline identified Stanley as an "LSD Millionaire").

700. Lovers, muggers, and thieves. The song was written by Ed Cobb who used to be in the Four Preps and who went on to write "Tainted Love" that Soft Cell painted the '80s with.

701. [d] The Cars' *Candy-O*. The band's drummer, David Robinson, was also the band's art director and an avid pin-ups collector was responsible for the idea but Vargas was 83 years old and retired. Fortunately, his niece was a fan of the Cars and gave him the necessary nudge. The model, whose name was Candy, even had a little fling with Robinson post-photoshoot.

702. "And I'm not a little boy" *or* "I'm not your little boy". Neville recorded the track for Par-Lo Records and it went to #1 on the R&B charts and #2 on the Pop charts, but the label went broke before Aaron saw a penny.

703. Because the "Eater" (it wasn't purple – it *ate* purple people) wanted to <u>be in a rock and roll band</u> – just like the rest of us! Sheb Wooley was the artist. Essentially, a Western kind of guy, he was in *The Outlaw Josey Wales, Giant,* and *Rawhide.* Even wrote the theme song for the TV's *Hee-Haw.* After "Purple People Eater" hit, others jumped on the bandwagon: Joe South did "The Purple People Eater Meets the Witch Doctor" (Big Bopper covered it on the flip of "Chantilly Lace"), and Bo Diddley did "Purple People".

704. "Peggy Sue Got Married". He recorded the song in his Manhattan apartment all by his lonesome and in December '58; then, studio cats did overdubs about six months later (or four months after he died). Don't be fooled by the version that Norman Petty did in '64 with Jimmy Gilmer and the Fireballs doing more of a surf guitar'ish track

behind Holly's vocal. The one you want is the one you hear in the *Peggy Sue Got Married* flick – the rare, unadorned, apartment version.

705. [a] The Wailers. Some think that Bob Marley wrote the song but he wrote Nash's *follow-up* "Stir It Up".

706. [a] "Something in the Air" by Thunderclap Newman, a band that Pete Townshend put together to play the songs of Speedy Keene, the Who's roadie and the guy who had written "Armenia in the Sky" on *The Who Sell Out*. Townshend produced it, did the string arrangements, and even played bass under the pseudonym of Bijou Drains. A 15-year old Jimmy McCulloch played lead guitar – the same Jimmy McCulloch who joined Wings and did the lead on "Juniors Farm". Ironically, he wrote the anti-drug song "Medicine Jar" on *Venus and Mars* and, then, wound up dying of a heroin overdose at age 26.

707. Well, I tried to be fussy by putting an underline on rock and roll act, and if I stick to my guns, [b] The Easybeats are the answer with "Friday on My Mind" in 1966, however the Seekers' – a *folk* act – were worldly a year before. Two of the Easybeats bandmates – Harry Vanda and George Young – produced the first six AC/DC albums (which featured George's younger brothers Angus and Malcolm), and wrote/produced "Love Is in the Air" by John Paul Young (no relation).

708. [a, b, *and* c] "Put a Little Love in Your Heart" (written with her bro, Randy Myers, and Jimmy Holiday), "Bette Davis Eyes" (written with Donna

Weiss seven years before Kim Carnes had a hit with it), and "Come and Stay With Me" (some say written with Jimmy Page who she was shagging at the time, but BMI doesn't listen him as a co-writer, nonetheless she did write two songs with Pagey, we do know that). She's married to Randy Edelman who wrote "Weekend in New England" for Manilow. More useless knowledge, more often.

709. "...I'm the son of a bitch that named you Sue!" It written by Shel Silverstein, who also wrote "Sylvia's Mother" and "Cover of the Rolling Stone" for Dr. Hook, "The Unicorn" for the Irish Rovers, and composed the soundtrack to *Ned Kelly* which starred Mick Jagger (with Waylon Jennings and Kris Kristofferson singing the songs). The inspiration for "A Boy Named Sue" came from humorist Jean Shepherd, one of Silverstein's buds and someone who knows what a drag it is growing up with a chick-sounding name.

710. [b] NBC's *Midnight Special*. For the most part, the show was hosted by a different artist each week – short of a nine-month stretch that Helen Reddy did – and Wolfman Jack's voice was the thread that ran true through all of 'em. The Wolfman was a hot commodity during that period, guesting on the Guess Who's "Clap for the Wolfman", Sugarloaf's "Don't Call Us, We'll Call You", Flash Cadillac & the Continental Kids' "Did You Boogie (with Your Baby)", as well as being canonized in Todd Rundgren's "Wolfman Jack" on *Something/ Anything?* Da Wolfman even released an album on Wooden Nickel in 1972. However, the single "I

Ain't Never Seen a White Man" bubbled under and never made it past #106. And why did *Midnight Special* go off the air? It was canceled at the request of Dick Ebersol as part of a deal for him to take over then-ailing *Saturday Night Live*.

711. The Stones *Beggar's Banquet* but only on the reissue. Both London (U.S.) and Decca (U.K.) were both steadfast on their thumbs-down on the toilet version and, after much wranglin', the Stones finally gave in. You're probably not aware of it, but for the first 30 years of the album's life, it played back at the wrong-o speed! There was a snafu in the mastering process and it was produced at a *slower* speed than it was recorded. On the 2002 ABKCO release, they corrected the mistake which also changes the timing of the album (shorter by about 30 seconds) and the key of each and every song.

712. You're close if you said [a] Dick Clark (*American Bandstand*), but it was actually [b] Dick's wife (Barbara, I believe) who did the name dubbing. When the chubby one did a session for Clark – one where he mimicked Fats Domino – Clark's wife asked Ernest Evans (his real name) what his name was and he said "My friends call me 'Chubby'". Given the impression of Fats he had just done, she said, "As in Checker?" So, with the wordplay of Fats v. Chubby and Domino v. Checker, you've got the story. Bob Horn? He was the original host of *Bandstand* but when he got popped for a DUI, Dickie boy took over.

713. [b] Tom Rush. He covered three Joni songs – "Circle Game", "Urge for Going", and "Tin Angel", as well as James Taylor and Jackson Browne tunes – on his '68*Circle Game* LP, long before those folks were on anyone's radar. Stepping a little to our right and donning our cowboy hat, George Hamilton IV's version of "Urge for Going" was Joni's first song to achieve *commercial* success, albeit on the C&W charts.

714. [a] "Fly Robin Fly" which has six unique words because the group was German and had trouble learning English so they kept the brain vise to a low roar by repeating the chorus of "Fly, robin, fly" three times and an ending of "Up, up to the sky!" "Hava Nagila" has 10; "In-A-Gadda..." and "Her Majesty" 34; "You Are So Beautiful" 31.

715. And, here are the A-Z's of one-hit-wonders...

    a. "Born to Be Alive " - Patrick Hernandez
    b. "Israelites " - Desmond Dekker & the Aces
    c. "My Boy Lollipop " - Millie Small - considered the first international ska hit
    d. "You, I "- The Rugbys
    e. "The Pied Piper " - Crispian St. Peters
    f. "Ballad of the Green Berets" - Sgt. Barry Sadler (and a real Green Beret)
    g. "Reflections of My Life " - Marmalade (the Brits will argue that Marmalade was not a one-hit wonder in their parts and they'd be right)
    h. "Oh, Happy Day " - Edwin Hawkins Singers

i. "Beautiful Sunday " – Daniel Boone (it's the biggest selling single of all-time by an international artist on the Japanese *Oricon* chart (their version of *Billboard*).
j. "How Do You Do" – Mouth & MacNeal
k. "I'm Easy" – Keith Carradine (from the movie *Nashville*)
l. "Gallant Men "- Sen. Everett McKinley Dirksen (written by CBS' Charles Osgood)
m. "Men in My Little Girl's Life – Mike Douglas
n. "One Tin Soldier " – Coven (or Original Caste)
o. "Lay a Little Lovin' On Me" – Robin McNamara
p. "Rubber Duckie " – Ernie (voice by Jim Henson)
q. "For the Good Times" – Ray Price
r. "Thunder Island – Jay Ferguson (originally in Spirit, but now doing music for TV/film [he did the theme to *The Office*])
s. "Chirpy Chirpy Cheep Cheep" - Mac & Katie Kissoon (Katie went on to be a backup singer for Van Morrison, Eric Clapton, Elton John, and Roger Waters)
t. "Desiderata" – Les Crane (married to Tina Louise – "Ginger" – on *Gilligan's Isle*)
u. "Day by Day – Godspell (yes, the same one that Ben Stiller uses as his prayer when asked to give the blessing in *Meet the Parents*)
v. "Good Time Charlie... " – Danny O'Keefe
w. "Hot Child in the City " – Nick Gilder

x. "Pop Muzik " – M

y. "Reach Out of the Darkness " - Friend & Lover (Jim Post and Cathy Conn [later Post]). The track was recorded in Nashville and features Joe South and Ray Stevens. BTW, Jim became a Chicago folkie, and legendary for being the first to record Steve Goodman's "City of New Orleans".

z. "Precious and Few" – Climax (Sonny Geraci was the lead singer for both Climax *and* the Outsiders ["Time Won't Let Me"] and a young Chuck Mangione did the chart arrangements for the Outsiders.)

Bonus question: Tommy Facenda with "High School U.S.A." It started with his home state (Virginia) version where he mentioned various local high schools, then Atlantic picked up on the notion and had him do localized versions for 27 other metros around the country, each mentioning local high schools. All the different versions were combined into one chart entry that hit Top 30 on both the Black Singles and the Hot 100 charts.

716. Oliver (last name "Swofford") with "Jean" and "Good Morning Starshine". After a couple of other tries – including an attempt to hook up, musically, with Karen Carpenter (who, I presume, is not Rock & Roll Heaven's caterer) – Oliver hung it up and became a pharmaceutical rep.

717. "Lady Marmalade". Fifty dollah, no hollah. One could write a whole tome on Crewe, but here's a thumbnail: Wrote/produced most of the 4

Seasons' hits, arranged Mitch Ryder's hits, had his own with "Music to Watch Girls By", owned DynoVoice Records (the Toys, *Barbarella* soundtrack), did the Oliver hits we quizzed you on earlier, created Disco Tex and the Sex-O-Lettes. He and Nolan also wrote "My Eyes Adored You" which the 4 Seasons recorded for MoWest but the label balked at releasing it, so Crewe bought it back for $4k and shopped it around until Private Stock bought it but would release it with only Frankie Valli's name, sans Seasons.

718. Buster Poindexter, whose "Hot, Hot, Hot" has been the opening theme for Jimmy Buffett's live gigs for years.

719. [b] Jerry Jeff Walker. Contrary to popular belief, the song ain't about the infamous Bill "Bojangles" Robinson, but rather an ambiguous alcoholic Caucasian, according to Walker. Jerry Jeff is immortalized in Waylon & Willie's "Luckenbach, Texas" and Jerry Jeff co-wrote "Railroad Lady" (from *A White Sport Coat and a Pink Crustacean*) while riding the last run of the Panama Limited with Jimmy Buffett. He's also the one who first took Buffett to Key West, cruisin' down in Walker's old Packard.

720. [a] Traffic and [b] Little Feat. Three Dog Night had Floyd Sneed who was an African-Canadian and the Allmans had Jaimoe. I know you Feat freaks are saying "what about Sam Clayton?" and the Traffic jammers are raising the question of Reebop, but Sammy didn't show up until the *second*

incarnation of Little Feat and Anthony "Reebop" Kwaku Baah joined Winwood and company in '71 for *Welcome to the Canteen*.

721. [a] WAR's "Cisco Kid"... and Renaldo (Cisco) doesn't "drink wine", either. He really is a teetotaler. The song came about because WAR's Howard Scott was lamenting that Hispanics had no heroes of their own. All of the cowboy heroes - Roy Rogers, Gene Autry, Hopalong Cassidy - were caucasian, but not Cisco.

722. I think Running Bear might have gotten lucky in Kentucky, but the answer is [b] "Hooked on a Feeling" - the Blue Swede version. The "ooka shaka" chant was not original to the Swedes, my little trivia students. Jonathan King ("Everyone's Gone to the Moon") was the first to do the chant in his version of "Hooked..." three years earlier, but Blue Swede liked it enough to cop the idea. In *Subliminal Seduction,* Key claimed "ooka shaka" is changed to "who got sucked off" at 0:33 into the tune, but you'll have to be the judge. Key sound familiar? He was one of the expert witnesses who testified in that case concerning Judas Priest, subliminal messages, and a suicide pact between two young men in Nevada.

723. [a] Rush: Trio; [b] Ramones: Quartet (but a trio during early rehearsals); [c] the Kinks: You get points for Quartet *or* Quintet as they started out as a foursome and added a fifth - a keyboardist - as they were recording "Lola"; [d] the Dells: Quintet; [e] The Band: Quintet; [f] Sex Pistols: Quartet.

724. Neil Young. He bought it from Tut Taylor around the time Neil was recording *Comes a Time*. Best as I can tell, Hank Jr. had traded the guitar to someone for some guns, then that someone (whoever it was), sold it to Tut who had a guitar shop in Nashville called "GTR" (now Gruhn's). Neil's friend Grant Boatwright (Nashville session cat), tracked it down to Tut, who, then, sold it to Neil. Side note: Neil loans out the guitar on occasion to people he think should play it, like the time he loaned Dylan his tour bus and left the guitar on his bed with a note to enjoy its company for awhile.

725. Paul Anka. Yes, he did all the things I mentioned: the *Tonight Show* theme (a reworking of a song called "It's Really Love" that he wrote for Annette Funicello), Buddy Holly's "It Doesn't Matter Anymore", etc. He even shows up as doing the music for the war film *The Longest Day*. Most of us (fondly or indifferently) remember him for "(You're) Having My Baby" with Odia Coates*. The song had good intentions as it was meant as an ode to his pregnant-with-child wife, but the National Organization for Women thought of it in a less than shining light and gave Anka the "Keep Her in Her Place" award. *Odia also did the vocals on John Denver's "Take Me Home Country Roads".

726. Miles, yes; Coltrane, apparently not. While you might question Miles' ethics for having done the deed, he did play a horn solo on Scritti Politti's "Oh Patti" on *Provision*, and as the lead on Toto's "Don't Stop My Now" on *Fahrenheit*. You'll see he and Coltrane sampled on some stuff, even listed

on Santana's *Milagro* LP, but our understanding is that those were old Coltrane recordings that they just laid in to the session.

727. "I Don't Like Mondays" by the Boomtown Rats. Bob Geldof wrote the song after reading a wire service report on the tragedy while he was hanging out at WRAS, Georgia State University's campus radio station. Balls-to-the-walls, the Rats debuted the song in San Diego less than a month later. It was a Number One single in the U.K., but most U.S. radio stations shied away from it because of its sensitivity and the fact that Geldof had said some rather pissy things about U.S. radio.

728. Points for getting *any* of the following correct... Georgio did/had/whatever'ed: Musicland Studios, a recording studio in Munich where Queen, Zep, Stones, ELO, Donna Summer, Deep Purple, T. Rex, Elton recorded ...co-wrote "I Feel Love", "Love to Love You Baby" for Donna Summer ... had a hit of his own with "Son of Your Father", the first U.K. #1 to prominently feature a synthesizer (played by Chris Thomas who produced INXS, Sex Pistols, Pretenders) ... did the soundtracks to *American Gigolo, Cat People, Midnight Express,* and *Scarface,* as well as "Take My Breath Away" on the *Top Gun* soundtrack.

729. [a] Jeffrey Osborne: L.T.D.; [b] Ben E. King: the Drifters; [c] Sam Cooke: the Soul Stirrers, the group that was also the incubator for Lou Rawls and Johnnie Taylor ("Who's Making Love", "Disco Lady"); [d] Marvin Gaye: the Moonglows; [e]

Lionel Richie: the Commodores (hey, I had to give you one easy one!); [f] Minnie Riperton: Rotary Connection.

730. [a] Billy J. Kramer who was managed by Brian Epstein and for whom John & Paul wrote "I'll Keep You Satisfied" and "Bad to Me".

731. Canned Heat, who were named after Tommy Johnson's 1928 tune, "Canned Heat Blues". No doubt you remember them from watching *Woodstock* or hearing "On the Road Again" or "Going Up the Country" in ads. Al "Blind Owl" Wilson (guitarist/singer named for his nearsightedness) was such a good Bluesman that Stephen Stills dedicated "Blues Man" to Al (Jimi, and Duane) on *Manassas*.

732. Asylum Records, the home of Jackson Browne, Carly Simon, the Eagles, Tom Waits, Linda Ronstadt, Joni Mitchell (he was the subject of "Free Man in Paris"), even Dylan for awhile. He co-founded Asylum with Elliott Roberts (an artist manager), then sold it to Warner who merged it with Elektra. Then, he started Geffen Records, got into backing Broadway shows like *Dreamgirls* and *Cats*, produced the flicks *Beetlejuice* and *Risky Business*, so on and so forth. He's said to be worth about $6.5 bil (with a "b").

733. "King(s)" – Evelyn Champagne *King*, Elvis - *King* of Rock 'n Roll, *King*ston Trio, and *King* Harvest.

734. <u>All</u> the answers are correct, babycakes! Here's the lowdown on the incarnations which is probably the one you missed: 1 - Sting, Stewart, and Henry

Padovani; 2 - Andy, Sting, Stewart, and Henry Padovani; 3 - and, finally, the lineup of Andy, Sting, and Stewart. Did I hear you scream, "Who is Henry Padovani?" Henry was the first guy Stewie approached to be in the band and was in the group long enough to record the band's first single ("Fall Out" b/w "Nothing Achieving"). At issue was Henry's ability on guitar (something Sting was insistent about), so they recruited Andy and he and Henry shared guitar duties for two months or so, then after a blown session with producer John Cale, Henry was asked to leave. But not all love was lost in the battle as Miles Copeland, the band's manager and owner of IRS Records, solicited Henry to be his Veep, which he did for a decade; and, secondly, he was invited to play "Next to You" with the current lineup during the encore of their final show in gay Paree.

735. The Twist was an invention of Mr. Hank Ballard (w/ the Midnighters) in 1959. He wrote it, invented the dance, but didn't have the hit (it came out on the flip side of his "Tears on Your Letter"). Chubby Checker released his version the same year, hit #1, took a year off, got re-released, and hit #1, again*! The first – and only – record in the Rock era to have successful bookends to a vacation on the charts. Back to Hank, now... His "Work With Me, Annie" was his (and the Midnighters') biggest hit (#1, R&B) but his follow-ups got him in hot water with the FCC and they banned "Annie Had a Baby" and "Annie's Aunt Fannie". That didn't stop him, though. He released songs like

"Open Up the Back Door", where there's the line "I want to make a little cream". Blowfly has nothin' on this cat. *Other songs to hit #1 more than once are "Go Away Little Girl", "Locomotion", "Please Mr. Postman", and "When a Man Loves a Woman" (yes, the Michael Bolton one did the trick).

736. [a] *West Side Story* (the movie soundtrack) – an astonishing 54 weeks at the top. If you're comparing apples to apples, *Thriller* did 37 weeks, *Rumours* and Harry Belafonte's *Calypso* did 31. *Dark Side of the Moon* was on the charts longer than any other, raking up some 741 weeks.

737. Isley Brothers "That Lady". "Who's That Lady" was the 1964 tune they updated for in 1973 for *3+3*, the album where the three original Isleys added two little brothers and a cuz and became a six-pack of burnin', churnin' funk.

738. "25 or 6 to 4" (Chicago). People have tried to lay drug references, Cockney slang for a hooker, even cricket scores on the phrase but, at the end of the day, Robert Lamm just couldn't sleep and wasn't exactly sure what time it really was.

739. Not that we can summon up Rick – or George – for verification, but we understand that he is alluding to George Harrison as "Mr. Hughes", a name he used as an alias when travelling. Rick was, after all, George's next door neighbor in L.A. and we assume George tipped him off to that little dodge. According to the grapevine, *"hid in Dylan's shoes"* refers to an album of Dylan covers Harrison was planning that was never realized. The line, "Wearing his disguise", is a bit murky, but in all

probability had something to do with Harrison's tendency of traveling incognito.

740. 73 – the number of keys on Mike Pinera's Fender Rhodes as he was writing the song.

741. Harry Truman. Harry Truman. "America needs you, Harry Truman" sayeth Chicago and "So long Harry Truman. Goddam, it's hard to find an honest man," sayeth Danny O'Keefe (from *So Long, Harry Truman* which was produced by John Boylan, the man responsible for those ten billion *Boston* albums and for introducing Linda Ronstadt to a bunch of guys who became her backing band and, then, turned themselves into a little 'ol cowboy band called the Eagles.).

742. [c] "Dreadlock Holiday". According to 10cc's Eric Stewart, "Justin Hayward and I had decided to go parasailing. That's when they strap a parachute to you and you're towed behind a speedboat, so it's almost like flying. There were three black guys with us and one turned to Justin and said. 'Hey man. I'll give you a dollar for your camera.' Justin said: 'Don't be silly.' This guy then offered to pay 50 cents for the silver chain Justin was wearing. When Justin refused, quite politely, this guy suddenly said, 'If this was Jamaica man, I'd cut your hand off.' It was at this point that my parasail took off, me with it, leaving Justin in the middle of the ocean with this bizarre situation."

743. [b] David Ruffin. And he sang lead on "Ain't Too Proud to Beg", "I Wish It Would Rain", "All I Need", "I'm Losing You", "Beauty's Only Skin

Deep", etc. Things started to unravel for David when he requested that the group should be called "David Ruffin & the Temptations" after Motown gave Diana Ross first position in "...and the Supremes" and his ego lost its wheels from there. Eventually, the Temps had enough and canned his butt. He had one hit ("My Whole World Ended"), then hit the drug skids, time in the big house for not paying his taxes, and died after a crackcapade. He was so broke when he died, Michael Jackson fed the tip jar to help pay for his funeral.

744. [b] Tokens. Neil and the band recorded two singles which flopped. Then, Neil met Howie Greenfield and four years and 40 million records later, the Tokens were just a faint memory. They, on the other hand, had their own serendipity with "The Lion Sleeps Tonight"* and, as producers, scored hits for Randy & the Rainbows, the Chiffons, the Happenings. *The song's origin? Some Zulu cat named Solomon Linda wrote "Mbube" (Lion) in the 40s, sold more than 100,000 copies, then sold the rights for 10 shillings (less than a coupla bucks) to his label. Musicologist Alan Lomax discovered the song, gave it to Pete Seeger who redubbed it "Wimoweh" and had a 50s hit with it with the Weavers. A guy named George Weiss then rewrote it into "The Lion Sleeps Tonight" and that's the Tokens version most know. After the tune made $15 mil for its use in *The Lion King*, Linda's heirs went to court and settled for their fair share.

745. Gospel was good to Elvis – it provided him his only Grammy awards. In the sessions and on-stage, he employed several gospel groups: Blackwood Brothers (the first people to convert a passenger bus into a tour bus for group travel), Imperials Quartet, the Jordanaires, J.D. Sumner &

the Stamps Quartet. We'll even give you a point if you said the Sweet Inspirations since they emerged out of the Drinkard Singers, a prominent '50s gospel group who were the first gospel group to make an album on a major label (*A Joyful Noise* on RCA), and counted among their members Cissy Houston (aka Emily Drinkard), Whitney Houston's momma. The Sweet Inspirations are on more records than you can shake a stick at – Hendrix' "Burning of the Midnight Lamp", Dusty Springfield's *Dusty in Memphis,* Van Morrison's "Brown Eyed Girl", Frankie Valli's "Grease", Aretha, Wilson Pickett, James Gang...

746. [d] *Shakedown Street,* the name given to the area where vendors set up their tents at a music festival. If you wanna quiz a Deadhead on what the only "disco" song the band ever did, the title track comes dang close given what Clive Davis was pushing the band toward in disco's heyday.

747. [a] Motown. Sister label Tamla's was "The Sound that makes the world go 'round" and sister label Gordy's was "It's What's in the Grooves that Counts"; [b] is STAX (an earlier version was a "stack" of records); [c] is Don "Sooooooo-ul Train" Cornelius. Soul Train Records included the Whispers and Shalamar (with Jody Watley, a *Soul Train* dancer). [d] Immediate Records was started by Andrew Loog Oldham, the Stones manager/ producer. The hit was "Out of Time" by Chris Farlowe, a chap Jagger gave first dibs to for "Paint It Black" and a few other tunes he and Keith penned. Immediate's very first single was a British

licensing deal for the McCoys' "Hang On Sloopy". They also had Mayall's Bluesbreakers for a single ("I'm Your Witchdoctor", produced by Jimmy Page) - which showcased Mayall's first appearance of Clapton, and the first attempt at a single ("Little Miss Understood") by Rod Stewart. [e] Monument Records. One of their places in music history is for discovering Leona Douglas, the first African-American female to record as a Country artist. They were also home to Boots Randolph who hit with "Yakety Sax" and does the sax yakkin' on Orbison's "Mean Woman Blues".

748. February 3, 1959: The "day the music died" (the Buddy Holly plane crash)... February 9, 1964: The first appearance of the Beatles on *Ed Sullivan* (and during the time 'Sullivan' was on that night, there was not one single incident of juvenile crime in the entire U.S.)... June 16, 1967: the Monterey Pop Festival starts... August 15, 1969: Woodstock begins... December 8, 1980: Lennon shot and killed... July 3, 1971: Jim Morrison's death... August 16, 1977: Elvis died.

749. [a] CSN/"Suite: Judy Blue Eyes"; [b] "My Way"; [c] "Desperado" by the Eagles; [d] from the soundtrack of Mary Poppins, it's "British Bank" (oh, c'mon - you've seen the dang movie and you know it. I think God likes Julie Andrews and you might wanna start liking her, too.); [e] "Goodbye Stranger" by Supertramp; [f] the track that Paul Simon wrote in the after effects of the JFK assassination, "The Sounds of Silence". It's a song some will remember as having two versions –the

low-fi, acoustic one on *Wednesday Morning, 3 A.M.* in the Spring of '64 and an electric version that came out a year later – the one that became a hit. After *Wednesday Morning's* bellyflop, the duo split up and Paul went to England. Fast forward a year or so where Tom Wilson – Dylan and S&G's producer – was wrapping up the production on "Like a Rolling Stone" and got the wild hair to beef up "Sounds of Silence" without consulting Paul or Artie. He brought in Al Gorgoni (the guy who did the lead guitar on "Brown-eyed Girl", all of the early Neil Diamond and 4 Seasons hits), Bobby Gregg (drummer on *Bringing It All Back Home* and *Highway 61 Revisited*), and Bob Bushnell (who also did the Neil Diamond hits as well as cutting his teeth with Elmore James) and gave the track some muscle – and enough incentive for Paul and Art to reunite.

750. "The End". And, this *is* The End, my only friend. The end.

Now, on to the bonus questions…

751. "Landslide", a song that Stevie Nicks wrote at a fork in her road – one where she was either going back to school or continuing on with guitarist Lindsey Buckingham following Buckingham Nicks being dropped by Polydor. She was hanging out in Aspen, Colorado, sitting in someone's living room when the idea struck by "looking out at the Rocky Mountains pondering the avalanche of

everything that had come crashing down on us... at that moment, my life truly felt like a landslide in many ways."

752. ELO (Electric Light Orchestra). The band claim that their music "picks up where The Beatles' 1967 song 'I Am the Walrus' left off."

753. "Marrakesh Express". The song comes from Nash's real 1966 Moroccan experience where he found First Class to be lackluster and moved back to where the fun with the ducks and chickens was. He offered the tune to the Hollies and they tried it out in the studio, but it never saw the light of day. That and other songs he offered but got panned was one of the reasons he left for CS&N.

754. His father's ashes. In an interview with *NME,* Richards sez, "He was cremated and I couldn't resist grinding him up with a little blow. My dad wouldn't have cared. It went down pretty well".

755. [b] Kurt Cobain and Krist Novoselic of Nirvana. Cross my heart. Yes, and that really was Lily Allen who, on her *It's Not Me, It's You* album, said that Creedence Clearwater Revival is 'His' (God's) favorite band. Hmm... a 737 just fell out of the sky.

756. The Kinks' "You Really Got Me", a song whose distinctive riff came about while Ray Davies was figuring out the chords of The Kingsmen's "Louie Louie". While the rumor is rampant that Page was responsible for the solo, the facts are while he did, in fact, play *rhythm guitar* on a few tracks from The Kinks' first album, the solo on "You Really Got Me" was played by then 17-year-old Dave Davies.

Page's contributions to the album came weeks *after* that session. Jon Lord - future Deep Purple'r - also played keyboards on the same Kinks album. One bit of clarification about "Heart of Stone" - Page played on the alternate version you hear on *Metamorphisis* not the single version.

757. Mad Dogs & Englishmen - the band that backed Cocker's magnum opus of the same name. Leon Russell was "The Master of Space and Time", Jim Price (trumpet) "The Price is Right", Don Preston (guitar) "The Gentle Giant", Claudia Linnear (vocals) "The Stellar Gypsy", and Bobby Keys (sax) "The Ruby-Lipped Essence of Lubbock Texas". I would've used "Delta Lady" as a clue but everyone knows that refers to Rita Coolidge and I simply wasn't going to make this a gimme. The name "Mad Dogs & Englishmen" came from a 1931 Noel Coward song of the same name.

758. Aretha Franklin - for "Respect", "Chain of Fools", "Share Your Love With Me", "Don't Play That Song", "Bridge Over Troubled Water", "To Be Young, Gifted, and Black", "Master of Eyes", and "Ain't Nothing Like the Real Thing". Only one of those was an Aretha self-penned original - "Master of Eyes (The Deepness of Your Eyes)". The others, in order, were Otis Redding's "Respect"; "Chain of Fools", which had been written by Don Covay as a child and sang when he was doin' gospel music with his siblings. It lay sleeping until Jerry Wexler asked Covay to come up with material for Otis Redding, so he did up a demo of himself playing guitar and overdubbing

all the vocals. When he played the song for Redding in Wexler's office, Wexler decided that the song would be better suited for Aretha Franklin; Ben E. King's 1962 R&B hit "Don't Play That Song"; Paul Simon's "Bridge Over..."; Nina Simone's "To Be Young, Gifted and Black" (that she had written in memory of Lorraine Hansberry, the author of the play *Raisin in the Sun*); and, finally, an update of Marvin & Tammi's "Ain't Nothin' Like the Real Thing".

759. Italian songs. What follows that line is a puzzler to all of us. It's a bunch of Italian-sounding nonsense words which appear in the printed lyrics as "?". Even the sheet music arrangements usually read "improvised Italian lyrics" in parentheses after the line.

760. [a] Frank Sinatra. Elvis sang Frank's hit "Witchcraft" and Frank did Presley's "Love Me Tender", a song adapted the tune of "Aura Lee", a sentimental 1861 Civil War ballad. [b] Madonna? Nope - Mariah Carey. It happened in 2008 when Carey hit the top with "Touch My Body". It was her 18th #1. Elvis had 17, Madonna 12.

761. Dean Martin hit #1 with "Everybody Loves Somebody" in 1964 and Sammy Davis Jr. topped the charts with "The Candy Man"* for three weeks in 1972. The "Candy Man" theme was created strictly for *Willy Wonka and the Chocolate Factory* but isn't in the original Roald Dahl book or in the later Johnny Depp version of the movie. Davis wanted to play Bill, the candy store owner, in the

movie but lost out to some other gooey, nutty confectioner. *"Candy Man" featured background vocals by the (California Lt. Governor's) Mike Curb Congregation, who had previously released their own unsuccessful version of the song.

762. [a] and [c] are the ones that are true. Let me 'splain... First, [a]: Arlo's on-site version of "Comin' into Los Angeles"was a bit too stoney and loosey-goosey, so they went back in the studio and beefed it up. If you listen to the version on the Rhino set (*Woodstock: 40 Years On: Back to Yasgur's Farm*) that came out in '09, you'll also hear that Arlo's mic wasn't even on for the first minute or so. "Sea of Madness" by CSN&Y was actually recorded a month *after* the festival at the Fillmore East and "Marrakesh Express" was taken into Atlantic Records' studios to do some overdubs. We were probably too busy getting ourselves "back to the garden" when the soundtrack came out to recognize the exception the producers allowed themselved because the title of the first album set was *Woodstock: Music from the Original Soundtrack and More* so these re-dos and beef-ups must've been part of the "More". [c] Artie Kornfeld who wrote those very songs, as well as 75 other Billboard chart tunes, was indeed one of the four guys who bankrolled the gig. He was also the one who convinced Warners to film the fest. Now, some background on the other falsies... [b] Joni was convinced by her manager that appearing on the *Dick Cavett Show* was more important, so she gleaned the lyric ideas for her song "Woodstock" from watching reports of the event

on the tube in her hotel room and from what her then-beau Graham Nash told her. [d] In total, promoters paid all the acts at Woodstock approximately $172,000. Creedence was the first to sign on for the fest and at a price of $10 thou. The reports on who got what vary, but the Lincoln Journal Star reports that Hendrix got $18k (plus another $12k for the movie), The Who got $11,200, Joe Cocker $1,375, The Dead and Santana $2,250 each. The little guys – like Quill – $375 buckeroos.

763. Zappa had only four chillun and Pilot Inspektor Lee wasn't one of 'em (although he is the son of Jason Lee from the sitcom *My Name is Earl*). FYI, Ian Donald Calvin Euclid Zappa is more well known to we earthlings as "Dweezil". Diva Thin is Frank's youngest and co-wrote "Chana In De Bushwop" with her father that's on *You Can't Do That On Stage Anymore Vol. 3.*

764. "Stand By Me". The flip was "I Am the Greatest". Came out in '64 and never got off the ropes.

765. "Along Comes Mary". The song was written by Tandyn Almer who gained later ink alongside Brian Wilson as a co-writer on a handful of Beach Boys tunes, including "Sail On, Sailor". Almer's most noteworthy contribution to our lives as hipsters may be the Tandyn Slave-Master, a waterpipe that was described in the stoner classic *A Child's Garden of Grass* as "the perfect bong".

766. Bill Clinton. Hillary proclaimed such on *60 Minutes* during Bill's inaugural run at the White

House. Standing by one's man wasn't Tammy's cup of tea, either – she was married five times.

767. There were several – the biggest would be the Pony via his #1 "Pony Time", then the Hucklebuck, the Limbo Rock, and the Fly. The Pony is the dance that you often see Cindy Wilson of the B-52s doing.

768. "Cold Turkey". All three had the experience of trying to get off heroin by going cold turkey. The song's first performance was at the Toronto Peace Festival (*Live Peace in Toronto 1969*) where Yoko introduced it as the newest song written by John; John then added that the band had never played the song together as a group before. It was the first song Lennon took sole credit for ("Give Peace a Chance" was originally credited to he and Paul but later changed to give John sole credit). The lineup included Clapton on lead and Klaus Voorman on bass on both the live and studio versions with Yes' Alan White on drums on the concert version and Ringo on the studio version.

769. [b] Mike Appel toiled in a variety of capacities in the '60s – as the writer/guitarist behind The Balloon Farm's mid-charter "A Question of Temperature", producer/writer for the heavy metal band Sir Lord Baltimore – but his day was made when one of his friends referred Springsteen to him. Bruce auditioned for Appel in '71 and Appel told him to come back when he had more tunes. A year later, when he shows up on his doorstep with serious tuneage, Appel signs him to

a production deal and drags his butt to New York City for an audition with John Hammond. Subsequently, he produced Bruce's first two LPs and some of *Born to Run* when he and the Boss got snitty with each other, sued, settled, (long pause), then eventually made up.

770. [a] "Good Morning Starshine" (Oliver); [b] "The Name Game" (Shirley Ellis); [c] (original version of) "Breaking Up is Hard to Do" (Neil Sedaka); [d] "Sweet City Woman" (The Stampeders); [e] "Get a Job" (The Silhouettes) That's the song where Sha Na Na got its name because the next line in the song is "Get a job Sha na na na, sha na na na na"; [f] "He's So Fine" (The Chiffons).

771. False. It's a long story, but the basic broadstroke version is that Jacko bought the *rights** to <u>most</u> of the Beatles songs for $47.5 mil in 1994 when he acquired ATV's song catalogue that Northern Songs (the publishing arm for the Beatles stuff**) was a part of. However, not everything! The holdouts would "Love Me Do,", "P.S. I Love You,", "Ask Me Why," and "Please, Please Me"that were published before Northern Songs was formed and were part of Paul's MPL Communications. *Paul and John's estate still get their songwriter royalties, trust me. **George's contract with Northern Songs expired in 1968 so he had the rights to his own compositions.

772. "Crossroads" by Robert Johnson. When Johnson released it in '37 on Vocalion, it was titled "Cross Road Blues". There's two different interpretations as to its meaning – one being he was selling his

soul to the Devil in exchange for fame as a famous Bluesman (another Johnson - Tommy [no relation] - claims to have done just that); the other being the fear that many blacks of that day felt about being out alone after dark and getting lynched. The song sat dormant for 30 years until Clapton and Cream did it on *Wheels of Fire* (didja know that EC borrowed some lines from "Traveling Riverside Blues" for this version and/or that Page & Plant added some of their own lines to "Traveling Riverside Blues" so they could get part of the songwriting credit?). *Guitar World* named Eric's solo the 10th best of all-time ("Stairway..." was first; Van Halen's "Eruption" second; then #3 "Freebird", #4"Comfortably Numb", #5"All Along the Watchtower", #6 "November Rain" [G 'n R], #7 "One" [Metallica], #8 "Hotel California", #9 "Crazy Train", then "Crossroads" @ #10). The rehab center Clapton built in Antigua is called Crossroads, too.

773. David Crosby. The kids' names are Bailey Jean and Beckett. Seems like Croz donated considerable seed. As a pup, Crosby fathered two children who were placed for adoption: a son James Raymond in 1962 (when David was 21) and a daughter Erika Keller in 1966. He's reunited with both as adults and Raymond even joined up with Crosby in a group called CPR (with Jeff Pevar) and sometimes appears on-stage as part of the touring bands for Crosby & Nash and Crosby, Stills & Nash.

774. [c] Bonnie Bramlett who was on tour with Stephen Stills when she encountered Elvis in a Holiday Inn

lounge in Columbus, Ohio. Elvis later said he was drunk and "it became necessary for me to outrage these people with about the most obnoxious and offensive remarks that I could muster" in order to bring the conversation to a hasty close.

775. Billy Joel's "The Entertainer"(from *Streetlife Serenade*). What Billy is alluding to is the shortening of "Piano Man" from 5:00 to 3:05 to fit radio's preference for short songs. The gotcha is that while the timing is printed on the 7" as being 3:05, the actual length was 3:48.

776. [a] Lovin' Spoonful from Hurt's "Coffee Blues" (serious double entendre about Maxwell House Coffee "good to the last drop"); [b] Jethro Tull (the agriculturist version invented the seed drill); [c] Procol Harum, although the real name of the breed is Procol Harun, but the band's Keith Reid wrote it down wrong; [d] Three Dog Night.

777. Toto. The big hit on the album – "Lowdown" – was requested by the producers of *Saturday Night Fever*, but Boz turned 'em down and gave permission, instead, to *Looking for Mr. Goodbar*. The drummers among you pull out your copy and slap on the earphones so you can hear one of the early instances of "dual drum tracking" and hard-panning where Jeff Porcaro's eight-note "hi-hatting" can be heard on one channel and his sixteen-note reading on the opposite side.

778. Neil Young/"Ohio". Let me bring in Graham Nash to put a ribbon on the package... "What other band would have a song like 'Teach Your

Children' racing up the charts and, then, immediately, kill it stone dead when four students were killed? Neil wrote 'Ohio' and we recorded it and put it out within 10 days. People in the business thought we were absolutely crazy."

779. It was Teddy, the man who started out as a drummer for The Cadillacs ("Speedo") and kept his seat behind the trap set when the band merged with Harold Melvin and the Blue Notes. Eventually, after doing vocals for the band as they were warming up, he got a chance to do lead and become the focal point. After a few years of people thinking he was "Harold", he demanded that the titling be changed to "...featuring Teddy Pendergrass". In 1977, he went solo and became a hot ticket via his "women only" concerts. In '82, the brakes on his Rolls failed and he suffered a spinal cord injury, leaving him paralyzed from the waist down. He died in January, 2010.

■ ■ ■

Bibliography

WHILE MUCH OF WHAT'S been boiled down to the ink in this book are curiosities I've collected from all my years of being, uh, curious, every author has their limitations. So, without further adieu, I tip my hat to those authors, publications, and websites that helped add some interesting fodder to this tome.

We've worked hard to fact check everything and actually found updated info along the way that changed some of the early data. However, Rock and Roll being what it is, there's always the potential of literary jaundice. That said, if you find *anything* that needs correcting, please let us know (garyworld@gmail.com) and we'll update it in a future edition.

Badhorn, Philippe. "Interview in Rolling Stone" (France). Rolling Stone, Feb. 2006.

Bennett, Bobby, Sarah Smith. The Ultimate Soul Music Trivia Book: 501 Questions and Answers about Motown, Rhythm & Blues, and More. Citadel Press, 1997.

"B.B. King, American Blues Musician". *www.jazzandbluesmasters.com/bbking.htm*

"B.B. King - Lucille Speaks". *www.worldblues.com/bbking/prairie/lucille.html*

"Blind Faith's Original Artwork". *www.angelfire.com/wi/blindfaith/vvcov69.html*

"Blues Terminology". *www.tabernablues.com/autores/terminologia/*

"Bob Dylan and Neil Young". *www.thrasherswheat.org/jammin/dylan.htm*

Bronson, Fred. The Billboard Book of Number One Hits. 5th ed. New York: Billboard Publications, 2003.

Buskin, Richard. Inside Tracks: A First Hand History of Popular Music from the World's Greatest Record Producers and Engineers. Quill, 1999.

Cashmere, Paul. "What George Harrison Thought of Allen Klein". *Undercover.com*, July 5, 2009.

Chapman, Rob. "Brothers Up in Arms". *www.davedavies.com/articles/mojo_0596.htm*

Chat room discussion with Ray Manzarek and Robby Krieger, July 3rd, 1996 *www.thedoors.com*

"Chips Moman". www.answers.com/topic/chips-moman

"Clem Catini". *www.codauk.co.uk/clem_cattini.htm*

Clemens, Fred. "Those Immortal Singing Dogs!" http://www.bobshannon.com/specials/dogs.html

Cohen, Rich. "The Sinatra Doctrine". *The Believer*. June/July2006

"Concerts for Boomtown Rats". *Concert Vault*. *http://concerts.wolfgangsvault.com/Concerts.aspx?stype=artist&id=896*

Creswell, Toby. 1001 Songs: The Great Songs of All Time and the Artists, Stories and Secrets. Da Capo Press, 2006

Dalvano, Rick. "Messing with the Mystic". *http://easyweb.easynet.co.uk/~rthomas/rexdal*

DeMain, Bill. They Call Me Mr. Big – Notorious Rock Managers. *Performing Songwriter*. January/February2006

"Easy Rider: 35 Years Later". Moviemaker.com. June 6, 2004. *www.moviemaker.com/directing/article/easy_rider_35_years_later_2921*

Einarson, John and Richie Furay. For What It's Worth: The Story of Buffalo Springfield. Lanham: Cooper Square Press, 2004.

Fletcher, Tony. Moon: The Life and Death of a Rock Legend. Harper, 2000.

Friedlander, Paul and Miller, Peter. Rock & roll: A Social History. Westview Press, 2006.

Friedman, Roger. "Joni Mitchell's '70s Suicide Attempt" *www.jonimitchell.com/library/view.cfm?id=1853*

Furay, Richie. Live concert from the Narrows Center for the Arts. August 29, 2009. www.mvyradio.com

"George Harrison and The Chiffons" *www.benedict.com/Audio/harrison/harrison.aspx*

Gambaccini, Paul. "The Rolling Stone Interview: Paul McCartney ". Rolling Stone. Issue 0153. January 31, 1974.

Gambaccini, Paul, Tim Rice, and Jo Rice. British Hit Singles. 7th ed. Guinness Superlatives, 1989.

Herzog, David Alan. Test Prep Your IQ with the Essentials of Music and Song. Peterson's, 2003.

Hewitt, Paolo, and John Hellier. Steve Marriott: All Too Beautiful… . Helter Skelter, 2004.

Heylin, Clinton. Bob Dylan: Behind the Shades Revisited. IT Books, 2003.

Holmes, John. Rock Star Babylon: Outrageous Rumors, Legends, and Raucous True Tales of Rock and Roll Icons. Plume, 2008.

Hotshotdigital.com/OldRock/PlattersBio.html

"In Ricky Nelson's "Garden Party, "Who is Mr. Hughes?" *www.straightdope.com/columns/read/2173/inrickynelsonsgardenparty whoismrhughes*

Israel, David K. "On Music: 7 Songs with Fewer Than 35 Words". *Mental Floss,* July, 2008.

Junior, Chris M. "Hop Aboard the Midnight Train to Georgia with Gladys Knight & the Pips". *Goldmine,* May 12, 2008.

Kaiser, Henry. "Jerry Garcia Live!", *Guitar Player,* October, 2007.

Kirkpatrick, Rob. The Words and Music of Bruce Springsteen. Praeger Publishers, 2007.

Konow, David. Bang Your Head. Three Rivers Press, 2009.

Lott, Rod. Crystal Blue Conversation. Hitch Publishing Company, 1995.

Manilow, Barry. "Advice Letter." *Playboy* Dec. 1965.

Marsh, Dave and James Bernard. The New Book of Rock Lists. Fireside, 1994.

McCracken, Mitch. "Sam Phillips selling Elvis' contract to RCA was no mistake". *Little Rock Examiner,* August 31, 2009.

Miles, Barry, Grant Scott, and Johnny Morgan. Greatest Album Covers of All Time. Collins & Brown, 2008.

Moog. DVD. Directed by Hans Fjellestad. 2004. Plexifilm.

Moriarty, Frank. Seventies Rock: The Decade of Creative Chaos. Taylor Trade Publishing, 2003.

Morse, Tim. Classic rock stories: the stories behind the greatest songs of all time. St. Martin's Griffin, 1998.

Motown Records. Lier Notes. 25 Years of Grammy Greats. Motown Records, 1983.

"Music Performer Nicknames". *www.amiright.com/names/nicknames/c.shtml*

Myscow, Nina. "Life is No Holiday for This Super Group". *www.minestrone.org/article004.htm*

Person, Craig. "Caesars Rocks!" *The Windsor Star.* June 19, 2008.

Poulson-Bryant, Scott; Fontaine, Smokey D. What's Your Hi-Fi Q?: From Prince to Puff Daddy, 30 Years of Black Music Trivia

"Rock of Ages" trivia board game.

"Rock Trivia Quiz". Rolling Stone. Issue 552, May 18, 1989. Page 94[c].

"Rust Never Sleeps". *www.thrasherswheat.org/tnfy/rns_album.htm*

"Saturday Night Live transcripts – October 11, 1975". *http://snltranscripts.jt.org/75/75a.phtml*

Simons, Dave. "Tales From the Top: The Rolling Stones' Sticky Fingers (1971)". *http://songwriter101.com/articles/30696_0_6_0_C/*

Skinker, Chris. "Neil Young: The Nashville Sessions". *CMT.com*, September, 1999.

www.SonnyCurtis.com

Sutcliffe, Phil. "Bustle in the Hedgerow". *MOJO*, April, 2000.

"Real Names " *digitaldreamdoor.nutsie.com/pages/realname.html*

"The Atlantic Story". *www.bsnpubs.com/atlantic/atlanticstory.html*

"The History of the Traveling Wilburys " *www.travelingwilburys.com/theband.html*

"The Midnight Special" (synopsis). *www.tv.com/themidnightspecial/show/2974/summary.html&full_summary=1 TV.com*

Trex, Ethan. "How Chuck Berry Became a Beach Boy (and other copyright infringement cases)". *Mental Floss*, June 2008.

Watson, Tom. "Beatles' 1964 Gibson SG and Keith Richards' 1959 Sunburst Les Paul: Results from Christie's Auction". *www.modernguitars.com/archives/000140.html*

Whitburn, Joel. Top Pop Singles 1955-1986. Record Research Inc, 1987.

Whitman, Andy. "Listening to Old Voices: Van Morrison - The Lion In Winter ". *Paste Magazine*, November, 2005

"Who's Next". *www.thewho.net/linernotes/WhosNext.htm*

Wilkerson, Mark. "Amazing Journey: The Life of Pete Townshend". *Lulu.com*, 2006.

Zappa, Frank, and Peter Occhiogrosso. The Real Frank Zappa Book. Fireside, 1990.

Also, the following websites were consulted between the dates of December 10, 2008 and September 15, 2009.

Wikipedia.org
IMDB.com
Billboard.com
classicbands.com
earcandymag.com
AmIWrong.com
www.inthe70s.com
halife.com/trivia/musichtml
TriviaOne.com

■ ■ ■

Acknowledgements

ALONG THE WAY, I've had the fortune of having many wonderful, patient, and as-curious-as-I shotgun riders. People who indulged me, pushed me, and loved me for all the good and bad of my music addiction.

I say a belated thanks to my mother whenever I can. Despite all the thanklessness I showed when she bought me a piano for Christmas at age 6, it was a gift that helped start my journey.

At the same time, my 66-year old father took a more nurturing approach and was the first to show me the joy that music can bring when he bought a record player, planted it outside my bedroom door, and started plying me with Mitch Miller sing-a-longs, Harry Belafonte's "Day-O" and Laurie London's "He's Got the Whole World in His Hands", followed by trips to Randy's Record Mart to buy the Everly Brothers, Elvis, Jimmie Rodgers, and eventually the Beatles and Dylan. It was he who first showed me that it's ok for someone to cry when a song touches them and I'll never visualize "God Bless America" any other way than remembering him with his hand over his heart singing along to Kate Smith on TV.

To my high school band director, Gene Hoggard, who was the first to show me how much fun it was to color outside the lines of music by having our marching band do routines to Dvorak and Sibelius (and winning two state championships with 'em, I might add).

To my longest-running music compadre, Gary Moore, who understands better than anyone that every locale generates its own soundtrack — one created by walking on both sides of the railroad tracks with your ears and heart wide-open.

To Chuck & Jane Tanner and Larry Horton — my 40205 "power trio" — who challenge me, share with me, and look at me funny (and lovingly). They're the local beta-testers for my discoveries and the reason I understand Blues, Americana, and "Der Kommissar" as well as I do.

To all my exes who live in Texas and parts beyond and my old roomies Bill Rieke and Mark Huffman for indulging me my musical whims, ga-gas, and roadtrips.

To Tom Grisham, David Munoz, and Hector Reyes — my San Antonio radio brethren — for showing me how to magnetize one of the most fascinating musical crossroads in America. Anyplace where the Ramones, Willie Nelson, Ted Nugent, Earth Wind & Fire, and Gino Vanelli show up in everyone's album collection is a great sandbox to play in.

To Don Meyers and Bill McMahon for letting me paint all I wanted to without taking the brush out of my hands.

To Sean Ross, who can recite chapter and verse on nearly every local or regional hit that ever got played on the radio and who can mine some of the most fascinating Soul records ever made. I pale in his shadow.

To Erik MacDonald, Freddie Pillot, Tommy Chaltas, Craig Brashear, Michelle Peacock, and the other record promotion people along the way who expanded my horizons, and showed me where the tangents were and how much fun it was chasing them.

To Brett Shepherd who keeps me younger than any Baby Boomer should be allowed to be. Thanks to him, I'm able to drop some "Fever Ray" schnizzle on those whipper-snappers who hold the door open for me and dare call me "sir". Punks!

To John Timmons, Randy Bolton, and Sean Bailey at ear X-tacy, my favorite record store people in the world. Anyone who can connect the dots from José Gonzalez to John Martyn's *Solid Air* and on to parts unknown deserves a standing-O. They still *get* it and they still *got* it.

To others along the way like Ian Ramsey, Darryl Diemer, Evan Thurmond, all the Nielsens, Ernie Garcia, Leslie Graves, Becky Tabb, David Meszaros, Weaks McKinney-Smith, Bill Purdom, Stephanie Bourassa, Rani Melby, and Joe Gallagher who shared music with me or schooled me on some things I might have otherwise missed. You know who you are and I thank you.

To David Emery, who helps keep my eyes open and my soul awake.

To Harry Nilsson for making me believe that even bank tellers have a song to sing, to Jefferson Airplane for introducing me to albums as a unit, to Jim Morrison for showing me the magic of unrepentant fervor, to Al Green and Bruce Springsteen for leaving everything on the floor, to Rodgers & Hammerstein for

The Sound of Music, and to Dar Williams and John Sebastian for always being handy to pump air into my heart with "After All" and "Darling Be Home Soon".

To every musician in the world who follows their own personal bliss whether it's on-stage in front of 10 or 10,000, playing guitar in their bedroom, on the side of a hill, or in a Holiday Inn lounge. And to every music fan who perpetuates the knowledge flow on the web thru blogs, 'pedias, and message boards. Thank you for your help in keeping the notion of music alive.

To my beloved Sheila Blandford who pats me on the head, doesn't ask what's going on between those earphones, or what the difference is between the Flaming Lips and Lipps Inc., and who keeps my feet grounded with the music most of America loves but not enough of us give credit to.

To my daughter, Taylor Lewis Guthrie, who looked up at me at age four and asked what was playing on the radio. "Jimi Hendrix," I said. "Ooh... that's *cooooool,* daddy!". I knew right then and there our musical expedition together was going to be long, fun, and enlightening. God bless you and the Ella Fitzgerald-meets-Kurt Cobain world you brought me — one I trust will carry on down our family line. With you, I know there's a heaven.

Which leads me to thank my Higher Power who gives me equal chances to succeed and fail, and for blessing me with a heart that can hear. He/she are (very) good to G^2 and G^2 is grateful.

■ ■ ■

ROCK
AND ROLL
HEAVEN
ENTRANCE
EXAM

ROCK AND ROLL HEAVEN
ENTRANCE EXAM

Before we do the reveal, wanna take a shot and see how many of these music-related logos (bands, labels, products, albums, etc.) you can get right?

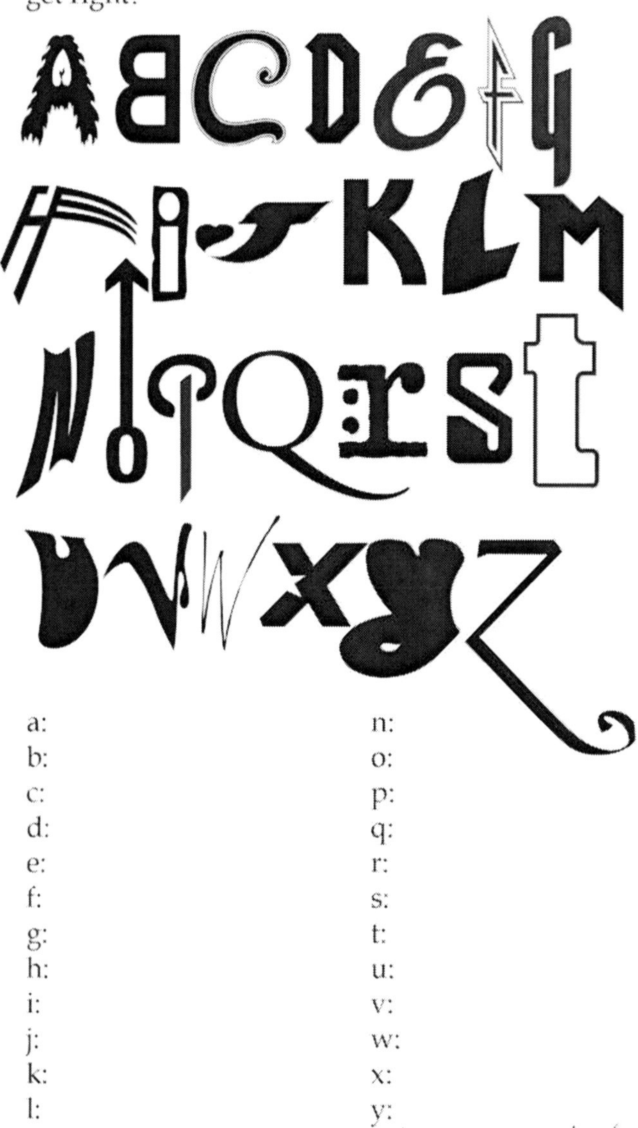

a:
b:
c:
d:
e:
f:
g:
h:
i:
j:
k:
l:
m:
n:
o:
p:
q:
r:
s:
t:
u:
v:
w:
x:
y:
z: Led Zeppelin (duh)

A AEROSMITH
B ABBA
C CHICAGO
D AC/DC
E ELO (ELECTRIC LIGHT ORCHESTRA)
F DEF LEPPARD
G GIBSON GUITARS
H VAN HALEN
I SEX PISTOLS
J JACKSON 5
K KISS
L BLACK SABBATH
M IRON MAIDEN
N MONKEES
O THE WHO
P DEEP PURPLE
Q QUEEN
R REPRISE RECORDS
S SCORPIONS
T STAX RECORDS
U RUBBER SOUL (BEATLES)
V VERVE RECORDS
W PINK FLOYD'S "THE WALL"
X INXS
Y YES
Z LED ZEPPELIN

About the Author

GARY GUTHRIE IS A TRIVIA QUESTION of his own, interestingly enough. He's the radio program director who stitched together solo versions of Streisand and Diamond's "You Don't Bring Me Flowers" turning the duet into Columbia Records biggest single of the '70s.

His penchant for new music has led to him to gold albums for Springsteen, Meatloaf, Meat Puppets, and others. His pioneering work in the Classic Hits and Smooth Jazz formats led to being saluted as the "Father of the Hybrid Format" at the National Association of Broadcaster's Breakfast of Champions.

He continues to follow his creative bliss with art commissions from folks like Mercedes-Benz and the E! network, producing the Randy Brecker-led *A New Kind of Blue* and *Before the Goldrush* with Neko Case and Swell Season, writing the score for *The Radio They Found Inside Cat Stevens' Head* performed by various modern dance troupes , and mvyradio.com's "On the Road" initiative where he's recorded close 500+ gigs from the Allmans to Elvis Costello to the Decemberists.

If you're into the six degrees of separation thang, his appearance in Robert Altman's *O.C. and Stiggs* renders him a mere three degrees separated from Pat Boone and two away from Ozzy Osbourne.

You can reach Gary a mere single degree away via garyworld@gmail.com.

ROCK
AND ROLL
HEAVEN
ENTRANCE

CPSIA information can be obtained at www.ICGtesting.com
Printed in the USA
BVOW07s0832191214

380124BV00001B/11/P